Sex, Lies, and Forgiveness

Hazelden Titles of Related Interest

Is It Love or Is It Addiction? Falling Into Healthy Love, Brenda Schaeffer

Answers in the Heart: Daily Meditations for Men and Women Recovering from Sex Addiction, Hazelden

Sex, Lies, and Forgiveness
Couples Speaking Out on Healing
From Sex Addiction

Jennifer P. Schneider, M.D.
Burt Schneider

A Hazelden Book
HarperCollins*Publishers*

FIRST HARPERCOLLINS EDITION PUBLISHED IN 1991.

Library of Congress Cataloging-in-Publication Data

Schneider, Jennifer P.
    Sex, lies, and forgiveness : couples speaking out on healing from sex addiction / Jennifer Schneider and Burt Schneider.
        p. cm.
    "A Hazelden book"
    ISBN 0–06–255343–7 (alk. paper)
    1. Relationship addiction. 2. Marital psychotherapy.
I. Schneider, Burt. II. Title
    RC552.R44S36   1991
    616.89'156—dc20   90–55844
                                       CIP

91 92 93 94 95 RRD 10 9 8 7 6 5 4 3 2 1

This edition is printed on acid-free paper which meets the American National Standards Institute Z39.48

All the quotes in this book are from real people. Identifying details have been changed to protect peoples' anonymity.

To our parents—who answered our questions.
To our children—who we hope will question our answers.

Contents

Acknowledgments

Many people contributed to the realization of this book. The following people read portions of the manuscript and made valuable suggestions: Cynthia Arem, Ph.D., Carol Evans, Ph.D., Linda Karl, M.D., Ruth Komarniski, Ph.D., Roger Ferris, Ph.D., Arnold Arem, M.D., Michael Hutchins, Ph.D., Dan Overbeck, Ph.D., Robert Kafes, C.S.W., Katherine Arnold, M.S., Sandra Szelag, M.Div., Anne Stericker, Ph.D., and Kinne Tevis, M.D.

To the many people who participated in the surveys and interviews with the belief that your experiences could help others—we thank you for your courage.

Finally, we thank our editor Rebecca Post for her encouragement.

CHAPTER ONE

Overview

As people recovering from the effects of sexual addiction, many of us erroneously believed that if our sexual and relationship needs were met, we could become whole people worthy of love. We abused ourselves and others to fill the void left by a hurtful childhood. And the paradox was that the more we got, the more we wanted. Some of us had already struggled with other addictions – alcohol and other drugs, food, gambling, spending – but we wanted to hang on to this one a little while longer. "It takes what it takes" is a slogan we heard in Twelve Step circles. For some of us, it took yet another affair, the end of our marriage, the termination of an unwanted pregnancy, a highly publicized arrest for soliciting a prostitute, the loss of a job because of sexual impropriety, or contracting a sexually transmitted disease before we admitted our behavior was unmanageable.

By meeting with others who struggled as we had, we began to regain our self-esteem. As we continued in recovery, we saw a glimmer of hope for our relationships too. We learned that we were dealing with an addictive process that affects the whole family, and that healing was possible if we committed ourselves to honesty.

Burt's Story
Maybe I am one of those people who should not be married. I just don't do relationships well, I said to myself as I prepared to marry for the second time.

The evidence supported the statement. My first marriage had ended partly as the result of my extramarital affairs, and I had post-

1

poned my marriage to Jennifer out of fear of commitment. Our three-year courtship had been marred by my sexual interludes with other women, and I seriously doubted my ability to remain monogamous. Despite these doubts, I did marry and for the first year found myself obsessing and fantasizing about other women. I had a brief sexual encounter with a married woman in my graduate program and went back to what I now know as *white-knuckle fidelity*. A year later, I was involved in an addictive relationship and felt hopeless about extricating myself. But somehow this time was different. I no longer wanted to be doing what I was doing. I was paying too high a price for leading a double life. I was depressed and not sleeping well. I was sick and tired of lying and cheating. On the outside I was a loving husband and father; on the inside I was dying.

When I tried to break off the relationship, the other woman threatened to tell her husband and my wife. I preempted her and in a tearful confession told Jennifer what had been going on. Even though I hoped this was to be my last affair, I could not be sure.

"These things just keep happening to me," I said.

Despite years of therapy, I had no explanation for my behavior. Shortly thereafter, I read about a program modeled after Alcoholics Anonymous for persons who were dealing with addictive sexual behavior. I read that I was not alone—that there were others who were feeling the same pain and loneliness that I felt. Although there were no Twelve Step programs for sexual addiction in my community, I began attending other Twelve Step meetings and changing the words in my head. When the members said "alcohol," I heard, "my sexual behavior." Despite the shame and embarrassment I felt when I spoke at a few meetings, I began to feel hope. I made contact with people in another city who had started a Twelve Step meeting for sex addicts and I attended one of their meetings. I was overwhelmed with relief. Here were people I could relate to and who understood me. What they did to cover up their feelings of worthlessness and shame may have been different from what I did, but we were all broken people who wanted desperately to get well.

I began a meeting in my city. For the first year, I often sat alone in a church meeting room waiting for another person to show up.

Many came and went, but eventually one other person stayed and the meeting grew. I began to work on my own recovery and hoped I could rebuild trust in my marriage.

Jennifer's Story

My gut was telling me something was wrong. I had a sinking feeling inside that I knew meant Burt must be involved with another woman. But when I asked Burt what was going on, he would brush me off.

"Nothing," he would say with a shake of the head. "It's just your imagination."

I began to doubt my own sense of reality. I was feeling the same craziness I had felt at other times during our tumultuous three-year relationship that led to our getting married – against my better judgment. I had all the clues that commitment was a big problem for Burt. When we got too close, he would suggest that we both needed to see other people. I knew this meant he was getting scared. And when he got scared, he put distance between us by dating someone else.

I reacted by immediately getting involved with another man. This made me more desirable to Burt, so he would intensify his efforts to get me back and all would be fine for a while. And the cycle would continue.

After our marriage there were no other men in my life, but I suspected that monogamy was not as easy for Burt. When he told me about his latest affair, I realized I wasn't crazy after all. I was hurt and angry, and divorce seemed inevitable. When he suggested I attend a self-help meeting for families and friends of alcoholics, I was incensed.

"You're the one with the problem and you want me to work on myself?" I asked.

But being the good people pleaser I was, I went – and got the message at the first meeting. Although alcohol was not a problem for us, I could relate to the women I heard speak. I heard that I did not cause Burt's problem, I certainly could not cure it, and I had no control over it. I could only heal myself and begin to set some boundaries on what I was willing to accept in our marriage.

Because the program asked me to examine my own past behaviors, I took a close look at my previous relationships. I pictured myself once again as a naive young woman in love for the first time—with a handsome extroverted young man who announced to me after the second time we made love that he was gay and preferred his boyfriends. It took me many months to get over the pain of that failed romance. I remembered the several disastrous relationships that followed, each with a man who was emotionally unavailable because of his compulsive work habits, his interest in other women, or his fear of commitment. All I wanted, I thought, was a man who could really love me, but I just could not seem to find him. Professionally, I had no trouble attaining whatever goal I set for myself, but in my personal life I seemed to make one bad choice after another.

When I finally recognized that I have some responsibility for being in the relationship with Burt, and that if I had not married him I would most likely be with another emotionally unavailable man, I became ready to forgive him and start work on my own recovery.

What Are Twelve Step Programs?

Although we did not have a name for our problem for several years, we were dealing with sexual addiction and coaddiction, and the Twelve Steps offered a path to recovery. The prototype of Twelve Step self-help groups is Alcoholics Anonymous, a fellowship founded in 1935 by a stockbroker and a physician who were alcoholics. In 1938, one of them, Bill Wilson, wrote *Alcoholics Anonymous*, a book in which he summarized the program in a list of Twelve Suggested Steps for recovery. The Steps encompass three elements essential to making changes: (1) recognizing that our life is intolerable as is, and that change is necessary; (2) deciding to do whatever it takes to implement the change; and (3) acting to bring about the change.

Alcoholics Anonymous is not a religious program, but it is a spiritual program. Implicit in the program is the belief that the addict does not have to act alone to change. Instead, there is faith in a "Power greater than ourselves." The identity of this Higher Power is left to each person to determine. For many, the Higher Power is

God. For others, it is nature or the collective strength of all recovering people.

Despite its simplicity, the Twelve Step program can be a powerful instrument of change. The Twelve Steps offer a constructive program for living. Twelve Step meetings are not therapy; there is no role-playing, no confrontation, and no direct giving of advice. Twelve Step meetings have some definite advantages over individual psychotherapy. Finding others who have the same problem combats the feelings of isolation and loneliness that most addicts and coaddicts feel. Many report, "I really felt understood" after attending Twelve Step meetings.

Being understood and accepted by others helps addicts and coaddicts overcome the shame and guilt that many feel. These meetings are often where an addict or coaddict feels safe enough, perhaps for the first time, to share with others some painful or shameful experience. When Twelve Step participation is combined with the right kind of therapy, positive change is not only possible, but is likely. Therapy and Twelve Step programs can work very well together when the therapist is supportive of Twelve Step participation.

What Is Sex Addiction?

There is no time when we are more vulnerable to another human being than when we open ourselves sexually to that person. However, we each bring different beliefs about sex to our relationships. Ideally, sex between two people who care for each other is but part of the relationship—a shared activity that enhances closeness, is fun, and is a reflection of the good feelings they have for each other. In reality, many people believe that sex is

- something they are entitled to regardless of their partner's feelings.
- a way to escape from problems and bad feelings.
- something given in order to get love.
- proof of being loved.
- something that can be refused or encouraged as a way to manipulate another person.

When sex becomes any of these things, it becomes distorted. Instead of helping to bind couples together, it can become a wedge driving them apart. This book will describe the problems encountered by couples who bring these mistaken beliefs into their relationships.

For some people, sex or the pursuit of the sexual high is so important that it becomes the most important thing in their lives — more important than their ·primary relationship, their jobs, or their health. They are as addicted to sex as the alcoholic is to the bottle. It is fairly easy for most people to understand how someone can be addicted to a substance, but some people find the concept of addiction to a behavior difficult to accept.

How Sex Addiction Is Similar to Alcoholism

To make this concept clearer, let us look at how psychiatrists define chemical dependency. Psychiatrists do not diagnose an alcoholic on the basis of how much he or she drinks or how often. Instead, the diagnosis is based primarily on the way the alcoholic behaves. The criteria for chemical dependency include the following:[1]

1. *Loss of control.* The substance is taken in larger amounts or over a longer time than the person intended. The person recognizes that his or her substance use is excessive and has attempted to cut down or control it, but has been unable to.
2. *Obsession.* A great deal of time is spent trying to get the substance, taking it, and recovering from its effects.
3. *Continued use despite adverse consequences.* Important social, occupational, or recreational activities are given up or reduced because of the substance use. With heavy or prolonged use, a variety of social, psychological, or physical problems occur. Nonetheless, the person continues the use.
4. *Tolerance.* There is a need for increased amounts of the substance to get the desired effect.
5. *Withdrawal.* When use of the substance is stopped, characteristic withdrawal symptoms develop, and the person resumes use in order to relieve or avoid the symptoms.

Not all drugs have withdrawal symptoms. In fact, the presence of only three of the five criteria is necessary to diagnose someone as chemically dependent. These criteria are familiar to any recovering alcoholic or family member of a recovering alcoholic. However, they can be applied equally well to people whose drug of choice is addictive sexual behavior. Take the case of the married minister who has a series of affairs with parishioners he is counseling. His wife becomes increasingly dissatisfied with their marriage because of the extra time he spends away from home, but he can't resist the lure of the clandestine meetings. Aware of the discrepancy between his public image and his secret life, he repeatedly promises himself to have no more affairs, but is unable to stop when the next attractive woman makes an appointment with him to discuss her problems. Eventually, his affairs are discovered and he loses his job. His wife threatens divorce.

The minister's behavior shows loss of control, obsession, and continuation despite adverse consequences—three of the five criteria. He was unable to stop even though he wanted to, was obsessed with other women to the point of neglecting his family, and continued the affairs although he risked losing his job and marriage. Despite his knowledge that being sexual with women in the congregation was not in his best self-interest, he was unable to stop.

Or take the case of a married woman who has a sexual fling on an out-of-town business trip. She feels a sense of power and excitement and decides to have other brief affairs, but only while out of town to avoid detection by her husband. After several brief affairs, the excitement wanes. Breaking her own rule, she begins an affair with someone in her own city. She is turned on by the intrigue of not getting caught. She ups the ante by having more affairs with local acquaintances, each a little riskier than the last. She arranges her work schedule around the affairs, taking time away from the office during her workday. At one point, she invites her lover for dinner at her home and enjoys sharing special looks with him in front of her husband. Her husband confronts her, then files for divorce. He tells her he has been aware for a long time of her preoccupation and her distancing from him.

Her behavior shows obsession, continued use despite adverse

consequences, and development of tolerance—three of the five criteria. Her preoccupation with the other men caused her to make poor decisions about her job and the affairs' threat to her marriage; she persisted in the affairs despite the potential loss of her marriage; and she found the need to take more risks to get the same effect.

Types of Addictive Sexual Behaviors
Any sexual behavior can be part of a sexual addiction. Carnes[2] has classified sexual addiction into eleven behavioral types, including

1. fantasy and masturbation
2. multiple sexual relationships
3. voyeurism and pornography
4. exhibitionism
5. receiving money or drugs for sex
6. paying for prostitutes or phone sex
7. rape and other intrusive sexual behaviors
8. anonymous sex
9. pain exchange
10. sex with children
11. cross dressing and fetishism

According to Carnes, addictive sexual behavior involves exploitation of others, is nonmutual, objectifies people, is dissatisfying, involves shame, and is based on fear.

Most sex addicts have at least two or three compulsive behaviors in their repertory. For example, lurking under someone's window may be the behavior that brings a man to the attention of the law, but careful questioning will usually reveal that he may masturbate excessively or spend significant sums of money on pornography. Therapists are now coming to understand that *all* areas of sexual compulsivity must be stopped if the addict is to recover. Otherwise, the addict just mentioned may temporarily increase his masturbation and pornography use only to relapse into voyeurism after therapy.

Married addicts sometimes talk of "acting out within the marriage." As one woman put it, "My body was there during sex, but my mind was elsewhere." For some addicts, fantasizing about other people or situations while having sex with their committed partner may be part of their addictive behavior.

Cycles of Acting Out

According to Carnes,[3] sex addicts follow a predictable cycle in acting out. It begins with *preoccupation*—when the addict is obsessed with thoughts of a sexual experience or a sexual partner. Next comes *ritualization*—an obsessive search for the sexual experience that heightens the excitement and is unique to each addict. For one person, the ritual may consist of dressing in special clothes, going to a bar, and looking over the potential sex partners. For another, it may be driving around looking for a victim to expose him- or herself to. For yet another, the ritual may include calling a lover to arrange a clandestine meeting or planning dinner with the lover at an out-of-the-way restaurant. The next step is the *sexual act*, which is where the addict loses control of his or her behavior. After the sexual act is completed, the addict typically feels *despair*, a sense of shame, hopelessness, and powerlessness about his or her behavior. The addict may vow not to do it again, but, in fact, the only way he or she knows how to deal with the despair is to tune it out with *preoccupation* . . . and the cycle begins anew.

The addiction model for sexual behavior is not universally accepted by sexuality experts. Some prefer to call sexual addiction an *intimacy disorder*. We believe that *all* addicts have an intimacy disorder. Other experts believe compulsive sexuality is a variant of *obsessive-compulsive disorder* (OCD). OCD is a psychiatric illness in which a person is plagued by intrusive thoughts that can only be relieved by repeatedly performing some action, such as hand washing or checking whether a door is locked. OCD is often treatable with specific drugs.

Because obsessive thinking and compulsive behavior are key components of all addictions, we believe that there is some overlap between obsessive-compulsive disorder and addiction. But the drugs that relieve OCD symptoms are less useful in the treatment of sexual addiction. The value of the addiction model for sexual behavior is that it suggests a treatment approach—the Twelve Step program and addiction counseling—that has proved effective for thousands of people who were unable to stop their problem sexual behavior on their own or with traditional psychotherapy. What is important is not how we label a behavior pattern, but how the pattern can be changed.

Family of Origin Issues

Sexual addiction is a problem affecting perhaps 6 percent of Americans. About 80 percent of members of Twelve Step programs for sexual addiction are men; however, sexually addicted women may be underrepresented because our society is more tolerant of men's sexual excesses than it is of women's. In our society, it is more shameful for women to come forward and admit their sexual addiction.

The seeds of sexual addiction are sown in childhood in a dysfunctional family that failed to provide children with adequate nurturing. This is often because one or both of the parents are addicts themselves, often alcoholic or sexually addicted. They also may be mentally ill or rigidly religious. They are almost always either physically, sexually, or emotionally abusive.

In a family where one parent is an addict, the nonaddicted parent focuses most of his or her energy on meeting the addict's needs and controlling the addict's behavior. As a result, the children in such a family are often left to fend for themselves and to meet their own emotional needs. Many of these children learn to soothe their pain through their own compulsive behavior or substance abuse. Why they choose one particular behavior or substance over another is an area of great scientific interest. Some researchers have pointed to intergenerational patterns suggesting a genetic or biochemical link.

What many of these families have in common is a set of rules that prevent the open expression of feelings. They are variations of *Don't trust* (especially outside the family), *Don't talk to anyone* (especially outside the family), and *Don't feel.*

Young children believe the world revolves around them, and that they are the cause of whatever happens to them and around them. If their parents do not treat them with love, they believe it is because they are not lovable. As a result, these children can develop a deep sense of shame about themselves and believe that they are not worthwhile people. If they are criticized repeatedly and made to feel as if they can never measure up to their parents' expectations, this shame is validated and reinforced.

Codependency and Addiction

Children in troubled families can acquire a set of personality traits called *codependency*, which is a pattern of painful dependence on compulsive behaviors and on approval from others in an attempt to find safety, self-worth, and identity.[4] Codependents have low self-esteem and look to others for their self-worth. At the same time, they believe they cannot depend on others to fulfill their needs.

Depending on his or her childhood experiences, each codependent finds a different way to feel good and to escape bad feelings. Some codependents begin using alcohol, food, or sex addictively. Others become workaholics or compulsive gamblers. Still others find themselves in addictive relationships with partners who are not emotionally available. Codependents who are in a relationship with an addict are often called coaddicts or relationship addicts. We believe that codependency underlies all addiction and coaddiction.

Most people have codependent traits, but before we label ourselves or others as codependent or addicted, we need to assess how these behaviors affect our life. The people in this book who identify themselves as addicts, coaddicts, or codependents are not just people who occasionally exhibited addictive or codependent behaviors; they are people whose lives became unmanageable because of those behaviors.

Persons who become sex addicts or coaddicts frequently received unhealthy messages about sexuality when they were children. Usually, there was either a highly charged sexual atmosphere or sexual repression in their home. Surveys show that a majority of sex addicts, and probably coaddicts as well, were sexually abused as children. Some experienced overt incest or molestation and learned that sex equals love and attention. Others were victims of covert incest—they were not touched inappropriately, but they may have witnessed adult sexual activities, were subjected to repeated comments about their bodies or their sexual development, or were exposed to pornography. Some children were taught that sex is bad or dirty and their parents shamed them when they were seen touching their genitals.

In some homes, discussion about sex was taboo. Girls may not have been told anything about menstruation and may have been rejected in puberty by fathers who were concerned by their own attraction to their developing daughters. Boys may have been taken to prostitutes by "helpful" older relatives or cheered on in their pursuit of sex as teenagers.

As a result of our childhood experiences, some of us developed a set of core beliefs about ourselves that included the belief that sex is our most important need or that sex is the most important sign of love. We tended to find partners whose core beliefs fit with our own. In our relationships, we used sex to relieve stress, resolve conflict, feel reassured, or get our way. Part of our task as recovering couples is to understand the meaning that sex has for each of us. We can then change the areas that cause us problems and work toward having healthier relationships.

Couples' Recovery from Sexual Addiction

In order to do this, we need to understand the nature of sexual addiction and coaddiction and its impact on the family. Therapists and treatment centers are increasingly recognizing the problem of sexual addiction and are providing inpatient and outpatient treatment. These programs for the most part deal with individual recovery. But as more is learned about addiction, more attention is being focused on the family system and the couple relationship. Unfortunately, very little is known about couples who are recovering from sexual addiction. What aspects of their recovery are the most problematic for them? How are they handling their problems? What happens to the sexual relationship during recovery?

To answer these questions, we distributed a fourteen-page anonymous survey to recovering couples all over the United States. We located them through Twelve Step fellowships for sex addicts or through other recovering couples. Each member of a couple filled out a survey individually and mailed it to us anonymously. The pairs of surveys were coded so that we could later match up those completed by husband and wife. Because the surveys were filled out separately, we believe we were able to get more honest answers than if the couple had worked on them together. Many people supplemented their answers with long personal comments at the end of the survey.

In reading our respondents' comments, it is important to remember that we are capturing their feelings at a particular time. Many of the couples were in early recovery when they completed the survey. Early recovery is notoriously a time of upheaval. Feelings run strong, and they may change from day to day. Some people undoubtedly answered the survey when they were feeling optimistic about the relationship; others may have just finished an argument.

In addition to the daily fluctuations in feelings, many couples experience more fundamental changes as they work on their relationship. Early on, there is often a lack of trust, a great deal of fear and anger, and much uncertainty about the future of the relationship. If the same couples were to complete the survey a year or two later, their feelings in several areas would undoubtedly be different. What looks hopeless today may look hopeful tomorrow.

The people who answered our survey were actively working on their individual recovery and on their couple relationship. We received a total of 142 surveys. In fifty-four cases, both members of the couple completed the survey. Although an additional thirty-four people completed the survey, none of their partners did. This gave us information about eighty-eight marriages of recovering sex addicts and coaddicts. In addition to the surveys, we interviewed in person or by telephone several couples in which the husband was gay or bisexual or the wife was sexually addicted. This book is based on the results of the surveys and interviews. In the next chapter, we will present an overview of who responded to the survey.

Who We Are

The hotel ballroom was decorated with blue and white balloons imprinted with the conference slogan. People were greeting each other warmly, often with hugs. This event could have easily been a sales convention or even a family reunion. And in a way it was a family reunion—a family of recovering people getting together to share their experience, strength, and hope in dealing with sexual addiction and coaddiction, topics that most people only whisper about.

Some people might be surprised at how "normal" sex addicts and coaddicts look. They are men and women, straight and gay. Some have children. They work in a variety of occupations, from architecture to zoology. Many have been to college and have professional training; others drive trucks or care for children.

What we share is an uncommon journey. It is our hope that through our participation in the research for this book, we will be able to help others who are just beginning on the road to recovery.

Young and Old; Men and Women

We found most of our survey respondents through Twelve Step programs dealing with sexual addiction and coaddiction. Many had attended national conferences of Sexaholics Anonymous (SA), Sex Addicts Anonymous (SAA), S-Anon, and Codependents of Sex Addicts (COSA). In some cases, respondents were recommended to us by pastors or therapists. Of the 142 people who completed the survey, 67 were men and 75 women. The age range was broad: the youngest respondent was 24 years old, the oldest was 71. Of the 67 men, 4 percent were 20–29 years old; 36 percent were 30–39; 36 percent were 40–49; 18 percent were 50–59; 4 percent were 60–69; and one addict was over 70. Of the 75 women, 12 percent were 20–29 years old; 44 percent were 30–39; 25 percent were 40–49; 15 percent were 50–59; and 4 percent were 60–69.

Addicts and Coaddicts

Because several people identified themselves as both addicts and coaddicts, we had a total of 76 addicts and 74 coaddicts. Of the 76 addicts, 84 percent were men. Of the 74 coaddicts, 89 percent were women. An additional eight addicts identified themselves as coaddicts as well. This was because of family of origin problems, however, rather than because their spouse was a sex addict. Because over 80 percent of the respondents believed their parents had at least one addiction, most people were in the role of coaddicts in their family of origin. Only after they had stopped their addictive behaviors did some people recognize that they had problems with a need to control others, please others, and with other coaddictive issues. Therapists typically suggest that addicts have at least two years of sobriety before they tackle any problems of coaddiction and codependency. Often, it is only after several years of sobriety that addicts even recognize their need to address these other issues.

In fifty-four cases, both partners filled out the survey. Of these, 11 percent were part of a couple where both were sex addicts, and in 4 percent only the woman was sexually addicted.

Addicted to Sex; Addicted to Drugs

When some people who are chemically dependent give up their drug of choice, they may be amazed to discover that they have other addictions. Sometimes the focus on one addiction can keep them unaware of others. For example, they may have considered any sexual acting out to be a result of their impaired judgment while intoxicated. Only when they became sober did they recognize that they were still obsessed with sexual activity—and that alcohol simply made it easier for them to be sexual.

Dual addiction to sex and drugs is especially common. According to Dr. Arnold Washton, more than 60 percent of cocaine addicts enrolled in his outpatient cocaine treatment program also had problems with compulsive sexuality.[1] For many in this group, abstinence from cocaine did not alleviate the sexual problems. Although their sexual activity was heightened by the aphrodisiac effect of cocaine, these patients were diagnosed as sex addicts too.

A study of one hundred women who were adult children of alcoholics found that more than half had a problem with alcohol. In *Aching for Love: The Sexual Drama of the Adult Child*, the authors wrote: "After being clean and sober for several months, some ACOAs suddenly begin to have affairs, switching one compulsion for another. 'I've used compulsive affairs and sex as another addiction to keep me away from myself,' said one participant."[2]

What this tells us is that it is important to be aware of all our addictions. Unless we are recovering from all of them, it will be very difficult to avoid relapse in any of them.

In our survey, only 17 percent of sex addicts and 39 percent of coaddicts believed that they had no other significant addictions. The remainder told us they were also chemically dependent (39 percent of addicts and 20 percent of coaddicts); had eating disorders (32 percent of addicts and 38 percent of coaddicts); were workaholics (38 percent of addicts and 25 percent of coaddicts); or were compulsive spenders (13 percent of addicts and 12 percent of coaddicts). Three addicts and one coaddict were also compulsive gamblers. Many were attending Twelve Step meetings for two or more addictions.

From Families Affected by Addiction
Like chemical dependency, sexual addiction can be a family illness. Recovering people may find it useful to look at their family history. Grandfather may have been a sex addict, their father an alcoholic, and an aunt married to a sex addict. Recognizing these patterns can help us understand our own vulnerability to addiction. This does not make us any less responsible for our actions or minimize the need for change, but it may relieve some of our shame. Often, it is only after we have begun the recovery process that we know what questions to ask of other family members.

Of the 142 survey respondents, only 19 percent said their parents had no addictions. At least one parent was chemically dependent in 40 percent of the respondents' families, and one or more parent was sexually addicted in 36 percent. Thirty percent of respondents had at least one parent with an eating disorder, and 38 percent had one or more workaholic parent. Compulsive gambling was present in 7 percent of families.

Married, With and Without Children

All except four respondents were currently married—those four were living with a partner in a committed relationship, and only two of these had never been married. Despite the turmoil in many marriages, 67 percent of all the respondents were in their first marriage. Twenty-five percent of respondents were in their second marriage, 4 percent in a third marriage, and 2 percent in their fourth marriage.

One-quarter of the respondents had no children. Thirteen percent had one child; 22 percent had two children; 17 percent had three children; and 20 percent had four or more children. On average, respondents had 2.1 children.

Well-Educated and Gainfully Employed

Alcoholics Anonymous, founded by a stockbroker and a physician, initially appealed to an educated group of people and gradually attracted more blue-collar workers. The same pattern is apparent among people recovering from sexual addiction. Self-help groups for sexual addiction began about fifteen years ago and are now in a position similar to where AA was in its early days.

Most of the survey respondents were well-educated. Of the 67 men, 42 percent had a graduate degree; 31 percent had a bachelor's degree; 16 percent had some college or trade school education; and 9 percent had a high school diploma. Of the 75 women, 23 percent had a graduate degree; 36 percent had a bachelor's degree; 33 percent had some college or trade school education; and 9 percent had gone through part of or all of high school.

The occupations of the respondents generally reflected their high level of education. There were several physicians, psychotherapists, nurses, attorneys, clergymen, technicians, and teachers, as well as business people, accountants, administrators, clerical people, housewives, and students. Other occupations represented were builder, truck driver, printer, woodworker, commercial artist, speech pathologist, police officer, writer, college professor, farmer, engineer, banker, chiropractor, real estate broker, and insurance broker.

In any large gathering of recovering sex addicts, the helping professions appear to be overrepresented. It may be that physicians, psychotherapists, and clergy choose careers in which they feel needed. These careers also provide frequent opportunities to meet with people who are vulnerable to exploitation.

Types of Addictive Behaviors

Carnes has observed that sex addicts have an average of three compulsive sexual behaviors, which was also true of those we surveyed. Nearly all respondents who are sex addicts listed compulsive masturbation and pornography in addition to their other addictive behaviors. Moreover, 68 percent had participated in extramarital sex; 28 percent had been sexual with those of their same gender; and 15 percent had frequented prostitutes. Several respondents mentioned that they visited peep shows, massage parlors, and had telephone sex. Usually, there was a combination of these activities. Eighteen percent of addicts reported involvement in voyeurism; 12 percent in exhibitionism; and 4 percent had touched others inappropriately. Several respondents reported engaging in serious antisocial behaviors, including four who admitted to incest; two to molestation; and one to molestation and raping his wife while she slept. All of the men who had engaged in criminal behaviors had also been involved in other addictive sexual behaviors.

Many Were Sexually Abused

Accurate statistics on sexual abuse are hard to obtain, for several reasons. People tend to repress traumatic childhood experiences of incest and molestation, which are often remembered only years later. When asked whether they had been sexually abused, many people will simply not be able to recall these experiences. Other people are uncomfortable with things that occurred to them in childhood, but do not classify those things as sexual abuse. That sexual abuse can occur even without touching is news to many people. Some behaviors are easily recognized as sexual abuse. These include

• fondling a child's breasts or genitals.
• having a child touch an adult's sexual parts.
• having sex with a child.

Abusive behaviors that do not involve touching include adult nudity in front of an older child or having a child observe adults' sexual activities. More subtle sexual abuse is present when a child's boundaries are crossed. Examples include

• not allowing a child privacy in the bathroom or in his or her own bedroom.
• frequently commenting on the size of an adolescent's breasts or penis.
• accusing an adolescent daughter of trying to seduce her father.
• calling an adolescent daughter a "slut" or a "whore" and predicting that she will go to bed with every boy she dates.
• sharing pornographic magazines or videotapes with an adolescent son.
• giving a child graphic descriptions of adult sexual activities.

Another type of sexual abuse that is often not seen as abuse is that involving a young boy and an older woman. In our society, when a thirty-five-year-old man seduces a fourteen-year-old girl, we agree that this is abuse, and the man may go to prison as punishment. But if a thirty-five-year-old woman seduces a fourteen-year-old boy, society and the boy may see it as a "conquest" or as "getting lucky." The movie *Summer of '42* is a good example of how this kind of abuse is romanticized.

A sexual relationship between two people is abusive when there is a power differential. Examples of relationships in which one person is more powerful than the other include

• a parent or other adult and a child.
• a clergyman and a parishioner.

- a therapist and a client.
- a physician and a patient.
- an employer and an employee.
- a teacher or professor and a student.

In all these cases, the less powerful persons are not in a position to make free choices about the sexual relationship. They may be anxious to please the more powerful person or may fear consequences if they do not. They are also susceptible to the belief that the more powerful person has their best interests at heart. They are all hostages rather than peers in a sexual relationship.

Despite the likelihood of surveys to underestimate the extent of sexual abuse, 45 percent of our respondents believed they had been sexually abused as children. It is generally believed that girls are more often molested than are boys, but in our survey 51 percent of men and 39 percent of women (52 percent of sex addicts and 37 percent of coaddicts) had been sexually abused. Based on his more detailed questionnaire, which listed specific types of sexual abuse, Carnes reports that 87 percent of sex addicts were sexually abused as children.

Their Recovery Experience

All respondents identified themselves as recovering sex addicts, coaddicts, or both, and almost all were attending at least one Twelve Step program. The fellowships that address addictive sexual behavior all use the Twelve Steps adapted from Alcoholics Anonymous. Where they differ is in their definition of "sexual sobriety." A pamphlet published in 1989 by the National Council on Sexual Addiction compares the major groups in detail.[3]

Sexaholics Anonymous, founded in California in 1978, has the clearest definition of sexual sobriety: "For the married sexaholic, sexual sobriety means having sex only with the spouse, including no form of sex with oneself." Unmarried sexaholics are advised to have no sex at all.

Sex Addicts Anonymous, begun in Minnesota in 1977 by a group of therapists, asks members to define their own sobriety and boundaries. They write: "We cannot abstain from our sexuality,

21

because it is part of our humanity. Instead, we abstain from the compulsive, destructive behaviors that rendered our lives unmanageable. Boundaries reflect both what behaviors we'll abstain from and those we'll embrace in a search toward serenity and sexual health."[4]

Members of Sex and Love Addicts Anonymous (SLAA), a fellowship begun in Boston in 1976, determine what their bottom-line sexual behaviors are—self-destructive sexual behaviors that are out of control—and commit to avoiding them.

Begun in 1982, Sexual Compulsives Anonymous (SCA) is attended primarily by gay men. Its members develop their own sexual recovery plan and define sexual sobriety for themselves. They say, "We are not here to repress our God-given sexuality, but to learn how to express it in ways that will not endanger our mental, physical and spiritual health."[5]

Following in the tradition of Al-Anon, the fellowship for families and friends of alcoholics, several programs now exist for family members and friends of sex addicts. These include S-Anon, Codependents of Sex Addicts, and Co-Sex and Love Addicts Anonymous (CO-SLAA). These programs are very similar. S-Anon supports a Twelve Step program for recovering couples called S-Anon Recovering Couples, which meets regularly in several cities.

Recovering Couples Anonymous (RCA) attracts couples who are recovering from any addiction, but many members are dealing with sexual addiction.

It is unusual to meet someone with over ten years' time in SA, SAA, or SLAA. In our survey, time in recovery ranged from one month to seven years, with a median of one to three years. Of the addicts, 3 percent had less than two months' sobriety; 13 percent had two to six months; 20 percent had six to twelve months; 35 percent had one to three years; 21 percent had three to five years; and 8 percent had more than five years in the program. Of the coaddicts, 1 percent had less than two months in recovery; 11 percent had two to six months; 27 percent had six to twelve months; 39 percent had one to three years; 17 percent had three to five years; and 6 percent had more than five years' recovery.

In the next chapter, we will meet a number of couples who tell in their own words what it was like before recovery.

CHAPTER THREE

The Quagmire Before Recovery

When I was eighteen, I had my first sexual experience and got pregnant, so I got married. Sam drank a lot, was gone much of the time, and when he came home we would usually fight. I felt so lonely and unappreciated. Sex between us was very bad, and during the pregnancy it was painful as well. After the baby was born, I had my first affair. When that relationship went down the drain, I had another affair. For the next twenty-five years, I was in and out of affairs. At one point, I became suicidal over one person, so I went to a psychiatrist who gave me Valium and antidepressants. As crazy as I was about my latest lover, I couldn't be faithful. When he wasn't available, I felt abandoned and would find somebody else to make me feel good. Each time, I swore I would never get into another affair like the last one, where I was addicted to the man, but I did. My husband just kept drinking, and seemed oblivious to what was happening.

— GAYLE

During my drinking days, I spent very little time at home. I had my drinking buddies and I had affairs with several women. I used to say that I had the best of both worlds—I was able to get out and run around and do my own thing, and I had a faithful wife and two loving children at home. Gayle and I never really knew what each other's life was like. Our interactions were mostly arguments over sex, my drinking, and the children. I never even suspected she was having affairs until the last few years. Our home was always well kept and she was very involved with the children's school activities. I thought everything was fine. I guess I never paid enough attention to her to even recognize that she was unhappy.

—SAM

Five years ago, when Jim, Sam and Gayle's son, was admitted to a chemical dependency treatment center for drug abuse, they agreed to attend family week—a program designed to give family members information about addiction and its roots in the dysfunctional family system. Jim had long been aware of his father's drinking and his mother's affairs, and he confronted them during family week. Gayle told us it was as if a "bomb had gone off" in the small group, but it was also the beginning of the recovery process for both parents. Sam now has several years' sobriety in AA, and Gayle has given up her affairs and is active in Sexaholics Anonymous (SA).

Like other addictions, sexual addiction has its roots in the family. It may be the primary addiction or may coexist with alcoholism or other compulsive behavior. In our survey, 40 percent of respondents had a parent who was chemically dependent, and 36 percent had a parent who was sexually addicted. Addictive patterns continue and are often repeated in the next generation. When we obtain help for ourselves, we begin to break the cycle for the next generation as well.

The Dysfunctional Marriage: The Addict's Perspective

Although we did not realize initially that we are sex addicts, most of us have always been aware of how important sex was in our life. We brought into our marriage the belief that we could not survive without sex. We demanded sex, not taking into account our partner's wishes. The bedroom may have become a constant battle-ground. Some of us were more interested in sex outside the home than with our spouse. In order to "protect our supply," that is, prevent our spouse from learning about—and attempting to control—our illicit sexual activities, we lied, cheated, covered up, manipulated, and kept secrets. Lying became second nature to us. And to make it less likely that our lies would be detected, we withdrew emotionally. We became vague when asked about our whereabouts. Some of us protected ourselves by taking the offensive, acting angry and lashing out. Our anger and resentment gave us excuses to "go back out there." We responded to questions with feigned virtue: "When have I ever given you reason to doubt me? You need help with your crazy suspicions. You'd better see a shrink." And often our spouse did.

Caught in the addictive cycle, we were subject to mood swings that our family could not understand. Knowing that we could not predict how we would feel tomorrow or the next day, we hesitated to commit to anything in advance. We kept our options open, in case something better came along. At times, we were overwhelmed with guilt and shame, so we withdrew or intensified our addictive behavior. We could see our spouse trying hard to understand us, taking the blame for the craziness in the relationship, changing him- or herself in every way possible in order to please us, but we were caught in a never-ending cycle. The more "helpful" our spouse became and the more responsibility he or she took for our behavior, the more guilt and shame we felt.

We often saw our husband or wife as the only obstacle to our sexual satisfaction, and we resented him or her. We believed that if only he or she were not in our life, we could pursue the perfect woman or the perfect man, or participate without guilt in the sexual smorgasbord that was waiting for us.

The Dysfunctional Marriage: The Coaddict's Perspective

Many of us feared displeasing our spouse or getting him or her angry. If it was a choice between trusting our gut feelings or accepting our spouse's word, we chose to believe our spouse. We wanted so much to trust our partner. Just the thought that he or she might be seeing another woman or man triggered our deep fear of abandonment. Rather than face the possibility that our spouse was lying and might leave us, it was safer for us to deny our own instincts. Many of us tolerated emotional abuse and colluded with our sexually addicted spouse, believing that we were the main problem in the marriage.

We accepted intolerable behavior and blamed ourselves. If our partner was attracted to others or sought sexual gratification outside the home, it was because we were deficient lovers. If our spouse was unable to account for large chunks of time, it was our fault for not giving him or her freedom.

Many of us *enabled* our spouse in his or her addiction, which means we prevented our spouse from experiencing the consequences of his or her behavior. If we suspected an affair, we did not confront our spouse. We feared he or she would respond with anger and leave us. Instead, we hid our pain and tried to win him or her back. We went on crash diets, bought sexy underwear, watched pornography, and engaged in uncomfortable sexual practices. We made excuses to our family and friends for our partner's absences, not wanting others to suspect we were being betrayed.

Because we believed that sex is the most important sign of love, we felt personally rejected when our partner turned away from us. When our partner was sexual with us, we felt affirmed. We used sex to end arguments. We were afraid of saying no, for fear of driving away our spouse. We believed it was our duty to sexually satisfy our partner.

We learned to use sex to manipulate. Granting or withholding sex became our method of reward or punishment. Sex was a pacifier in the wake of unpleasant news.

We spent hours obsessing about and trying to understand our spouse's unpredictable behavior. When he or she turned on the charm, we were lulled back into complacency. One caring act could erase ten hurtful episodes. We did not realize that we, too, were being manipulated. We clung to good memories and tried to ignore reality. We believed that all we had to do was try hard enough.

The Dysfunctional Family: The Child's Perspective
Children who grow up in a family affected by sexual addiction experience much of the same chaos as children who grow up in a family affected by alcoholism. One woman remembered:

When I was ten, I was molested by my older brother. That started the shame and the guilt. Whenever I heard the word "sex," I got so tense and scared. Sex was not talked about in my house. I had to find out for myself about having periods.

During the whole time I was growing up, my dad was having affairs. I knew about it because I was always the one with my mom. I remember once, when I was about eleven, my dad took the car. Mom got into the truck and asked me to go with her. We drove past this one lady's house and my dad's car was there. Mom started screaming.

I thought Dad was just there visiting, but it was quite obvious to Mother that he was having an affair with this lady. We were driving down this real long hill and my mom picked up a big wrench from the floor of the truck and started beating her head with it, screaming about Daddy not loving her and not loving us and how could he do that to her. I remember trying to get the wrench away, trying to control the truck, and her screaming and yelling. Finally, we ran off the road. We didn't hurt ourselves, but I was scared to death.

I guess the banging of the truck through the ditch finally brought my mom back to reality. She started up the truck, went home, and we never discussed it. Daddy came in later and we never talked about it.

Dad also got letters from other women. I would be the one that would get the mail and take it to my mom. Then she would fuss and curse at me because I had given her the letters. Well, I had just gotten them out of the mailbox—it wasn't my fault!

Another woman recalled:

> *My father had many girlfriends. My parents were not married to each other. My mother was my father's mistress, so my father was never really there for me. At Christmas, he was always with his other family. Growing up, I never felt I was good enough. I was raised like a junior mistress for my dad. He would give me lots of things, but I wasn't good enough to call him at home. I wasn't good enough to spend Christmas with.*
>
> *His other family knew about us. His wife would call over to our house to ask for him if she needed to get hold of him.*
>
> *I was a bastard, and I grew up in a small town where there was a lot of cruelty. I had an abortion at eighteen. I swore I'd never have a bastard child.*

The messages children receive in a family where one or more members are sexually addicted can affect them in significant ways as adults. The former wife of a sex addict was molested in childhood by a family friend. When she told her mother, her mother said, "Well, you're a very sexy little girl." She was subsequently molested by others. She later married a man who said he was not sexually attracted to her. She thought, *He must really love me if he wants to marry me and not have sex with me.* It turned out he was a sex addict and gay. Another woman recalled that when she told her mother that an uncle had molested her as a child, her mother told her, "That's how some men are." She eventually married a sex addict who later molested their children. When she told her mother, her mother's reaction again was, "That's how some men are."

Life in a family where one or more members are sexually addicted is a tangled web of lies, denial, and crises. In our survey, some couples described a chaotic existence; others simply told of a gradual erosion of good feelings, deteriorating communication, and an impaired sexual relationship between the husband and wife. Anger and resentment became the dominant themes in these relationships. What follows are excerpts from some of the surveys.

Generally, the comments reflect the difficulties couples had in the quagmire before recovery.

The Addiction's Toll on the Sexual Relationship
Often, one partner was more interested in sex than the other, and this caused frequent arguments. One woman wrote:

My demands drove my husband further away, and he got angry, so I withdrew into my fantasy world. This drove us further and further apart and away from communication and intimacy.

Several men reported a pressure to perform which led them to withdraw even further. One wrote:

Her attempt to fix the problem with more sex was threatening to me, because I did not desire it.

Another wrote:

Since my wife believed (and still believes) that the number of sex acts in a given week indicates how well the marriage is going, we had constant arguments.

Getting a sexual "fix" is the number one priority for addicts. Two addicts wrote:

. . . My addiction has been the major stumbling block in our marriage. It reduced my sexual desire for my wife and despite great satisfaction with the marriage, I fantasized about no longer being married so I could live out my sexual fantasies more fully.

. . . I was not willing to learn to relate to a real woman; the addiction was easier. Each sexual release made a sexual encounter with my spouse seem unnecessary for a while. But my secret life built its own wall of fear and resentment.

Two coaddicts responded:

> . . . *We had no sex after the first few years, probably because of his addiction. My theory is that the shame and secrecy he was feeling before he understood his addiction inhibited him. When he did understand, it had been so many years with no sex in the marriage that neither of us was interested.*

> . . . *He was often tired and emotionally unavailable. Sex with me was just a substitute for masturbating to porno movies. We fought about sex more than anything else.*

One sexually addicted woman described her husband as a caring, sensitive lover with whom she always enjoyed having sexual relations. Her husband, however, described problems. He wrote:

> *Toward the end, I suffered from impotence. I would think about her with someone else and would not be able to have sex.*

Feelings of Shame, Guilt, and Low Self-Esteem

Not getting his or her needs met in a relationship can worsen an addict's feelings of being flawed. But acting out only adds to his or her shame and guilt. Often, the addict's partner unnecessarily takes the blame for the addict's dissatisfaction and withdrawal, lack of sexual interest, and other relationship problems. As a result, both partners sometimes turn their anger inward and suffer depression or physical problems. Several addicts described the effects of the addiction on their self-esteem:

> . . . *My addiction caused me to lie and sneak around. I felt guilty. I lost all respect for myself and it was hard to function as a rational person.*

> . . . *I was frequently dishonest. I felt isolated and my self-esteem was low. I wanted to change my dysfunctional behaviors but did not know how. I felt inferior to my spouse. These feelings made it impossible for me to become intimate.*

Often the addict reported feeling shame about his or her behaviors, while the coaddict's self-esteem plummeted because of the addict's withdrawal. Coaddicts wrote:

> . . . *Although I was a competent professional psychotherapist, I felt ugly, stupid, worthless, and incompetent. I began to isolate myself from friends and drank often to cover up the pain.*

> . . . *Since I had been told by my husband, "My men friends are more important than you," I didn't feel important, sexy, or pretty, even though I dressed nicely and fixed myself up each morning. I didn't understand why there was no affection or love. My self-esteem came from satisfying him with sex, and I couldn't.*

Several coaddicts described what happened to their self-esteem: "I became isolated, dependent, clinging, and had low self-esteem." . . . "I felt I was not good enough for him. I did everything I could to keep him from getting angry." . . . "I gained twenty pounds in the two years of our relationship. I felt I couldn't say no to sex, I felt angry and of very low worth." . . . "I always thought I wasn't exciting enough." Another explained:

> *I increasingly withdrew to the point that it was as if there was only one person in the marriage—him. My whole purpose in life was always to agree, never conflict, always sacrifice.*

Emotional and Physical Withdrawal

Both addicts and coaddicts withdrew from the relationship. They did this to avoid further hurt or to avoid being found out. Whatever the cause, emotional withdrawal, physical absence, or both, were dominant themes in these marriages before recovery. This contributed to a cycle in which communication became more difficult and conflict resolution less likely. Several addicts reported: "My withdrawing would cause my wife to cling more, which would make me withdraw more." . . . "My addiction removed me from the needs and wants of my spouse. I focused more on sex than on other aspects of our relationship." . . . "I couldn't handle intimacy. I needed to escape and did at times of stress."

Coaddicts, too, withdrew emotionally and physically. They said: "I now see that years of denial made me stuff all my feelings. I withdrew emotionally and physically from the marriage." . . . "I wouldn't express emotion and began working longer hours and isolating myself."

The Addict Became the Center of Attention
Until the addict begins recovery, he or she is usually the focus of all family members. One addict was able to see this pattern. He wrote:

> *Generally, I wasn't present. My wife raised our kids. They all walked on eggshells around me. Even when they didn't know what was wrong, or if anything was wrong, life revolved around me. While my wife didn't exactly know what was going on, I created a lot of self-doubt in her.*

Coaddicts believe they are responsible for and can control others. When they perceive a problem, they believe they can find a solution if only they work hard enough. Coaddicts share in the delusion that they are responsible for the addict's happiness. Their goal is to fix the addict and make things right. One coaddict reported:

> *My life was focused on him. I constantly attempted to track his needs and wants. The more needy I seemed, the more he withdrew. I tried to have a lot of sex because I feared he would act out.*

In trying to fix everything, coaddicts can sometimes make life very uncomfortable for their partner. One addict reported, "I felt that I was living under a microscope. She was always trying to find a cure for me." Another reported:

> *We seemed to fuel each other's addiction. Her codependency would lead her to attempt to fix me, which would lead me to feel more inadequate. This would result in more sexual acting out.*

The Addict's Deceit

Lying is an integral part of addictive behavior. It is the chief source of distrust in addicted families. In the words of several addicts, "The addiction caused us both to lie. I was living one and she had secrets too." . . . "The addiction allowed me to continue the highs from lying and feeling superior." A typical coaddict's response went something like this woman's:

I have no trust in him now, although it's beginning to grow again. His addiction caused him to tell many lies and be emotionally unavailable, causing me to distance myself from him.

Blaming the Coaddict

It is easy to blame someone who is willing to accept blame, and coaddicts are masters at accepting responsibility for other people's problems. Coaddicts may instead develop emotional or physical problems. One addict recalled, "I blamed my wife for failing to fulfill my needs." Another remembered:

My head always told me my wife was the problem, that she couldn't do anything right. When I was fantasizing, I didn't want to be interrupted. I was crabby and often depressed.

The coaddict usually accepted the blame. One woman said, "He blamed me for his addiction and I believed him." Another reported:

My self-esteem was always low, so his affairs validated my worthlessness. He also rationalized his affairs by saying I was too fat, too thin, too flabby, too old.

The Coaddict's Enabling and Denial

When coaddicts enable by failing to confront the addict with their suspicions of an ongoing affair, it is likely that the addict will continue the affair, telling friends, "What he doesn't know won't hurt him" or "She doesn't suspect a thing." But if the addict knew of the coaddict's pain, the addict would have to consider the consequences of prolonging an affair. The husband of a sex addict who had multiple affairs related:

> *I enabled her by tuning out. I really allowed her to do just about anything she wanted. I never gave her a budget and I scarcely denied her anything that we could remotely afford. I didn't want to get her angry by telling her she couldn't have some things. I didn't ask her where she'd been when she stayed out late so many nights. It was my fear—I feared to get her upset. I was afraid of the emotional damage I would take. I was so busy protecting myself that I wasn't willing to confront her.*

One recovering sex addict recognized that his wife had enabled him. He wrote:

> *She made it easier for me to act out. Even when she caught me doing things, I would weave fairy tales that she believed because of her codependency.*

Other enabling behaviors include making excuses or lying to others for the addict, giving him or her money to spend on pornography, and "swinging" with the addict. But denial of the addict's problem is also enabling. One coaddict wrote:

> *I permitted my husband to act out because I did not follow my hunches. He flirted and I got jealous, but I did not ask any questions. When I noticed him looking at my daughter as if he were attracted to her, I did not question him. I stuffed my uncomfortable feelings.*

The Coaddict's Lack of Boundaries
When coaddicts accept intolerable behaviors, they pay with resentment, anger, hurt, emotional shutdown, and loss of self-esteem. One coaddict who wrote that she had lost self-esteem also wrote:

I had sex even when I didn't want to in order to be validated. I thought it was my job to make him happy and meet his needs. I obsessed about where he was and with whom when he was gone.

A coaddict's partner may lose respect for him or her because of his or her lack of clear boundaries. One addict wrote, "She put up with too much." Another wrote, "I lost more and more respect for her for allowing me to be abusive."

An Overall Chaotic Marriage

When the addict's behavior is governed by a secret obsession or compulsion and the coaddict is obsessed with trying to understand and control the addict, the result is often chaotic. Several respondents described their lives as chaotic. Two women wrote:

. . . *He was lying to me constantly, and I knew it but he would never admit it and I was never able to say, "You're lying to me" because my self-esteem was too low. It made me crazy. I was always reacting one way or another to his moods, needs, and wants. This was my job—right!*

. . . *His behavior was erratic—happy one minute, depressed the next, with no explanation. He also was late a lot. He spent a lot of unexplained time in the car.*

In a chaotic marriage, strong emotions such as jealousy, obsession, anger, and resentment fuel an already volatile situation. One man who married a sex addict and who was himself a sex addict wrote, "I was insanely jealous of her former husbands and lovers, and fantasized about her cheating." Wives of sex addicts wrote that they were so obsessed with their spouse that they neglected other responsibilities: "I was so preoccupied and worried I became nervous, overtalked, asked too many questions, and quit caring, doing laundry, cooking, etc." . . . "I was angry at the emotional abandonment and expressed that anger in many subtle ways. My addiction to him kept me in the marriage way beyond when I should have left, and that promoted even more anger."

The Sexual Relationship Before Recovery

When asked to rate their sexual relationship before recovery, more than half of the men and women rated their sexual relationship as poor. Still, 37 percent of men and 40 percent of women thought their sex life was good or excellent before recovery. Husbands and wives generally agreed in their assessment. Here are some of the reasons people gave.

Why Sex Was Poor

For some couples, the problem was that one person was much more interested than the other in sex. One couple wrote:

> HUSBAND: *We had sex often, but it was never enough for me. She was hardly ever present, other than physically. I wanted her to be satisfied, but I thought it was her fault she wasn't.*

> WIFE: *He was so sexually demanding and forever critical of me that I had lost all self-esteem. I finally felt as though I didn't want him to touch me.*

In some cases, the coaddict was more desirous of sex. Obviously, this created serious problems for the couple when there was extramarital sex. One man wrote:

> *I believe my wife is a sex addict even though she feels more comfortable calling herself a coaddict. She always uses sex to gauge our marriage. The more sex acts, the better. Ten sex acts a week means everything is super, even if we aren't speaking. I was acting out so much I avoided my wife out of fear that she could sense my just having had sex. Since she equates quantity of sex with love, we have many arguments about sex.*

To want sex from their spouse for reassurance is typical of coaddicts, who often mistake sex for affection and believe that sex is the most important sign of love. The differences between addiction and coaddiction in women will be discussed in greater detail in Chapter Eleven.

Often, sex was bad before recovery because of the addict's focus on sex outside the marriage. A woman addict wrote:

> *One of my excuses for my addiction was that sex in the affairs was more exciting than sex in my marriage. My husband and I had gotten to such a miserable place in our sexual relationship that we couldn't seem to fix it. But I now realize it was a vicious circle— How can you fix your sexual relationship at home if you're out sleeping with other people?*

Some couples rarely had sex before recovery. One woman reported that she and her husband had no sex with each other for fifteen years. Both assumed it was because of her, but later learned it was a consequence of his addiction.

Some respondents reported arguing, not being able to communicate, and feeling angry and resentful over sex. One man said, "There was lots of tension, anger, shame, and an inability to talk about sex." His wife wrote, "I often said yes to sex when I didn't want to."

Several couples noted that extramarital sex eroded their sexual activity. One addict wrote, "Our sexual relationship was poor because I would feel guilty about my past sexual behaviors and it would inhibit my performance." Another man wrote: "I wasn't present. In sex, I needed fantasy or dangerous activities." His wife responded: "I felt intimidated sexually, always judged and felt wanting. I felt incompetent sexually, so I avoided sex." Yet another man wrote: "She wasn't that satisfying. My sexual attraction to her was limited." His wife responded: "He preferred to masturbate rather than have sex with me. I felt like he did not desire me." Both women felt sexually undesirable while the men preferred their addictive sexual activities.

Why Sex Was Good
One man wrote, "We experienced much joy together." His wife concurred, "We shared mutual pleasure and he was prepared to satisfy me in ways I enjoy most." Another woman wrote about her sex addict husband: "He was always a very caring and concerned

lover. He read all sorts of books about how to please a woman and got very good at it."

Several coaddicts who enjoyed their sexual relationship before recovery felt in retrospect that there was something missing. They wrote: "Ignorance is bliss! I rated our sexual relationship excellent because if I received sex often and with great intensity, then I felt great and loved." . . . "I feel we had an excellent sexual relationship throughout our marriage, physically. Emotionally, I knew he was preoccupied and I took it personally." One man wrote, "Sex was generally playful, fulfilling, frequent, and mutual." His wife responded, "Sex was frequent, orgasmic, and helped mask problems neither of us was able to deal with."

Making love to a "perfect" person or to a mother substitute—roles common to coaddicts—is difficult. As one addict noted: "Sex was regular and pleasant. However, I had times of impotence due to feelings of inadequacy. I felt I had married a saint, so I had some performance anxiety."

Uncomfortable Sexual Practices

In attempting to please their partner sexually, many coaddicts engaged in sexual behaviors contrary to their values, often because they hoped it would prevent their partner from being sexual with others. One woman wrote:

> *I tried to become what I thought he wanted. I prostituted myself and did things in bed that made me feel very uncomfortable. I kept thinking if I tried hard enough to be good in bed, he wouldn't do the other things.*

Others coaddicts believed they had no choice—that it was their duty to give their partner whatever he or she wanted sexually. For some, it may have been easier to give in than to constantly fight about sex. One woman wrote, "I felt it was my 'job' to control him sexually, to be available so he wouldn't rent porno flicks or masturbate all the time."

Two-thirds of coaddicts wrote that they had participated in uncomfortable sexual behaviors. Several reported having sex when they did not want to. "I did it to keep the peace," said one man. Some coaddicts reluctantly agreed to have sex in places other than in the privacy of their home. "We had sex at sex clubs and where people could see us, like on our balcony," according to one woman.

Some coaddicts agreed to participate in sexual activities that they didn't like, such as oral sex, anal sex, bondage, using pornography, or including a third person in sex. Several coaddicts allowed their partner to photograph or videotape their sexual activities. One woman wrote:

> *We read* Playboy *magazines. He thought it would help me expand my sexuality. We had anal intercourse. We watched X-rated movies during sex. He kept trying to bring me into his fantasies to help him live them out. I kept saying, "It's not right" and he kept saying there's nothing wrong between consenting adults. I felt emotionally abused.*

Alcohol and other drug use were often part of the picture for several couples. One addict wrote: "I had sex with a lot of different men, every week. I can't even remember most of their names or faces because I drank a lot too." A coaddict wrote:

> *Nothing seemed uncomfortable at the time, because I was drinking then and blocked out a lot. I have always been uncomfortable with sex any time. It's shameful and humiliating. But he never did or wanted anything weird or kinky.*

Participating in uncomfortable and unwanted sexual behaviors may contribute to coaddicts' low self-esteem. They may conclude they are "as bad as them" or wonder if they are also sex addicts. As a result, coaddict resentment often increases.

Using Sex to Manipulate

Even though most coaddicts did not realize their spouse was sexually addicted, most were aware early on how important sex was to their spouse. Two-thirds of coaddicts reported having used sex to control or manipulate their partner. Some did it to get sex in order to feel loved. One wrote:

> *If he wasn't talking to me, I tried to seduce him. I would buy sex toys thinking I could turn him on and he would have sex at home. In my eyes, sex was equivalent to love.*

Other coaddicts believed they could prevent their partner from acting out by being sexual. They wrote, "He was going to prostitutes, so I tried to have more sex with him." . . . "I believed if I could get him to be sexual with me then he won't want others." . . . "Before either of us left town on business, I tried to have as much sex as possible. I thought that would keep him from wanting to be with other women while we were apart." Another woman recalled:

> *When we fought, I would use sex to make up. And when he would confess to me, we would have lots of sex. I felt the more we had sex, the less likely he would go elsewhere.*

Some coaddicts had sex to please their spouse, not because they themselves wanted to. They wrote: "I said yes to sex to please him, though I didn't want to have sex." . . . "I tried to be cute and seductive, but it did not work. He had no interest in sex with me because he was acting out outside the marriage. I could only assume I did something wrong."

Some women used sex as a reward or punishment. They wrote: "I withheld sex if I was mad or upset, and used sex to make him happy if he was down." . . . "If there was something I wanted, I promised to deliver sex in trade for whatever it was."

Despite dysfunctional patterns, some couples are able to maintain equilibrium for many years until the relationship is stressed to the point where one or both seek help. This often happens as a result of crisis or disclosure—a process referred to in the recovering community as "hitting bottom."

Crisis and Disclosure

As we have seen, long before the underlying problem was identified as sexual addiction, most marriages were being adversely affected by the addict's sexual acting out and the coaddict's response to it. In some marriages, a single crisis occurred that led to disclosure and identification of the addiction. Other couples went through a series of events or crises that gradually revealed the problem. The addict's acting out may have continued during this time or it may have stopped through the use of sheer willpower and determination. In disclosure, some couples were open with each other about extramarital sexual activities, but did not recognize those behaviors as part of an addictive pattern. Some coaddicts did not suspect anything and found out only when the information was volunteered or came out after the addict had a scrape with the law; other coaddicts learned of the addict's acting out only after the addict was already in a recovery program. In our survey, we asked coaddicts: *When you first suspected your spouse was acting out sexually, what did you do about your suspicions? How did you learn definitely about it? What were your reactions?*

The twenty-eight-year-old wife of a man who had a long history of excessive masturbation, pornography use, and voyeurism suspected nothing until her husband told her about his problem after five years of marriage. She wrote:

> He had told me about several things before we were married, but I didn't realize the seriousness of the situation. I didn't realize it was an addictive behavior—he had thought it was just a bad habit. I was scared and confused and didn't know what to do. I really don't want to know anything else because the little I know now makes me scared, especially when I think about having a family.

After twenty-five years of marriage, a woman who learned that her husband was having an affair wrote:

> I had my suspicions, but because of his religious background and his strong stand against adultery, I couldn't believe he'd do this. Even when it was evident to my children, I would say that he

would never commit adultery, although I knew of two times in the past when he had kissed other women.

After seven months of suspecting something, I broke into his desk at work and found one hundred sexy, loving cards and letters from his mistress. We went into counseling and I began to trust him again. Then, I found he'd been with her again. Later, he told me of other affairs. This last time, I knew he was seeing someone, but it took eight weeks before I spied on him and found out.

I hated myself for staying with him. I felt old and ugly because he said he wanted a young body, even though I know I look pretty good for my age. I asked him everything. He got very angry when I asked him. I kicked him out. I found Sexaholics Anonymous meetings for him. I wrote to two of his old mistresses about his addiction and advised them to get an AIDS test. I got tested myself. I told his mother. I saw a lawyer.

Her husband wrote, "She cannot forget what I have done. . . . I have to prove I am worthy of being forgiven." At the time they completed the survey, each had been in a recovery program for only a short time. Her anger and hurt were still very evident. They were not optimistic about the future of their marriage, but were willing to work on it.

A thirty-four-year-old woman, married ten years, wrote:

Two years into our marriage, my husband was arrested for voyeurism. I tried to ignore it and minimize it by saying it was no big deal. I didn't realize that his masturbation and use of pornography was abnormal. I believed my uncomfortable feelings about it meant there was something wrong with me. I always considered myself sexually inexperienced because I had never done the things that I read or that he told me about, so he became my sexual teacher. I kept trying to convince myself it was okay no matter how bad my gut felt about it. Thank God I procrastinated indulging in most of his sexual wish list.

He had an affair four years into our marriage, and then several other sexual experiences, but they were all kept secret until eight months ago when everything came out in a joint therapy session. At first, I went numb because it hurt too much. I thought I was stupid, that I should have known better. I criticized myself for not listening and acting on my gut feelings when things were happening and my husband was lying to me. I was repulsed by him. He was dirty, sick, and yet at the same time I saw a scared little boy who didn't know any better. I hated him for hurting me, yet I was concerned and compassionate for him and all he went through.

I asked him who he had his affairs with and who knew about it. He gave me the information. I knew after the therapy session that he wanted to end the lying. We had the support we needed from our therapist to work through it all.

I ritually cleaned my house—threw out sheets (his last sexual encounter was in my home and in my bed) and became driven to work through and recover from my "disease" as well. I read books, went to S-Anon, spent time alone, went away with my sister, and dealt with major issues in group therapy.

Both members of this couple reported a greatly improved sexual relationship, were working on rebuilding trust, and had optimism about their future together.

A thirty-three-year-old man, married twelve years, had extramarital affairs and also masturbated excessively with pornography. His wife, the mother of several small children, wrote:

After four years of marriage, I found pornographic magazines in the house and confronted him. He promised he'd never do it again. Later, he confessed he had committed adultery and other sexual acts throughout our marriage. I was shocked at first. As the numbness wore off, I got extremely angry and went off like a pressure cooker. All the feelings I'd stuffed for eight years came out. I cried a lot, screamed and yelled, stabbed soap boxes, and pretended it was him. I took long walks alone, and cried every time I saw infidelity on TV. I thought, What had I done wrong? Why was this happening to me? Could I have done something to stop him or make him happier? I felt like my world was falling apart.

He said to ask questions and he would answer them as honestly as possible. I asked him how often it had happened and with whom. Was it anyone I knew?

I went to a Twelve Step program to find out how to fix him. That was over three years ago.

Her husband gave her the information she requested but wrote, "I was scared to death that when she really knew me she would hate me like I hated myself." At the time they completed the survey, both rated their relationship as excellent and were committed to a future together.

A thirty-nine-year-old woman married twenty years had a series of affairs. Her husband wrote:

I knew about an affair after seven years of marriage. Later, after sixteen years, I became suspicious again, but I believed her story and suppressed my suspicions. Of course, I wanted to believe she would end the affair and choose to love me. As long as I didn't openly know about it, I ignored it. Finally, I confronted her and she confessed, but she lied to hide her present relationship. I believed she was revealing a past but not present affair. After four months of unrest, I figured it out.

I felt abused, used, manipulated, angry, foolish, inadequate, unloved, and rejected. I questioned her love. I doubted she wanted me in her future. I asked her for information about her feelings, the seriousness of the relationship, handling of birth control and disease concerns, and number of sexual encounters, but she wouldn't tell me much about her activities or feelings. I stopped having sex with her and insisted she go to counseling.

When this couple filled out the survey, they were in early recovery and still dealing with fundamental issues of rebuilding trust.

These are stories of betrayal, anger, and deteriorating relationships, but they are also stories of efforts to restore a marriage. Reconciliation appears to happen more quickly when an honest exchange of facts and feelings occurs.

Discovering the Addiction

When the addict's sexual behaviors are understood as an addiction, the couple can move to another level of healing and begin recovery. In our survey, we asked how this awareness came about. Often the addict sought professional help, and then a therapist or chemical dependency counselor suggested the diagnosis. One woman sex addict wrote: "Our marriage counseling separated into individual counseling and my psychologist diagnosed me as a sexaholic and gave me *Out of the Shadows*. Reading the book convinced me." Men addicts wrote: "Fourteen years into my first marriage, I attended a family program at a treatment center and recognized my addiction then." . . . "After I was arrested for soliciting a prostitute, I went to a therapist who identified my sexual addiction. I sought therapy for obsessive sexual thoughts."

Coaddicts wrote: "After two years of marriage, information about his affairs came out. We went to counseling and our counselors told us to read *Out of the Shadows*." . . . "He was undergoing therapy for his overeating and was confronted by his therapist about his sexual addiction."

Several addicts did not realize they were addicted until their spouse took action. Coaddicts either decided to leave, insisted that the addicts seek counseling, or supplied them with information about sexual addiction. Addicts wrote: "My psychotherapist had been telling me for a year that I was sexually and alcoholically addicted, but I didn't believe him until my wife left me. That was after twenty-seven years of marriage." . . . "My wife showed me information and invited me to go to meetings." . . . "My husband confronted me and forced me to go to treatment." . . . "My therapist suggested I had a compulsive problem and recommended SA after my wife threatened divorce." One couple reported:

HUSBAND: *After my last affair, she threw me out of the house, so I attended an SA meeting, read Carnes' book and Sexaholics Anonymous, and realized the symptoms described me.*

WIFE: *After twenty-eight years of marriage, I found out about yet another affair and kicked him out of the house. He said it was like an addiction, so I contacted AA and found out there were SA meetings for him, S-Anon for me.*

Some addicts recognized their addiction only when their lives became unmanageable. They bottomed out in dramatic ways: "After twenty years of marriage I was arrested and went to counseling." . . . "His last affair became public knowledge at work, where he was a counselor." . . . "He was arrested for soliciting a prostitute." . . . "I was arrested for exposure."

In the past few years, sexual addiction has garnered increasing attention in the media. Some addicts recognized themselves as addicts after addictive behavior was described on TV. This was the case for several of our survey respondents, who wrote: "My wife saw Patrick Carnes talk about sexual addiction on TV." . . . "I knew I had a problem before we got married. I couldn't stop masturbating. One reason for marriage was that I thought it would cure me, but it didn't. The problem was progressive. I saw a program on TV that identified this behavior as sexual addiction."

Other Twelve Step programs are excellent sources of information about sexual addiction. A large number of sex addicts attend Alcoholics Anonymous, Narcotics Anonymous, or Overeaters Anonymous. Addicts wrote: "I kept putting the sexual stuff into my Fourth Step in OA, and finally a counselor there mentioned sex addiction." . . . "I was nearly arrested for my sexual acting out. I heard mention of SA at an OA meeting, so I started going."

Spouses of sex addicts who attend self-help groups, such as S-Anon or Codependents Anonymous (CODA) meetings, may get information there about sexual addiction to recognize the addiction in themselves. One woman wrote, "When I began attending S-Anon, I realized from their descriptions of sex addicts that I was one."

Discovering the Coaddiction

Identifying coaddiction often comes about after the recognition of a family member's sexual addiction. According to several women: "I began to become aware of my coaddiction after my husband told me about his gambling addiction—he was a 'closet' addict with both sex and gambling. Gam-Anon made me aware of how deeply I was focused on my husband's life and problems." . . . "I found out he was a sex addict and realized that I must be a coaddict." Some coaddicts became aware of their coaddiction only when their spouse urged them to attend Twelve Step meetings. One woman wrote:

> *When my husband began attending SA, he suggested to me that I attend S-Anon. I was incensed—it was bad enough that he had put me through the pain of his betrayal. Now, I was supposed to get myself fixed! I didn't think there was anything wrong with me. But in order to please him, I went to the meetings. It didn't take me long to recognize that I was a coaddict—that I had felt responsible for his happiness, that I had given him all the power for my happiness, and that I took the blame for the problems in our marriage.*

Some addicts recognized their own coaddiction after months or years of recovery from addiction. One man wrote, "Only recently in my recovery from sexual addiction have I begun to recognize my coaddiction." (The relationship between addiction and coaddiction in the same person is discussed in greater detail in Chapter Eleven.)

Dealing with Disclosure

Either before or after the addict recognized that his or her problem sexual behaviors were an addiction, the spouse was given some information. This disclosure is an important step in healing the relationship because it sets the stage for a new relationship based on honesty and respect. This was the experience of Alice, a forty-two-year-old research scientist quoted in *Back from Betrayal:*[1]

> *When my husband first told me about his affair, I felt a tremendous need to put the pieces together. I asked for specific dates, for details on the ups and downs of their relationship. It was painful to hear the answers, and my husband kept trying to end the dialogue. But I insisted, and he answered everything I asked. There were things I didn't ask, because I didn't want to know.*
>
> *The answers I got to my questions provided explanations for so many puzzling things that had happened, so many times I'd*

thought I was crazy. Now I knew why he had been so hurtful on a particular vacation. I had said, "You're so good to me," and his guilt over the affair, which was at its peak at that time, made him unable to accept the compliment; he needed to prove to me on the spot that he wasn't good to me. . . . Now I knew that I hadn't been crazy after all, that I had been right those times when I'd had a strong gut feeling that something was wrong, that he had been lying when he'd told me, "You're just imagining things."

I realized that on one level I had been aware all along of what was happening with him. To have him tell me the truth was to acknowledge the validity of those feelings. And another thing: Over the years I had begun to distrust him. Things just didn't add up. Not to have told me would have kept the distrust going. By answering all my questions, my husband began to rebuild trust in the relationship. This was a process that took many months. It is true that "the best amends is a changed life over time." But for me, the first step toward renewed trust after all the deceit was to receive honest answers from him. Honesty was crucial to the survival of our marriage during that crisis; I am glad he told me about his past.

In our survey, we asked how couples handled disclosure. Nearly all coaddicts requested some information from their spouse. A few wanted to know every detail, large and small, from beginning to end, including graphic descriptions of their sexual activities.

In the AIDS era, many spouses asked their partner for information about sexual activities that would put them at risk, especially if the activities had been with gay men or prostitutes. Since the HIV virus is transmitted via body fluids, unsafe sexual practices are those in which any body fluids are exchanged. Anal intercourse is particularly dangerous because the lining of the rectum is easily torn and semen or blood containing the virus can be absorbed. Vaginal intercourse can also be unsafe. One woman wrote, "I wanted to know with whom, how often, how much actual intercourse, and how much I was at risk for contracting AIDS."

How Coaddicts Felt

Some spouses wanted to understand why the extramarital sex happened. They wrote: "I wanted to know who, what she looked like, generally what took place, where, when, and WHY, WHY, WHY." . . . "How many times were you with her? Do you love her? Does her husband know? Were there others?"

Several spouses also wanted information that could help them sort out the past. They asked for verification and whether or not what they had suspected was real. This kind of information they needed to validate their own sanity. Respondents wrote: "I asked her when she had had the affairs, in order to connect them with suspicious events." . . . "I wanted to know how many affairs? When did they happen? How long did they last? What was going on at the time?"

Most spouses reported that they were given at least some of the information they requested. Some recalled that the addict was very open with them and willing to answer all their questions. These respondents wrote: "She told me almost everything I wanted to know. She lied about who the men were, but she confessed this the following day." . . . "He told me whatever I wanted to know. I needed that! It hurt, but at the same time was very cleansing for me."

Some addicts cautioned their spouses against asking for too much information. One woman wrote:

> He said, "I will tell you what you want to know but be sure you really want the details as then you will have to live with them."

Some addicts were reluctant to give information: "He would tell me what I asked. I'm sure he didn't tell me everything, but enough to satisfy me and make me feel like he was being honest." . . . "He told me some, not all, thank God."

Some addicts lied, made excuses, or refused to give any information: "She said she was not doing anything." . . . "He told me, 'I have been told it's not good to say too much in the beginning. I really would rather not tell you.' " . . . "He told me, 'It's none of your business. I will take care of it myself in my own time.' "

Some addicts were willing to give more information than their partner was ready to hear: "I didn't want to know about his homosexual activities, but he began to tell me and invited me to go with him to meet his gay friends. I said no. It tears me up to hear any of it."

How Addicts Felt

We also asked in our survey how the addicts felt about disclosure. Some addicts never shared specifics; others revealed every detail. Some addicts volunteered information; others spoke only under duress. One man told us: "She guessed many times and I would deny. I would confess only to what I found out she already knew and even then I would lie." Eventually, he told his wife the truth.

Other addicts, too, tried to reveal only the minimum. Other men told us: "My wife is aware of the nature of my illness in general terms. I never shared specifics." . . . "I felt vulnerable. I did not want to tell her. There are still some minor things I have not fully disclosed." . . . "I haven't told her all because I feel it would destroy her."

Several addicts were fearful or reluctant to disclose their behaviors but did it anyway, with mixed results. They wrote: "I felt sad, ashamed, depressed." . . . "She demanded to know all the details. Upon hearing them, she called me the lowest thing on earth. It was the first time in my life that I considered suicide." . . . "I was afraid she would leave me." . . . "I wish I hadn't told him—it made him trust me less." . . . "I thought it would fix everything, a confessional kind of thing. I thought she would immediately forgive me, but she let me down by acting hurt. I thought she had promised me that she would understand. I realize the codependency of that now, but then I just felt like she had broken my trust."

Many addicts were glad they had spoken with their spouse. Some comments were: "I felt very good. It helped both of us." . . . "Relief! Like a terrific weight was lifted off of me." . . . "I felt good but uneasy because of fears I would be rejected and thought of as a pervert or freak."

Some addicts waited to tell their spouse until they had been in a recovery program for a while. In one case, the revelation was not intentional. As part of his Twelve Step program, a man had written out an inventory of his past behaviors. He wrote, "She found two of my Fourth Steps and demanded an explanation. I was relieved."

In several cases, the disclosure was not news — the spouse was already aware that there was a problem, but had believed it was not ongoing. Addicts wrote: "She knew I had been arrested in the past for indecent exposure, but I downplayed my addiction as not active." . . . "She knew that I was bisexual and had acted out prior to the marriage. Being honest about the continuing behavior was hard, but I felt it was necessary for my recovery."

Concern About AIDS

We asked men and women if they were concerned about the threat of AIDS and other sexually transmitted diseases. Since the early 1980s, the number of AIDS cases in the United States has increased exponentially. More than 120,000 cases were reported by 1990 and an additional one to two million people are infected with the HIV virus but not yet showing symptoms. Women comprise approximately 9 percent of AIDS patients.

In our survey, most addicts were not concerned about their risk of catching AIDS. Several men and women who were having multiple affairs did not believe they were at risk. Two men who were sexual with other men knew about safe sex but practiced it only some of the time. One reported, "I didn't act out as often and sometimes wore condoms."

A young woman who had multiple affairs recalled:

> I have a brother who's HIV-positive. It's a real issue for me. I do AIDS counseling and I work with AIDS patients. It didn't stop me from acting out, though. I didn't even insist my partners use condoms. I told myself that I was special, different, and that I'm too selective or careful to contract the virus.

Other addicts also talked about their denial: "I was too far gone to even think that it could happen to me." . . . "As sad as this may sound, I did nothing to prevent the disease. I became convinced that I was going to catch AIDS and die. I even worked out a plan to commit suicide when it was confirmed that I had the virus. I hated myself for this but still couldn't stop."

One man handled his fear of transmitting AIDS to his wife by withdrawing sexually from her altogether. One woman told us, "I gave my husband venereal warts but denied it was me who gave them to him."

Spouses of sex addicts were generally in less denial than the addicts about the risk of contracting the AIDS virus. Many asked their partner to get tested for AIDS and several set very clear boundaries. One woman wrote:

> *We didn't have sex until after he got a negative result, then we used a condom until after receiving his six-month negative test. He just got a one-year negative test.*

Others thought about the possibility and decided their partner had not engaged in sexual activities that put them at risk. A few coaddicts were clearly in denial. For example, a man who had had multiple homosexual encounters wrote he was sure he must have caught AIDS—but chose not to get tested. His wife said, "I don't want to know."

* * * * *

Many people who told us their stories were in the midst of the crisis of disclosure. Some marriages appeared to be headed for dissolution. But most relationships somehow survived. How did they do it? Where did they get help? This is the focus of the next chapter.

CHAPTER FOUR

Getting Help

"I was in the midst of another affair and I went to see a psychiatrist. I knew my sexual behavior was out of control. I kept getting into relationships with people who I didn't really want to be with. After all, I was married, had several kids, and felt really lousy about what I was doing. Anyway, Dr. Crow was this traditional shrink who did nothing but listen and nod. I didn't quite tell him the truth. I told him my affairs were a thing of the past because I thought I could stop anytime I wanted to. I did a lot of talking, but nothing changed.

"About a year later, I decided that if I could only feel better about my marriage there would be no need to see other women. My wife and I went for marriage counseling. We were never asked about our sexual relationship, nor about outside affairs. Even when I was not involved in an affair, I was thinking about who among the women I knew could be a potential romantic partner. Although I enjoyed sex with my wife, I continued to masturbate and read pornography, and occasionally sneak off in the afternoon to an adult movie theater. Anyway, we worked on communication and talked about feelings, but I continued seeing other women.

"During my last messy affair, I was seeing a psychologist who had been highly recommended to me by a friend. I don't think I used the word addiction to describe my sexual behavior, but I told him that women were like alcohol for me, that I would just empty the bottles and toss them out. He never understood what I was trying to say. According to him, I just had to understand my family of origin issues and go through a 'redecision process.' So we talked about my childhood and I continued sleeping with other women. When I found a Twelve Step program for sex addicts, I told him about my discovery and what I had learned about my behavior. He was noncommittal and I got the impression that he really didn't want to be confused with the facts. I know several other men who are struggling with problem sexual behavior and are seeing the same psychologist—they aren't getting any more help than I did. I feel really angry about this."

This account, given to us by a married man who has had no more affairs since beginning his recovery from sexual addiction over six years ago, is unfortunately typical of the experiences of many who seek counseling or traditional psychiatric help for problem sexual behavior. The fact is, the vast majority of those we surveyed—96 percent of addicts and 87 percent of coaddicts—did seek therapy for problems related to the addiction.

In this chapter, we will report the experiences this group had with therapy and will describe for therapists and potential clients what treatment approaches appeared to be helpful to couples who are struggling with sexual addiction and coaddiction. We will also discuss the role of Twelve Step programs in facilitating recovery.

Sexual Addiction Treatment Programs

There are few inpatient programs specifically for sexual addiction. New ones are, however, being developed. In addition, there is an increasing understanding of the relationship between chemical dependency and sexual addiction. A number of chemical dependency treatment programs routinely include a sexual history as part of their assessment. If it appears that patients are sexually addicted, they are sometimes referred after treatment for chemical dependency to a facility that offers treatment for sexual addiction. But all too often, the belief is that once patients get clean and sober, sexual problems will be healed as well. There is some debate among chemical dependency counselors as to whether sexual addiction is real and should be addressed at all. Some counselors who deny the validity of sexual addiction may want to avoid looking at their own sexual issues. In any case, most treatment programs do not have staff with extensive training in sexual addiction and recovery.

Inpatient programs generally consist of four to six weeks of group therapy sessions, some individual therapy, educational lectures, and usually an introduction to Twelve Step programs. Relatives of patients are often asked to attend a family week where they are given information about addiction and the role families play in the process.

Patrick Carnes, who developed the first inpatient program for sexual addiction, has said that the risk of relapse is greatest for the patient whose family members do not themselves get involved in the recovery process. Simply stated, family members need to look at and work on their own feelings and behaviors as well. Recovering persons need a healthy family system in which to grow.

Another important element of the inpatient program is formulation of an aftercare plan. It is less difficult to abstain from drugs or addictive behaviors while in a treatment center that supports recovery. But what happens when people return to the real world with its stresses and temptations? Clearly, the inpatient program is only the beginning of the recovery process. The real test comes in the following weeks and months.

Whether inpatient programs are actually better than outpatient is a widely debated question. Some studies show no significant difference in the outcome of inpatient or outpatient chemical dependency treatment. No similar studies are yet available on the outcome of treatment for sexual addiction.

A knowledgeable therapist can help in this decision. You are likely to benefit from inpatient treatment if (1) you have tried counseling or outpatient treatment along with attendance at Twelve Step programs but cannot stay sexually sober, (2) the people you live with do not support your recovery or may be addicted themselves, and (3) your behavior is so dangerous—to yourself or others—that it must be stopped immediately.

Among the people in our survey, 9 percent of addicts had been through an inpatient program for sexual addiction. All said it was a positive experience and none subsequently relapsed. One man rated his treatment excellent for both educational and therapeutic value and wrote that "the main shortcoming was the lack of availability of aftercare counseling."

Eleven percent of sex addicts and 5 percent of coaddicts in our survey went through inpatient treatment for chemical dependency, with generally positive results. Several of these people reported that chemical dependency treatment led them to look at their sexual behavior.

Codependency Treatment Programs

Seven people in our survey had inpatient treatment for codependency. A forty-five-year-old woman who went through codependency treatment wrote:

> I learned a great deal about sexual addiction. I felt the coaddict program was much weaker. They need to really work on this program and address codependency in all their lectures. Also address what is sobriety for a coaddict.

If you are considering inpatient codependency treatment, ask what proportion of lectures and groups are conducted jointly with addicts. Try to determine if the program addresses codependency as a primary disorder or focuses on addiction. Many treatment centers subscribe to the theory that "addiction is addiction is addiction" and have patients who are chemically dependent in the same groups as codependents, sex addicts, and those with eating disorders. We believe there need to be specialized lectures and groups for codependents.

An even more basic question is, How do you decide if you need inpatient codependency treatment? When will outpatient treatment suffice? The following are stories of two women who chose inpatient treatment and are glad they did.

. . . Suzanne, fifty, was well known in her community for her many volunteer projects and boundless energy. What her admirers did not realize was that Suzanne's husband, a high-powered attorney, bullied and intimidated her and made no effort to hide from her his multiple affairs, which he claimed were a consequence of her personality failings and unattractiveness. When Suzanne learned of a support group for spouses of sex addicts and began to attend, her husband escalated his verbal abuse in an attempt to prevent her from going to the meetings.

The information and support Suzanne obtained at the meetings allowed her to stand up to her husband for the first time in their thirty years of marriage. As a result, her home situation became increasingly tense. Her husband did not want other people knowing about family problems and insisted Suzanne stay at home.

At this point, Suzanne decided she needed a safer environment in which to begin working seriously on her codependency and arranged admission to an inpatient treatment program. Her husband, now fearful that she might leave him, agreed to attend family week, and after her treatment ended, agreed to go to counseling with her. She says he is still very much in denial about the seriousness of his behavior, and she is not optimistic about the future of their marriage, but for the first time she feels empowered and recognizes she has choices.

Suzanne's home environment was too hostile to permit her to work on her own recovery. In the safety of the treatment center she was able to work on her own recovery and give her husband the message that she was very serious about making changes in her life and her relationship with him.

. . . Lorraine, thirty-four, the mother of three small children, fell apart when her suspicions of her husband's infidelity were confirmed. After he told her the truth, she first began having nightmares and then actual memories of childhood incest. Depression made it impossible for her to care for her children. She came across Patrick Carnes' book Out of the Shadows *and decided her*

husband was a sex addict. Her next step was to check into an inpatient treatment center that also treated sex addicts.

After a month of treatment for sexual coaddiction and incest, Lorraine returned home much strengthened and announced to her husband that she would not stay married unless he, too, went for treatment. She obviously meant it. Presented with this clear message, her husband chose treatment over divorce.

Now, five years later, Lorraine and her husband are both active in Twelve Step programs and are committed to their relationship. Lorraine considers her inpatient treatment a major turning point in her life.

Lorraine was too overwhelmed by the disclosure of her husband's affairs and the new awareness of her own incest experience to be able to function effectively. A time-out in inpatient treatment allowed her to begin healing.

Outpatient Addiction Treatment
Outpatient treatment may consist of one-on-one counseling and attendance at Twelve Step meetings, or it may be more formal, consisting of lectures and therapy groups three or four times a week for four to twelve weeks. Outpatients may also be encouraged or required to attend a minimum number of self-help meetings. Such programs often offer aftercare that typically involves attending weekly meetings for up to a year.

Of those responding to our survey, 5 percent had gone through some type of outpatient chemical dependency treatment. (It is interesting to note that although 29 percent of respondents said they were also recovering from chemical dependency, only 13 percent had obtained professional help. Most apparently obtained recovery through AA.)

Twelve Step Programs
The value of Twelve Step programs is widely accepted for recovery from chemical dependency. Fellowships modeled after AA are

now helping people with other addictions such as compulsive gambling, eating disorders, and sexual addiction.

Since we drew most of our respondents from Twelve Step programs dealing with sexual addiction, we were not surprised that 79 percent of addicts were attending meetings for sex addicts. Twenty-nine percent were involved in Twelve Step programs in addition to Sexaholics Anonymous (SA), Sex Addicts Anonymous (SAA), or Sex and Love Addicts Anonymous (SLAA). For example, 19 percent of addicts were also attending AA. Sex addicts in our survey were also attending Overeaters Anonymous (OA), Al-Anon, and Codependents Anonymous (CODA). Ten percent of addicts were attending no Twelve Step program at the time they filled out the survey, 8 percent were attending only AA, and 5 percent were attending only OA or Al-Anon. Several addicts who had been in recovery for years stated they used to attend SA, AA, and other programs but had stopped.

Most coaddicts (71 percent) were attending S-Anon or Codependents of Sex Addicts (COSA). Others stated that these programs were not available in their city, so they were attending Al-Anon, OA, CODA, SA, AA, Gam-Anon, or other programs. Ten percent were attending no Twelve Step program. Several told us that they had attended such programs in the past.

Nearly half were currently attending a Twelve Step couples' group, such as S-Anon Recovering Couples or Recovering Couples Anonymous (RCA). These meetings differ in format from other Twelve Step meetings by encouraging both members of the couple to share one after the other. Typical topics for discussion include learning to fight fairly, learning to trust again, how to avoid monitoring our partner's recovery program, forgiveness, changes in our sexual relationship, intimacy, and talking to children about our recovery program. The goal of these meetings is to promote couple recovery. They fill a gap in traditional Twelve Step programs, which are for individual recovery. Like the individual meetings, the couples' meetings are not confrontational and no advice is given. Couples learn by hearing how others are dealing with the issue at hand, the mistakes they have made, and what works for them. A therapist we know encourages some of her clients to attend to see how other recovering couples deal with specific issues. "It's wonderful for them to see role models," she said. Those who attended couples' meetings said they were very valuable. Some comments from our survey were: "Extremely valuable. It helps my husband and me work on communication and intimacy." . . . "We hear much about our feelings and others' feelings in recovery." . . . "It's very valuable for our relationship and our social life. We feel like we're part of life again." . . . "Invaluable contact with other couples. Nonsexual contact with the men in the group has helped me to make a male friend, I think the second in my life."

Counseling and Psychotherapy

Most respondents had at some time obtained counseling or therapy. Individually, as couples, or in a group setting, they saw psychiatrists, psychologists, psychotherapists, social workers, master's level counselors, clergy, marriage counselors, family counselors, sex therapists, and addiction counselors. We will use the term "therapy" to describe the services provided by all these professionals. Most respondents (79 percent of addicts and 69 percent of coaddicts) had seen more than one therapist.

Positive Results with First Therapist Were Rare

A successful therapeutic outcome in the first attempt is uncommon for people affected by sexual addiction. Nonetheless, a knowledgeable therapist with training in sexual addiction may be able to identify the problem. For example, a thirty-year-old nurse sought therapy after her husband, a physics professor, was arrested for soliciting a prostitute. She believed that her husband's interest in prostitutes was her fault, and that the primary marital problem was that she had lost all interest in sex. In therapy, it was learned that the husband had a long history of extramarital sexual activity and frequent masturbation. The couple wrote:

HUSBAND: *I went to the therapist because my wife was referred. The therapist diagnosed sexual addiction in me. I accept this diagnosis and agree with it. I am still in individual therapy with this therapist.*

WIFE: *I first went to deal with my sexual problem. I am now continuing for this and for codependency. I feel therapy is helping my progress, but it's still slow. Changes I'm trying to make in myself aren't easy.*

Both were attending Twelve Step meetings and both believed it very likely they would remain together.

Many therapists are trained to recognize chemical dependency. Only a few, however, have been trained to recognize sexual addiction. Most therapists do not consider the possibility of sexual addiction, even in clients in whom they have identified chemical dependency. Often, therapists who do identify sexual addiction are led to the diagnosis by their patients.

A young man and his fiancé consulted a therapist because they wanted a compatibility check. The man wrote: "My chemical use was recognized but not my sexual addiction. After over two years in AA, I finally recognized my sexual addiction and sought help in SA."

A forty-year-old housewife, a recovering alcoholic who had been sexually abused by her father, wrote:

After codependency treatment, I went to a women's group for five months, with excellent results. I knew that I was a sexual coaddict, a codependent, and felt desperate for help. There was no S-Anon here at that time and Al-Anon was not helping me fast enough. The treatment gave me healing and solutions and hope and strength.

Several other people who sought therapy after they had begun attending Twelve Step programs believed counseling had been beneficial. A man in his thirties, recovering from chemical dependency as well as from sexual addiction, reported:

I went to therapy to deal with issues in my life that I felt were at the root of my sexual addiction, and to deal with my codepen-

dency. After I had stopped acting out sexually, I needed guidance to teach me how to live noncompulsively.

A young social worker and her husband sought marriage counseling after the husband identified himself as a sex addict. The wife subsequently attended an incest survivors group for three months. She believed both experiences were helpful and wrote:

I feel the counseling in conjunction with Twelve Step groups was vital to my recovery. The marriage counseling helped identify patterns of communication that were dysfunctional. We learned how to support one another, listen, and talk intimately. And I don't think I could have worked through the molestation without counseling.

Dealing with childhood incest or rape usually requires professional help. Depending on the severity of the unresolved trauma, this may range from brief group therapy to long-term intensive individual and group therapy lasting two years or more. Because incest survivors often have sexual problems, sex therapy for both members of a couple may be necessary as a final step following the work with the partner who was molested.

Most Had Both Good and Bad Experiences with Therapy
A man who had as part of his sexual addiction engaged in affairs, masturbated excessively, and read pornography was separated from his wife as they worked on their individual recovery and on couple issues. Both said they were still committed to the relationship. In describing their therapy history, they wrote:

HUSBAND: *I went to counseling on and off over a three-year period. I went to try to salvage the marriage after my wife found out about one of my affairs. I felt uncomfortable and did not really want to go. I felt my behavior was compulsive, but the counselor did not identify it as such.*

WIFE: *We also went to couple counseling for two and a half years. The therapist was a nice man, but he didn't recognize addiction.*

*My husband lied to both of us and would not do any of the things
the therapist suggested.*

The same couple reported better results with subsequent treatment. They wrote:

HUSBAND: *I changed to a sexual addiction counselor because of his
specialty. I felt I made some progress with him, but I had to stop
going due to lack of insurance coverage.*

WIFE: *I went to a codependency group for four months. The group
was too large and diverse for me, but the therapists were good. The
result was that I realized I was seriously codependent. I recognized
my dysfunctional family of origin, my shame-based soul, and my
husband's.*

This couple's experience demonstrates two points. First, addicts
who go to therapy under duress (for example, "to salvage the marriage") rather than because they recognize the need to make
changes, may lie to the therapist about their sexual activities. Even
if they don't do this deliberately, it is likely that because of denial
they will underestimate the seriousness of their problem. Unless
therapists are skilled in recognizing addictive patterns, they will
miss the diagnosis. Second, treatment is likely to be most effective
when addicts realize they need help. When this man was finally
ready to own up to the nature of his problem, he sought a therapist
familiar with sexual addiction and made progress in treatment.

*Therapists Not Familiar with Sexual
Addiction Are Often Ineffective*
When a couple comes to therapy because of problems with extramarital affairs or other sexual problems in the marriage, therapists
should take a complete sexual history from each partner individually, since privacy will increase the chances of getting honest answers. If the history suggests sexual addiction, it might be advisable
for therapists to refer the couple to someone experienced in this
area.

A therapist who recommends masturbation or other sexual exercises without understanding the full extent of a client's sexual problems can do more harm than good. For example, a forty-nine-year-old man saw a marriage and family counselor for help with family problems. The man had a history of excessive masturbation with pornography as well as extramarital affairs. He wrote: "The therapist, knowing nothing about sexual addiction, encouraged me to masturbate when my spouse did not want to be sexual. This compounded my pain and shame."

Attitudes about masturbation have come full circle in the past fifty years. For generations, masturbation was looked upon as immoral, unnatural, and likely to lead to blindness, mental deficiency, loss of manly vigor, pimples, cancer, insanity, and a score of other ills. Now, however, masturbation is recognized by therapists as a healthy activity that is practiced by most men and women.

For most people, masturbation is self-nurturing. But for persons who have a history of excessive masturbation—people whose frequent masturbation has caused them injury or interfered with their relationships and work—more masturbation is not the answer. In fact, they may need to have a respite from it. Nor is masturbation a good idea for those people whose sexual acting out has included masturbation, while making obscene phone calls, for example. For these people, the fantasies that accompany masturbation may lead to a loss of control and an increased risk of other sexual acting out.

A couple in their thirties and married for ten years were several months into recovery. The husband's previous problem sexual behaviors included excessive masturbation to pornography, multiple affairs, voyeurism, and exhibitionism. He was eventually arrested for voyeurism. He wrote:

> *I was ordered by the court to go to traditional individual therapy for six months. My addiction was not recognized. The therapy taught me to use "acceptable" voyeurism. As a result, I became sneakier. Later, I went to another counselor, who recognized my addiction and had me check out SA. I'm now getting individual and group therapy.*

Despite court-ordered therapy for the man's voyeurism, he did not stop acting out. Instead, he simply became better at avoiding arrest. In other words, even when the therapist is not handicapped by the patient's denial, treatment may be ineffective unless the behavior is recognized as being part of an addictive pattern. Traditional therapy that consists of behavior modification techniques is likely to result in only superficial changes, and the client is likely to act out again in the future, particularly when feeling stressful.

Survey respondents who engaged in antisocial addictive behaviors such as exhibitionism, voyeurism, and inapproriate touching were particularly likely to have had a history of ineffective therapy with a long string of therapists. For example, a thirty-nine-year-old technician in SA for four months had seen five therapists. This man was arrested several times for voyeurism and exhibitionism. His fourth counselor recognized the addictive nature of the behavior and resigned from the case, feeling unqualified. Finally, the fifth counselor worked with the client in conjunction with the Twelve Step program.

One young man in recovery in SA for over a year without a relapse saw three therapists before his addiction was recognized. He told us:

I was in therapy for three years before my sexual addiction was recognized. I started going before I got married to get help for my drug dependency and to stop patronizing prostitutes. My marriage was seen as the successful culmination of therapy. I stopped therapy one year before I started acting out during my marriage.

Later, I sought treatment for my sexual addiction, working with issues of self-esteem and examining the addictive cycle. This is still ongoing.

This man's therapist apparently assumed that the presence of a steady sexual partner would fulfill his client's needs that were previously met by prostitutes, pornography, and masturbation. The therapist apparently did not realize that people who are sex addicts may prefer nonmarital sex.

Sex, Lies, and Forgiveness

A young businesswoman in her first marriage wanted sex several times a day, fantasized around the clock, flirted excessively, and tried to convince her husband to "swing." She wrote:

I first went to a counselor because I had had sex with a stranger while I was living with someone who I was going to marry. I sought help to try to understand why I was behaving this way. I loved the man I was living with. I went to counseling for two months, but my addiction was not recognized.

Later, my husband and I went to a psychologist for marriage counseling. It was not effective and we chose to see the therapist individually. My psychologist diagnosed me as a sex addict and gave me Out of the Shadows. *Reading the book convinced me that I was addicted to sex.*

A homemaker and mother of small children knew for years that her husband was seeing prostitutes. She wrote:

I saw the first counselor because I had lost a baby and was suffering depression, but the real problem was my husband's addiction. The therapist was the first person I told about my husband's addiction, but he didn't understand it at all. He just got me through the crisis. With the second counselor, I was still depressed and my husband was acting out a lot. We just talked through the crisis. I was sent by clergy to see the third counselor. He understood some, but still didn't know it was an addiction.

I'm now seeing a counselor who's a recovering coaddict and totally understands the Twelve Steps and addiction. It's like the difference between night and day. We're dealing with my issues, not my husband's. It's helping me understand myself and how I respond to his addiction. We're also seeing a marriage counselor. This counselor understands addiction and is dealing with changing the way we talk to and perceive each other. He's helping us communicate and deal with our emotions.

66

When the Coaddict Is Depressed
Depression is a common symptom of codependency, and there is often an event that precipitates depression. But when depression is chronic and seems unrelated to a specific event, consultation with a psychiatrist and antidepressant medication may be appropriate. For many people, though, traditional therapy combined with self-help group participation may bring about enough change to relieve the depression.

When Only One Is Seen as the Problem
When addiction tears apart a marriage, it is frequently the woman who seeks help for herself. This can lead to positive change in the marriage, and sometimes the man will agree to counseling because the woman sought help. But if the therapist perceives that the woman is the primary cause of the problems, the marriage will not improve and no real changes will occur. Effective counseling requires looking at the role of both partners. This idea was made clear by a homemaker in her thirties who had problems with therapists who perceived her as the primary cause of problems in her marriage. She wrote:

> *For my husband, sex with me was just a substitute for masturbating to porno movies. We had no intimacy. I went to several counselors. Every single time my husband and I went to counseling, it was because I had a problem that was hampering our marriage and we couldn't get it worked out by ourselves. Truly, I was the "identified patient." For example, when we went to a marriage counselor for three months, my husband's masturbating was seen as a "stress reliever." I did and still do have childhood issues that impact our life together, but it took a counselor who was a recovering person to spot my husband as having an equal part. The counselor recognized the addiction and got us into SA and S-Anon. I'm currently in a therapy group as well, working on codependency, inner child work, and shame reduction.*

Therapists Need to Be Willing to Learn from Clients
Because the concept of sexual addiction is relatively new, most therapists have had no training in this area. Yet some therapists are so entrenched in their own beliefs that they are unwilling to consider new approaches; other therapists are ready to try. Some survey respondents were fortunate enough to consult therapists who were ready to try. A middle-aged art teacher in recovery for eight months wrote that he found help with a psychotherapist whom he had seen for three years. Before this, he briefly saw two psychiatrists whom he did not find helpful in stopping his pattern of using pornography, patronizing prostitutes, and having affairs. He wrote:

I went to therapy originally for being "obsessed with sex," in my own words. No one recognized me as an addict until I heard of the SA program and went myself to find out if I belonged there. I read Out of the Shadows *as recommended by my mate and strongly identified with it. Meanwhile, my present therapist has become familiar with Twelve Step programs and now my therapy is geared to complement my program.*

What is interesting in this case is that the art teacher was in therapy for approximately two years before he identified himself as a sex addict. And rather than feel threatened by this, his therapist recognized the value of a different approach, learned about it, and incorporated it into his treatment plan. The result was a grateful patient who was succeeding in changing his behavior.

Therapists do their clients a disservice when they are unwilling to consider a diagnosis because they are unfamiliar with it. When therapists distrust self-help groups and discourage clients from attending, they impede recovery.

A physician who was recovering from sexual addiction and his wife were attending a Twelve Step group and found it very helpful. But they stopped attending the meeting on their therapist's advice. She had expressed concern that a meeting not led by a professional might get out of hand and do more harm than good.

Therapists who actively discourage clients from attending Twelve

Step meetings are forcing them to choose between therapy and the self-help group. This may cause clients, who feel they are being helped by the group, to doubt their own judgment. After all, the therapists are being paid to be experts, and clients often want to please their therapist.

Pleasing others is important to most people. In addition, many people have difficulty dealing with authority figures. They fear being assertive with people in power. In a therapist/client relationship, the therapist is inevitably the one with more power. When therapists discourage clients from attending Twelve Step meetings, many clients will most likely stop going.

Therapists who have clients attending Twelve Step meetings might take the opportunity to learn more about Twelve Step programs. In addition to reading about the Twelve Steps and talking with the client, it would be informative to attend an open meeting to see firsthand what happens at these meetings. Therapists who can work along with the Twelve Step program are powerful allies in the recovery process.

For Some, Therapy Never Helped

Although most respondents who went to several therapists eventually found one who was helpful, some only reported negative experiences. A forty-year-old man in his second marriage recalled what happened when he went for counseling during his first marriage. He wrote:

> *Originally, my first wife and I attended some joint marital counseling, but she was very resistant and ultimately refused to go. After that, I attempted some individual counseling and some clinical testing was ordered, but my sexual addiction was not addressed since the main clinical psychologist who did psychological evaluations denied such addictions existed.*

There is now an acceptance by the medical profession that the most effective treatment program for chemical dependency takes place largely outside the realm of medical professionals. The same applies to the diagnosis and treatment of other addictive behaviors.

If a client says to his or her therapist, "My sexual behavior seems out of control. Could it be an addiction? I think I may be a sex addict" or "My friend goes to a Twelve Step group and has been able to stop the same behavior. Should I try going too?" the therapist needs to explore this possibility with the client or refer him or her to someone who can.

Crossing Boundaries:
When Therapists Are Sexual with Clients

A middle-aged administrator in our survey who had engaged in excessive masturbation, pornography, and bisexual activity outside his marriage reported that his psychiatrist tried to seduce him.

Sex between therapists and clients is a widespread problem that occurs far more often than reported. A 1986 survey of American psychiatrists found that 6.4 percent acknowledged having sexual contact with their patients.[1] One-third of the offenders, all male, had been involved with more than one patient. In 1973, 7.2 percent of a random sample of 460 male physicians admitted to having sexual intercourse with at least one patient.[2]

The Hippocratic oath prohibits sexual contact between physicians and patients. The American Psychiatric Association's code of ethics prohibits sexual contact between psychiatrists and patients. The APA in 1985 dropped coverage for sexual misconduct from its liability insurance plan. It also voted in the same year to establish a work group to develop an educational program to reduce or eliminate sexual activities between psychiatrists and their patients. All professional societies of therapists acknowledge that a sexual relationship between a therapist and a client is harmful to the client.

Psychiatrist Peter Rutter in his book *Sex in the Forbidden Zone* explained why this is so. He wrote:

> The forbidden zone is a condition of relationship in which sexual behavior is prohibited because a man holds in trust the intimate, wounded, vulnerable, or undeveloped parts of a woman. The trust derives from the professional role of the man as doctor, therapist, lawyer, clergy, teacher, or

mentor, and it creates an expectation that whatever parts of herself the woman entrusts to him (her property, body, mind, or spirit) must be used solely to advance her interests and will not be used to his advantage, sexual or otherwise.

Under these conditions, sexual behavior is always wrong, no matter who initiates it, no matter how willing the participants say they are. In the forbidden zone, the factors of power, trust, and dependency remove the possibility of a woman freely giving consent to sexual contact. . . . And because the man has the greater power, the responsibility is his to guard the forbidden boundary against sexual contact, no matter how provocative the woman.[3]

Although Rutter wrote specifically about women clients and men in positions of power, the same dynamics apply to male clients who are seduced by their therapist. Because of their beliefs about sex, the opportunity for sexual exploitation is great among sex addicts and coaddicts. Sex addicts believe that sex is their most important need and may relate sexually to the therapist as they do with most other people. Coaddicts believe that sex is the most important sign of love and may either approach the therapist sexually or be vulnerable to the therapist's sexual advances. What the therapist needs to recognize, according to Rutter, is that

a patient trying to seduce a therapist may be repeating past injuries but is also most likely searching for a response that will discourage this repetition. The therapist draws these feelings out of clients because of the power he has either to reinjure his patients or to relate to them in a way that will free them from the wounds of the past.[4]

The imbalance of power between therapists and clients is similar to that between parents and children. Just as children cannot freely consent to sex with an adult, so clients cannot freely consent, in the adult sense, to sex with their therapists. Clients need to be in a warm, supportive, nonsexual relationship with their therapist.

Some therapists have their own unresolved sexual problems and may seek validation, including sexual validation, from their clients. Some therapists may not perceive that sex with clients is exploitative, harmful, or inappropriate. In the 1985 survey of psychiatrists, those who admitted to having had sex with their patients believed that 83 percent of the patients found the sexual contact "caring," "therapeutic," or "helpful."[5] The researchers who conducted the survey, on the other hand, believed that in all cases the sexual contact was harmful to the patients.

Ethical therapists agree that therapeutic treatment is no place for sex. It often takes years of therapy to undo the betrayal of trust and other damage done by a sexually exploitive therapist.

The Need for Honesty in Therapy

Active sex addicts will often deny or hide their behavior from family members and therapists in their attempts to sabotage therapy. While the addicts often lie to therapists about their sexual behaviors, many therapists do not know about sexual addiction, and so do not consider its presence or know the right questions to ask to discover its presence. Because of this, it is not surprising that so many of our survey respondents reported therapy was not initially helpful.

For example, after a middle-aged woman found out about her husband's affair, he agreed to see a marriage counselor with her. The relationship did not significantly improve despite three years of counseling. They wrote:

> HUSBAND: *I felt uncomfortable, did not really want to participate. I felt my behavior was compulsive, but the counselor did not identify it as such.*

> WIFE: *My husband was still in an affair and neither the counselor nor I knew that. The therapist trusted my spouse, as I did.*

To placate his wife, the husband halfheartedly agreed to counseling. He was unwilling, however, to end his affair. Therapy could not succeed under these circumstances. This man had a long history of affairs, excessive masturbation, and pornography use. After his wife discovered the latest affair, she asked him to leave. He wrote, "I then attended an SA meeting, read *Out of the Shadows* and *Sexaholics Anonymous*, and recognized that the symptoms described me."

In situations where the addict and the coaddict are seeing a therapist separately and as a couple, addicts might sometimes disclose to their therapist extramarital sexual behavior but ask that this information not be revealed to their spouse. This brings up two separate issues for the therapist. The first is the difficulty of doing effective counseling when an affair is ongoing. This is particularly important if the behavior is part of an addictive pattern. Until the extramarital activity ceases, no other issues in the marriage can be effectively addressed. If clients are unable to stop the behavior, they might benefit from individual counseling that will help them recognize their problem.

The second issue is honesty. Secrecy and lying are integral parts of addiction. Secrecy and intrigue add to the excitement of addictive behavior. Addicts become so accustomed to lying that many frequently lie even in situations in which there is no reason to do so. Addicts often find that talking honestly about secrets takes away the power of their addiction. A fifty-year-old businessman with a history of having affairs wrote:

> I've been in a recovery program for five years without a relapse, but I still find myself occasionally attracted to young women. I don't tell my wife about this every time it happens, but if I find myself obsessing about a particular young woman for days, planning my whole day around seeing her, and becoming resentful of my wife for preventing me from acting on my feelings (after all, if I weren't married, I could date the woman), then I know it's time to talk with my wife about it. Just telling her what I'm going through takes some of the energy away from it. Bringing it out into the open makes it less exciting. Once the secrecy and intrigue are gone, the desire becomes less strong.

Therapists will want to encourage honesty between partners. At the same time, confidentiality must be honored. A couple in their thirties described how their therapist handled this dilemma. The husband had been involved in voyeurism, multiple affairs, and frequently masturbated to pornography. They wrote:

> HUSBAND: *The therapist suggested our relationship is only as healthy as our secrets. She set up an appointment with my wife and me to open up and discuss secrets.*
>
> WIFE: *Initially, my husband had lots of secrets—his affairs, etc. But in therapy we have a self-care contract not to be sneaky or lie, and although we saw the same therapist in individual sessions, she did not break her confidentiality with him but supported him to tell me the truth, which he did in the third month of therapy.*

Since beginning recovery, this couple considered their relationship to be excellent and believed they would definitely be together in five years.

When a Therapist Becomes a Partner in Dishonesty

Therapists who support clients in lies are enabling them. When addicts do not experience the natural consequences of their behavior, they have little motivation to change. There is also an ethical dilemma for therapists who have information about one partner's sexual activity that the other partner does not know. How can a therapist maintain confidentiality with one client and not withhold relevant information from the other? One solution to this dilemma is for the therapist to work with only one of the spouses. Therapy with the partner who is sexually addicted might focus on understanding the problem sexual behavior and stopping it. Therapy with the other spouse might focus on codependency issues and self-esteem.

One clergyman who responded to our survey had affairs with parishioners that eventually cost him his job and resulted in financial and legal problems. His wife wrote:

> *My husband and I both went to the same counselor, but separately. My husband told the therapist a lot of things that were*

*kept from me, and I resented it when I found out because I felt the
therapist minimized the problem and let me believe it was not so
serious.*

The wife lost trust and confidence in her therapist. If, in the
course of individual therapy with marriage partners, a therapist ob-
tains information from one partner that is highly relevant to the
other partner's therapy but cannot be revealed, it may be better to
refer one of the partners to a different therapist. Otherwise, divided
loyalties can seriously affect the outcome of treatment.

Suggestions for Therapists
Most people reported that their self-help programs were crucial
in their recovery. Those who attended recovering couples' meetings
also found them particularly helpful. And despite many negative
experiences, most people still believed in the therapeutic process as
an aid to recovery. In fact, two-thirds reported that they were in
some form of therapy. Of those who were in recovery for two years
or less, an even higher proportion were in therapy.
Here are some suggestions for therapists:

1. Chemical dependency and other addictions affect a huge
   segment of our population. Chances are that, whether you
   know it or not, most of your clients have probably been
   affected in some way by addiction. Becoming informed
   about addiction will undoubtedly be an asset in your practice. Do some reading and attend open meetings of AA, Al-
   Anon, or other Twelve Step meetings so that you can speak
   about these programs with some familiarity.
2. When clients seek help for sexual problems, consider the
   possibility that sexual addiction or coaddiction may be an issue. Obtain a detailed sexual history separately from each
   member of the couple. Most likely when addiction is present, you will not be given all the facts. Monitor a client's
   body language and level of anxiety about topics under
   discussion.
3. When an affair or other nonmarital sexual activity is ongoing

(this includes masturbation so frequent that it interferes with a couple's relationship), couple therapy will not be effective, particularly when the problem sexual behavior is part of an addictive pattern. A contract to stop the behavior for a specific time should be considered. When an affair is ongoing, there should be no contact with that person during therapy. If a client cannot or will not stop the affair, then therapy will be most useful if it shifts focus to the unmanageability of the behavior and the need for addiction treatment.

4. A couple's relationship is only as healthy as the individuals in it. In recovery from addictive behaviors, individual recovery must precede couple recovery. Both members of the couple need to work on their own issues. Our belief is that part of this process is best accomplished when both members of the couple work a Twelve Step program.

5. In addition to the individual, the couple relationship also needs to heal. A couples' support group can break the shame and isolation felt by most couples affected by sexual addiction and provide them with opportunities to hear how other couples are handling some of the same problems they are having. Since each couple in these groups is in a different stage of recovery, the support group gives people a view of the recovery continuum. Hearing the "other side" of various issues can also be helpful for recovering couples.

6. Many therapists have found that the therapeutic process is aided when they are able to accommodate themselves to the client's belief system. For example, a religious client would need an atheistic therapist to adjust his or her words to the client's beliefs. In this case, a therapist who cannot work with a religious client should refer the client to one who can. Similarly, therapists who cannot support the sexual addiction concept should refer such clients to therapists who can.

In the next chapter, we will look at specific issues facing couples recovering from sexual addiction and coaddiction.

CHAPTER FIVE

Intimacy, Trust, And Forgiveness

Sitting in an elegant restaurant with their old friends, Bob and Sharon ate, laughed, and shared stories from the crazy days before they got into recovery from their sexual addiction and coaddiction. Bob recalled the time he'd had a fight with Sharon just before he was to go to Las Vegas to attend a trade show. Because of their fight, Bob went alone. He recounted to his friends how, finding himself alone in a motel room in a strange city, he felt lonely and decided to find female company. He had gone through the tabloids that carried thinly veiled ads for prostitutes and nervously made a call.

Having heard the story before, Sharon interrupted at this point, ". . . and when the woman came to his room, she was so unattractive that Bob paid her one hundred dollars and sent her away."

Bob looked at Sharon as though she were crazy and asked, "Whatever gave you that idea, Sharon? I'd never have done anything like that—I would never have sent away a prostitute."

Sharon recalled clearly the version of this story that Bob had told her and realized how naive she'd been to believe him. He had obviously felt he needed to explain the hundred dollar credit card charge to "ABC Services" and had given her a sanitized version of the events.

Another lie, she thought as she sat fuming and furious through the rest of the meal. When Sharon and Bob were again alone, she confronted him on his lie. His answer gave her pause for thought. "Sharon, I'm sorry this came up and spoiled your evening. I honestly didn't remember what I'd told you about that occasion. The fact is that during our first few years together I told you so many lies that I no longer remember when I was honest and when I lied. It's likely there will be other times in the future when you will learn about another lie of mine from the past. But there is one thing I can guarantee—in the two years since joining SA I've been rigorously honest."

Thinking it over, Sharon realized it was true. For two years, Bob had bent over backwards to be honest and reliable. He could not undo the past with its lies and betrayal, but he was doing his best to win back her trust. She realized she needed to let go of her anger about the past and focus on the present. She felt great sadness at the realization that their first several years together had been so full of deceit, but she also felt joy at the new life they were building together—a life characterized by honesty and consistency. This experience was but another episode in the important task that Sharon and Bob were addressing on an ongoing basis—rebuilding trust in their relationship.

When asked to name the single most important relationship problem in recovery, half of the survey respondents listed rebuilding trust, forgiving, or developing intimacy. These tasks are closely related.

Becoming Intimate

Intimacy is the willingness to let our partner really know us, to exchange feelings and thoughts without fear of being judged or criticized. Intimacy requires vulnerability. Generally, we are willing to be vulnerable only if we trust our partner.

With the long history coaddicts have of being hurt and disappointed, coaddicts may be understandably reluctant to let down their guard and be vulnerable to another person. This is why establishing intimacy is *the* challenge for couples in recovery.

Being trustworthy means being predictable, dependable, and faithful. Predictable partners can be trusted to behave the same way in the future as they have in the past. Dependable partners are those who can be counted on in important matters. Faithful partners act in the relationship's best interest no matter what the circumstances.

Because secrecy and dishonesty are integral parts of addiction, most addicts have lied, covered up, manipulated, and hidden their secret lives from those close to them. No wonder coaddicts find it difficult to trust. Most coaddicts have felt anger and resentment toward their partner. To resent means to feel again. When coaddicts resent something their partner did, they rehash it over and over in their mind, each time feeling anger and unhappiness. Only when coaddicts have worked through their anger and resentment and are willing to let go can they move on to develop intimacy in relationships. To coaddicts, forgiving means being able to remember the past without feeling the pain all over again.

Trust is an issue for addicts too. Addicts need to trust that they won't be judged or criticized. They need to trust that what they say will not be inappropriately shared with others.

Forgiving and rebuilding trust are both prerequisites for establishing intimacy. In this chapter we will look at how recovering people are accomplishing these tasks.

Rebuilding Trust

How Addicts Trust

In our survey, most addicts (81 percent) and half of coaddicts trusted their spouse mostly or completely. Generally, addicts were more trusting of their partner than were coaddicts. "No reason not to," said several respondents. "She's never strayed," wrote another addict. One wrote, "I have never had reason to doubt her fidelity or love." We did not ask respondents to define trust, but most interpreted it narrowly to indicate sexual fidelity.

Some addicts, however, defined trust more broadly. For example, a young businesswoman married five years and in recovery for almost a year wrote: "My husband is a man with high integrity and honesty. I married him in part because these were qualities I wanted but didn't have."

A thirty-three-year-old man in recovery one year wrote, "I don't always trust that she accepts me for who I am." Along the same lines, an architect in recovery several months wrote, "I trust she won't go acting out, but I don't know if I can trust her to be accepting of how I feel." An administrator in his forties and in recovery almost four years had very little trust in his wife. He told us: "I don't believe she will understand where I come from. I feel distance from her and her fear of me." Some addicts believed they could not risk vulnerability for fear of being misunderstood. Part of this fear may have been an accurate perception of their spouses who, after all, were struggling with their own codependency. Another part may have been a reflection of the addicts' general distrust of themselves and others. Both themes were clearly stated by other respondents.

A counselor in recovery a year found his trust in his wife increasing. He wrote, "As I learn to trust and accept myself as someone to be loyal to, I trust my wife more." A writer in his sixties in recovery over a year trusted his wife nearly completely. He wrote: "I think she has been quite honest and open. I simply cannot trust anyone 100 percent. That is part of my problem." An attorney in recovery one year wrote, "I cannot trust her completely because I do not completely trust myself yet."

The converse of this was expressed by a middle-aged scientist who has been in recovery almost two years. He said, "I trust my wife completely because I want to, because she deserves it, and because I'm secure enough now."

The addict's perception of his or her partner's codependency decreased the level of trust for several respondents. A consultant in recovery over three years wrote that his level of trust in his wife was low but getting better as she learned to let go. A physician in recovery almost five years wrote, "She still has issues of trust and abandonment not related to my sexual addiction."

Many couples in recovery can recall the craziness of the past, when crisis was the norm and they were in constant upheaval. The ingrained patterns of responding to constant crisis are hard to change and they often continue into early recovery. A retired professor with a year and a half in recovery related: "Six times in the past year my spouse ordered me to leave our house and to get out of her life. There was much abuse, name calling." Not surprisingly, he trusted his wife only moderately. In contrast, his wife wrote that she trusted her husband completely. "He is working a strong Twelve Step program and is in a supportive sex therapy group that I am in also. One day at a time," she said.

Finally, several addicts showed real empathy for their spouse. A male nurse in recovery a few months wrote, "She shares feelings, has consistent caring behavior." A forty-three-year-old clergyman in recovery almost a year wrote: "She is very wounded and still recovering from codependency. She also stayed with me through real hell."

How Coaddicts Trust

Like addicts, coaddicts typically focused on their spouse's sexual behavior as the basis for trust. Only 14 percent of coaddicts trusted their partner completely, compared with 42 percent of addicts. Here is how those who had a high level of trust explained their faith. A housewife in recovery three years wrote, "His program is his priority—his spirituality and growth and protecting his health." An editor in recovery five years said: "He's very truthful and we talk about when he's having lust problems. It keeps me from wondering and being suspicious." A research assistant in recovery one year wrote, "He will tell me if he is having problems that should cause me to trust him less." A husband and wife had been recovering together from sexual addiction for over four years. The wife wrote: "We are recovering together. He is willing to deal with issues, risk being intimate, and be involved in Sexaholics Anonymous (SA) recovery."

What do these respondents have in common? Most described a

real commitment to recovery by their spouse and a long-term commitment to a Twelve Step program. Several mentioned their spouse's honesty. Finally, most of these coaddicts were in recovery themselves for a long time. They have improved their own self-esteem and have developed a willingness to risk trust. As one of them said, "If it turns out that my trust is unwarranted, then I know I'll be okay alone."

A third of the respondents trusted their partner a great deal, but not completely. Many of them gave "once an addict, always an addict," as their reason for holding back. A sixty-seven-year-old counselor told us:

> *We are very open with each other. Our love continues to grow. We share ideas and feelings and I trust him completely—then I remember that he could relapse at any time. He is in his fourth year of therapy and I doubt this will happen, but I have to face the fact that it could.*

The memory of her husband's lying diminished the trust of a woman, who wrote, "He was a chronic liar and it has been only two and a half years since he stopped." Another woman attending Codependents of Sex Addicts (COSA) for a year wrote, "I didn't know he was engaging in this behavior during our marriage—how would I know now?" Her physician husband had been in a recovery program for one and a half years without a relapse.

If after a year or more of consistency and honesty from the addict you, as a coaddict, are still unwilling to trust, you need to look within yourself for the reasons. If as a child you couldn't rely on the significant people in your life, you may not be able to do so as an adult, even if that trust is warranted. In addition, if you cannot trust your own feelings, you may not be able to know if someone is trustworthy. Additional work on yourself may improve your willingness to risk vulnerability.

A homemaker in recovery almost two years wrote:

> *I respect his program, his honesty, but he is an addict and only has recovery this day. I will never "completely trust" him again.*

Nor do I view that as a desirable goal. I need to "completely trust" my Higher Power and the voice of my inner child.

A forty-five-year-old counselor in recovery ten months told us:

I know the addict part of him will never totally disappear, but if he does act out he will hurt himself more than anyone else. I also know that if he acts out I will not die.

These responses underline a major recovery theme for coaddicts: As they accept that there are no certainties in this world, except for their relationship with a Higher Power, they become more comfortable living with uncertainty in their day-to-day relationships. As this happens, coaddicts realize that they cannot rely on their partner to make them whole, and that they can be okay with or without their spouse. Paradoxically, only when their spouse ceases to be their Higher Power do coaddicts become free and secure enough to risk trusting him or her.

A second reason for many coaddicts' lack of trust is their unresolved hurt and fear of abandonment. Several coaddicts recognized that their lack of trust related more to their own fears than to their spouse's behavior. According to one woman: "His behavior demonstrates I can trust him more than I feel I am emotionally able to do right now. I have a hard time trusting anyone including myself."

Some coaddicts withheld complete trust because of realistic concerns about their partner's current behavior. According to a self-employed woman in recovery three months, "He always says he is very truthful; however, he sometimes stretches the truth."

Several coaddicts were not able to trust because of actual relapses. A housewife with seven months' recovery was unable to trust her spouse because ". . . he cannot stay sober over twenty-eight days at a time." A physician husband was trusted only slightly by his wife because he had a couple of relapses and admitted that honesty is difficult for him.

Several coaddicts in early recovery wrote that they could not trust their spouse because they did not have enough information about their spouse's addictive behavior. "I feel there is more he hasn't yet told me about his addiction," wrote an accountant. A real estate broker in recovery a few months said, "It's still too soon—I'm not sure exactly where he is with his addiction."

Although an obsessive need to know every detail and every feeling can be a part of a coaddict's unhealthy need to control, the fact is that most coaddicts have a legitimate need for information in order to make sense of their world. In the past, an addict's lies and distortions, coupled with a coaddict's uncertainty about trusting his or her own feelings, combined to create confusion and a feeling of craziness for many coaddicts. Information about their spouse's past feelings and behaviors can confirm for coaddicts that they are not crazy.

When we share our ongoing struggles and feelings with one another, we are vulnerable human beings working on overcoming our addictive problems. Sharing feelings promotes feelings of intimacy. Without open discussion, partners feel distant and trust and intimacy are difficult.

What Needs to Happen to Increase Trust?

When we originally asked respondents how much they trusted their spouse, we expected that the longer a couple had been in recovery, the more likely they were to trust. This turned out to be true for coaddicts, but not for addicts. The length of time in recovery had little influence on addicts who appeared to trust their spouse to a great extent no matter how long they had been in recovery. In contrast, coaddicts tended to increase their trust with the time they and their spouse were in recovery. For example, of coaddicts in recovery six months or less, almost half had very little trust and only 21 percent trusted greatly or completely. In contrast, of coaddicts in recovery over three years, none indicated very little trust and 83 percent had great or complete trust in their partner.

We asked both addicts and coaddicts, *What needs to happen in order for you to increase your trust in your partner?*

How Addicts Responded

Addicts who already trusted their spouse nonetheless often found room for improvement. Among their suggestions were: "Work the Steps." . . . "Take risks. Put more consistent effort into being trustable." . . . "Follow through on commitments." . . . "Show greater sensitivity to my feelings."

Addicts who did not trust their spouse had definite suggestions that would enhance trust. These included: "She could have more acceptance of me and be less emotionally distant." . . . "She could show a little more love and intimacy aside from anger, hostility, and distancing. We need better communication of *all* these feelings." . . . "We need to resolve some conflicts. She needs to deal with her rage better. I need to be not so nice."

Some addicts recognized that working on themselves would enhance their trust in their spouse. They wrote: "I have to be honest. We have to talk more." . . . "I have to feel stronger in myself, not relying so much on her opinion of me." . . . "Work on my fears." . . . "I need to become more willing to be vulnerable."

Becoming less judgmental and more accepting of their spouse was listed by several addicts as a help in increasing trust. One husband realized he needed to "be honest and give her the opportunity to have her own reactions. I need to not decide in advance how she will react so I give her a chance to act differently."

Greater willingness on the part of the spouse to be vulnerable is another factor that aids trust, according to addicts. A man who hardly trusted his spouse when it came to feelings wished for her to admit her own wrongs as they come up and share current struggles without a tough facade. A printer in recovery over four years had limited trust in his wife. He wrote:

> *She would have to open up more and let me know more about her inner feelings. We always talk about me and my recovery. I want to know more about her.*

Our willingness to share our inner lives with our partners tells them "I trust you" and makes them more likely to risk vulnerability in return. When our feelings are treated with respect and sensitivity, we are more likely to risk sharing again in the future. This is the process on which intimacy is built. We have found that asking *why?* about feelings can be a sure block to open communication. How can we answer that question when we often don't know the answer ourselves?

How Coaddicts Responded
Many coaddicts recognized the connection between trust and time in recovery. A woman in recovery for three months wrote that she would trust her husband more if he had continued sobriety. She also said, "I need to see a decrease in his anger and denial, and hard work on his program and on the marriage." Another woman who had only moderate trust in her husband because of her fear of a relapse wrote, "Time, with no lies, seems like what will prove he is no longer falling back into the old patterns."

Dependability and consistency are two behaviors that can rebuild trust. Most coaddicts did not have a dependable or consistent spouse during the years of active addiction, when their feelings ricocheted from high highs to low lows depending on what was going on in their lives.

Working on themselves was another major aid to restored trust. An administrator who trusted her husband very little after several months in recovery wrote that she needed to continue to develop her own self-esteem. "Time is needed to heal old wounds," wrote a woman in recovery over three years. Another woman in recovery three years echoed this. She wrote: "I need to work on myself in my own Twelve Step program. I see my own issues interfering with trust." A housewife who was married thirty years when she learned of her husband's addiction faced the same problem. She wrote:

> I used to trust him completely, but at this point in time I don't expect to ever trust anyone completely again. Time, sobriety, and working the program will help me to have more trust in him.

Although she may mean that *his* continued working the program will help restore her trust, the fact is that continuing to work *her* program is likely to help her become more willing to again risk vulnerability with her husband.

Improved communication, an aspect of increased sharing, was mentioned by a dozen respondents. A homemaker in recovery over a year said: "Keeping the lines of communication open is so very important for us. I call him when I need to or ask him to call me when he is away. I do wish that he would check in on a feeling level every day."

Some coaddicts may have unrealistic expectations of their spouse. For example, a man who is also a recovering alcoholic wrote that in order for him to completely trust his sex addict wife, ". . . she would need to verbalize to me that she has had the same spiritual experience that AA members speak of when released from their obsession."

In early recovery, coaddicts often have a great need to know. They may feel that if they know everything that is going on in the addict's mind, hear about every relapse into addictive thinking, and how the addict deals with every temptation, they will somehow be able to control the situation. Later, they learn that this is part of their own illness. Coaddicts need to look to the addict's commitment to the program, attendance at meetings, and a changed attitude as signs of recovery, rather than focusing only on specific behaviors. For example, a homemaker in recovery two years wrote:

Time needs to pass by. I need to trust myself and my perceptions more. I see his commitment to recovery (he did inpatient work and now has weekly group therapy, SA meetings) and a changed attitude as the crux of how I will increase my trust in him.

A good summary of what most respondents would like in order to increase trust in their addicted spouse was provided by another homemaker in recovery a short time. She wrote:

He needs much more sobriety, lots of surrendering, and less denial. I need to get through more of the anger and hurt and have additional positive experiences with him being sober, with both of us trying to build an intimate, good relationship.

How Does Each Spouse Become More Trustworthy?

After asking our survey group what they would like their spouse to do in order to increase their trust, we asked them, *What changes could they make in themselves that would aid their spouse's trust in them?* We found several common themes in the answers. The most common answer was for each member of the couple to continue working on his or her individual recovery. Many respondents believed their individual growth would promote trust.

How Addicts Responded

Addicts' responses included: "Be honest and don't have any sexual encounters outside of my marriage." . . . "I'll have to have a year or two of solid sobriety under my belt, SA style." . . . "Sobriety over the years and changing patterns that distress me or her."

Increased consistency was also mentioned by several addicts who wrote: "I think that being consistent in my behavior and whereabouts, checking in, and being sober over time helps." . . . "Reliability and predictability. Also, keeping her current on my recovery, both my successes and my slips."

Increased honesty was mentioned by several addicts. They recognized that their spouse wanted them to share their feelings.

How Coaddicts Responded

Coaddicts recognized the need to be less questioning and more supportive. "I have to tear down the walls I've built." . . . "I need to disengage myself from trying to direct his recovery."

Coaddicts also wrote about being less judgmental. They wrote: "I need to stop criticizing him as much as I do." . . . "I need to be less controlling." . . . "I need to listen to him without judgment or giving advice." . . . "I need to be careful not to throw things in his face that he has told me."

Ingredients for Intimacy

Providing an atmosphere of acceptance so that each person feels free to be vulnerable is the crux of intimacy. One couple wrote:

HUSBAND: *I need to reveal more to her about the status of my addiction and the feelings that I'm having.*

WIFE: *I need to not flip out when he opens up to me. He needs to trust that I won't leave him or use what he says against him. Actually, I never have left him, so I don't think it's my responses that have made him pathologically afraid to open up—someone else got to him early on! But I need to stop reinforcing his fear.*

A counselor in recovery over four years told us that to increase her husband's trust in her, "I will have to share my weaknesses and struggles with him."

Talking about feelings; being honest with each other; going regularly to meetings, going to marriage and individual counseling, or sex therapy; spending more quality time together; doing fun things together; and improving communication were often mentioned by survey respondents as ways they worked on rebuilding trust.

A twenty-eight-year-old man whose wife had had multiple affairs described how an agreement on friends of the opposite sex helped rebuild his trust. He wrote:

When I clamped down on her male friends, that made me happier. I said to our counselor, "Would you like it if your husband brought female friends home when you weren't home? How would you feel?" She said, "Well, I wouldn't be too hot on it." "See," I said to my wife, "why don't you make some female friends?" I told her I've never had female friends as close as my male friends. I told her I believe there's no such thing as male/female "friends." As soon as it starts getting close, there's the sexual element. I know how men think!

With time, this young husband may change his views about whether it is possible to have friends of the opposite sex. In the meantime, his wife agreed to avoid meeting alone with her male friends.

Some couples admitted they were not yet ready to work on joint issues. In recovery six months, one woman wrote:

At this time, we don't seem to be ready to work on "us." We are looking at ourselves and not each other. Sometimes I get angry at this. I feel the "we" still needs to be addressed.

When does the focus on "I" need to change to "we"? A healthy relationship requires healthy individuals. It is natural in early recovery to focus on individual rather than couple issues. For coaddicts, this may be particularly difficult, since their fear of abandonment is triggered when they see their partner getting more involved in his or her individual recovery program. Coaddicts who choose to stay in a marriage with the recovering addict have the difficult challenge of changing the nature of their relationship with their spouse while working to improve their own self-esteem. Detaching from their partner's addiction and recovery must also be done simultaneously with work on their own recovery. Coaddicts need to understand that the addict's first priority in early recovery is sobriety, not the couple relationship.

The necessity of working individual programs was recognized by a couple in recovery for one year. They wrote:

HUSBAND: *We are changing our behaviors in accordance with program principles—working on dependability and praying together.*

WIFE: *My spouse is working his Twelve Step program and trying to be more reliable and dependable. For me, trust in our relationship is directly related to my working my Twelve Step program and especially trusting in my Higher Power to lead me on my own path, not focusing on my spouse's program.*

Increased honesty is an important ingredient of rebuilding trust. One woman related: "He shared with me his last secret regarding his past acting out. We are being more open with each other, even if sometimes we have to agree to disagree on certain problems."

As a coaddict's recovery progresses, he or she has less of a need to know all the details of the spouse's addiction. "I want to know about my husband's struggles and near relapses only when they begin to affect our relationship. I don't want to know about every lustful thought he had during the day or about every woman he saw that he found attractive. If it's a problem for him, he can talk with his group about it," said a woman who has been in recovery for several years.

Telling each other everything all the time may work for some couples, but most find they need to share only what is truly important. The key to recovery is balance. For those of us who have seen life in only black-and-white terms, the many shades of gray hold some wonderful surprises.

Forgiveness

To forgive is not to forget. Forgiving means being able to remember the past without experiencing the pain all over again. To forgive is important primarily for ourselves, not for the person we forgive. The opposite of forgiveness is resentment. When we resent we experience pain and anger all over again. Serenity and resentment cannot coexist. Resentment is a strong trigger for relapse.

A recovering sex addict told us, "I made a decision to forgive the people who hurt me, and I've forgiven them, but I'm still very angry at them and resentful about the things they did." He has not truly forgiven them.

The process of forgiveness begins with acknowledging that a wrong has been done to us. Next, we have to recognize that we have strong feelings about what happened and we need to feel those feelings. We are entitled to be angry or hurt. Ideally, we can share those feelings with the person who has hurt us. If that is not possible, then we can share the feelings with our support group, a therapist, or a friend. After that, we can choose whether to stay in a relationship with that person. In either case, forgiveness does not imply permission to continue hurtful behaviors. As part of our own recovery, we need to decide which behaviors we can accept in our relationships and which we cannot.

Finally, we make a decision to let go of the hurt. We know we have truly forgiven if we can think about what was done to us without reexperiencing the pain. The primary goal of forgiveness is to heal ourselves.

In a marriage affected by sexual addiction, forgiveness is aided by evidence of each partner's changed behavior and commitment to a recovery program. These are also elements in rebuilding trust. For many couples, forgiving and learning to trust again go hand in hand. Both take time.

What About Forgiveness?

We asked our survey respondents, *Have you forgiven your spouse?* Seventy percent of addicts and 63 percent of coaddicts said they had mostly or totally forgiven their spouse.

Several addicts, but no coaddicts, found themselves unable to answer the question. The most common reason for this was expressed by a man with nine months of recovery who said, "She is not the addict." He did not recognize that both partners have some responsibility for the dysfunction in an addictive relationship. The view that only the addict bears responsibility for problems, and is therefore the only one who needs fixing, is likely to lead to ongoing resentment and stress in the relationship. Both partners will likely need to work on themselves, make changes in their behavior, and make amends to each other.

A recovering addict wrote: "I don't have much to forgive her for. I don't hold her responsible for not being able to accept my homosexual orientation. I can't accept it very well myself." A sex addict married to another sex addict said: "We have nothing to forgive each other for. We both stopped acting out with others when we met. We practiced our sexual addiction on each other."

A homemaker in recovery three years forgave her husband completely because, "If I believe he is addicted, then I must believe in his powerlessness." A sex addict in recovery for two years who is married to a recovering alcoholic wrote: "There is nothing to forgive. She has the disease of alcoholism. But for the grace of God, there go I." In recovery for four years, a counselor said, "Understanding addiction, I feel there is nothing to forgive."

We do not agree. Being addicted does not absolve a person of responsibility for his or her actions. The same line of reasoning would suggest that alcoholics who drive drunk and kill and maim are not responsible for their actions and do not deserve punishment

Intimacy, Trust, and Forgiveness

because they are alcoholic. We believe an addict has the responsibility to get help.

As they did with granting trust, most addicts had forgiven regardless of their length of time in recovery. In contrast, coaddicts tended to be more forgiving the longer their time in recovery. It was only after three years of recovery that most coaddicts forgave their spouse, which demonstrates that addicts should not expect instant forgiveness.

How Does Each Spouse Become More Forgivable?

Because only 44 percent of addicts and 28 percent of coaddicts had completely forgiven their spouse, we wanted to learn what they thought it would take for them to be able to forgive. We asked, *What do you think needs to happen in order for you to forgive your partner?*

Most said time. "Time to forget and time to build new relationships." . . . "Longer length of sobriety, some amends made, and good length of time being responsible at work, at home, and with his own life." . . . "Years of working the program and going to counseling together."

Other respondents asked for more sharing and acceptance, more open communication, and more sincerity. Several people wrote that the same changes they asked of their spouse in rebuilding trust would also help them forgive.

For many respondents, working on themselves was the key. Some wrote: "I need to fully explore my hurt, my sense of betrayal. Some of it is too painful and I haven't dealt with it yet." . . . "I still need to get in touch with and express my anger, then I need to develop my own better sense of well-being and serenity."

Forgiving themselves was also mentioned by several respondents. Another common wish was for the spouse to make amends or ask for forgiveness. They wrote that forgiveness comes more easily when the person who caused the hurt acknowledges his or her wrongdoing.

Forgiveness does not mean that feelings of anger or grief will not resurface from time to time. A coaddict in recovery over three years wrote, "I think I have forgiven, but now and then something happens that shows me I still have some resentment over the past."

Some respondents seemed to have unrealistic expectations and hopes for change. A middle-aged addict in recovery for a year wrote that in order for him to forgive his wife completely he wanted ". . . totally free and uninhibited sex and spontaneity." Another addict wrote, "She is unable to let go at all sexually. She is so controlled. I don't see that changing—ever. And I get resentful about it." If an addict's forgiveness of his or her spouse hinges on attaining the sexual fulfillment he or she found with other partners while acting out, then resentments are likely to persist and forgiveness is unlikely. Unrealistic expectations can only lead to continued unhappiness.

Feeling Forgiven
   We also asked respondents, *How much do you think your partner has forgiven you?* Although, as expected, coaddicts believed they were forgiven more often than addicts, many perceived their spouse to be relatively unforgiving. How accurate were these perceptions when compared with what the addict actually told us? Coaddicts had reasonably accurate perceptions of how much their spouse forgave them, although most coaddicts who had been completely forgiven by their spouse believed that they had not been completely forgiven.
   Coaddicts tended to forgive their spouse less easily than addicts forgave their spouse. This was expected, since most coaddicts tended to believe they had more to forgive than did addicts. When coaddicts had in fact forgiven their spouse, addicts tended to think that they had not been forgiven. On the other hand, when coaddicts had not forgiven their spouse, the addict appeared to be aware of this. One possible conclusion is that addicts tended to believe that their spouse had not forgiven them, whether or not this was true.
   Overall, the responses showed that many respondents who had been forgiven did not realize this. Forgiveness might be a fruitful topic of discussion for recovering couples.

Feeling Forgivable
   We also asked, *What do you think needs to happen in order for your partner to forgive you?* Since most respondents did not believe their

spouse had fully forgiven them, this question was designed to find out what changes people believed they needed to make in order to make them more "forgivable."

Typical answers suggested that time, making amends, continued recovery, and trustworthy behavior would aid forgiveness. Another common suggestion was that the spouse needs to work on his or her own recovery. Improved communication again came up as a factor that would aid forgiveness. One man wrote:

> *We take a daily morning walk together and sometimes talk then. We stop for breakfast and a chat. When we return, we read a meditation book selection, Bible passages, do check-in, and pray. In the evening before retiring, I read a chapter from a recovery book and we pray together. We do work tasks together—yard, garden, meals, etc. I guess I'm trying to say we're working at recovery— together, fortunately.*

As we have seen, trust, forgiveness, and intimacy are closely related. Each of these qualities takes time to fully develop, and all require active participation by both partners. By working on our individual recovery and giving time to our relationship, we begin to restore good feelings. Improved communication and a willingness to risk sharing feelings are also key elements of this process.

Finally, recovering couples need to learn how to have fun together and enjoy each other's company. Recreation with other couples can help put joy back in the relationship. Healthy sexuality, too, is part of couple recovery, and this is the focus of the next chapter.

CHAPTER SIX

Sexuality in Recovery

The silence in the room was broken only when someone nervously asked, "You mean we are going to talk about sex with my husband here and in front of everyone?" The setting was a hospital meeting room where some dozen couples met twice monthly to share their experiences as recovering couples. Previous topics had included rebuilding trust after an affair, forgiveness, and what to tell the children. But no topic got to the heart of the couple relationship more than sex.

We are all sexual beings. How we deal with our adult sexuality has a lot to do with what we learned and didn't learn as children. When we were born, the first question that our parents asked about us was, "Is it a boy or a girl?" In some families, boys were valued more than girls or vice versa. How our family viewed boys and girls affected our identity and how we reacted to people of the same or opposite sex. As infants, we derived pleasure from our body. Some of us learned early on from our caregivers that exploring our body was shameful; others of us were exploited sexually and learned to associate pleasure with pain. Some of us who were not overtly sexually abused may have been inappropriate confidantes or surrogate partners to our parents; others of us received negative messages about sex that caused us problems in adulthood. Mothers may have told daughters that "sex is all a guy wants." Fathers may have told sons that "if a girl doesn't put out, she's not worth your time." Boys may have been warned about getting too close to other boys because "there are a lot of queers out there." We learned about sex on the playground or in the locker room. And much of the information we got was wrong.

Some of us were never told anything about sex. This is also abusive. One woman from our survey wrote: "My parents were almost asexual. To them, sex was dirty, touching ugly." Not surprisingly, this woman later had difficulty accepting her own sexuality. Those of us who grew up uninformed about sexuality often feared sex and were particularly vulnerable to exploitation.

In childhood, many of us suffered some emotional, physical, or sexual abuse. Consequently, we became shame-based people with a set of troublesome beliefs about ourselves. These included: *I am worthless, I am unlovable, and I will always be abandoned.* Some of us came to believe that sex is the most important sign of love. Children who are sexually abused by someone they love naturally conclude that sex is equivalent to nurturing and love. Others began to use sex to reduce anxiety and escape stress, and eventually decided that sex is their most important need. The degree and style of nurturing we got as children affected our capacity as adults to nurture the significant people in our life. Some of us who were deprived of love as children spent many years looking for that love in a series of unfulfilling relationships. We brought guilt, shame, and other powerful beliefs about sex into our adult relationships.

Now, discovery of our addiction and codependency, treatment, and attendance at Twelve Step meetings has resulted in enormous changes in our feelings and behaviors. These changes affect all facets of our relationships, causing major upheavals in many areas, particularly sexuality.

In this chapter, we will look at what happens to a couple's sexual relationship when they begin recovery. We will contrast what couples said their sexual relationship was like before recovery and what it was like at the time of the survey. We will discuss specific sexual problems that respondents said have occurred since beginning recovery, and how couples are dealing with such problems. We also asked couples what changes they would like to make in their sexual relationship.

Sex Since Recovery

Respondents had a wide range of opinions about their current sexual relationship. One-third of the group rated their sexual relationship as poor, one-third as average, and one-third as good or excellent. When the responses of both members of the couples were compared, more than 90 percent substantially agreed with their partner's assessment.

Some people may be discouraged to learn that a significant number of couples in recovery rated their sexual relationship as less than ideal. However, when asked to rank the most important current problems in their marriage, only 8 percent of men and 5 percent of women listed sex first. Even more telling is that only one-third of men and 28 percent of women ranked sex as one of the top three problems.

When asked to rate their current sexual relationship as better, the same, or worse than before recovery, 71 percent of addicts and 68 percent of coaddicts believed it was better; 7 percent of addicts and 14 percent of coaddicts thought it was the same; and 18 percent of addicts and 11 percent of coaddicts felt it was worse. The remaining respondents said their relationship was neither better nor worse, but different.

Some Said Sex Was Better

The majority of respondents believed their sexual relationship was better in recovery than before. For example, a couple in their thirties who have been married for nine years rated their prior sexual relationship as poor and their current one as good or excellent. They wrote:

HUSBAND: *We now have more intimacy. She is more willing to initiate. She is coming into her own sexuality. We have better understanding and communication.*

WIFE: *We have increased intimacy. When my husband makes love to me, he is here with me psychologically. I can feel his presence. I feel that we are close, more open and vulnerable with each other, and I'm no longer performing to satisfy his needs or being on the defensive to avoid sex. I'm actually starting to tune into my own sexual drive where I never had a chance to before. My husband is more intimate, loving, and caring, but it is new. The "old" ways don't work anymore so I'm learning what sex is about all over again. The problem is that there isn't a lot of information about what a healthy sex life truly is. I know what it isn't, that's for sure.*

Two sex addicts who were married and in recovery said their sexual relationship had gone from good to excellent. They wrote:

HUSBAND: *Since my wife began recovery, our sexual relationship is more honest, less fantasy-oriented, based more on what we feel now rather than a seeking of some mythical inebriated sexual high. We have a very open and active sexual relationship. It just gets better the longer we are in recovery and the more we grow together.*

WIFE: *I'm much more relaxed and present and aware of my feelings during sex. I love myself more. I used to think of my father or past men — now I don't. I don't feel such a need to satisfy or perform for my partner. Our sex is more playful and fun. We talk more about our feelings.*

A couple married for thirteen years and in recovery for almost four years also reported a better sexual relationship. They wrote:

HUSBAND: *Our sex is less frequent, but better. What sex we have is satisfying, but neither of us has the drive that we once had. I think that among other things this reflects the time and energy we put into recovery.*

WIFE: *We're working very hard at showing mutual respect and communicating our feelings, wants, and needs in regard to sex. We've learned that sex does not equal love and that sex is optional. We're both learning to love ourselves and feel good about ourselves, which frees us up to be loving and caring to others. We're both committed to making our marriage work.*

This couple's focus on sex appeared to be diminishing in favor of an emphasis on the total relationship. This is common among couples who are beyond the early recovery period and reflects a more balanced role that sexuality plays in the relationship.

A minister and his wife who believed their sexual relationship had improved wrote:

> HUSBAND: *The difference is like night and day. The emotional and spiritual components are more important than the physical or strictly sexual.*
>
> WIFE: *He's more emotionally present with me. We have sex more often. He turns to me rather than himself. Less lustful, more love. Our lovemaking is more normal and we both like it and feel close to each other.*

That recovery has helped both members of a couple be more emotionally available during lovemaking was reported by several respondents. Outside the bedroom, too, recovering couples find they are generally more tuned into each other's needs.

Another couple who had good sex during their thirty-one years of marriage before recovery, found sex even better six months after beginning a recovery program. The wife explained:

> *Our sexual relationship is more honest and intense than it has been for over twenty years. Before recovery, he used sex to reward himself, to "make up" when I was upset, and to act out. I withheld sex to try to get him to face problems, promising to reward him with sex when our problem was solved.*

Before recovery, this couple used sex as a tool to manipulate each other. Removing this role for sex from their lives increased their intimacy.

Some Said Sex Was Worse

There are many reasons for the sexual relationship to worsen in early recovery. Addicts or coaddicts may have feelings that were previously numbed by sexual activity. Or they may want to isolate themselves rather than let their partner see them out of control.

Also, coaddicts may be concerned about catching sexually transmitted diseases when told by the addict about extramarital sex. Couples can work through these problems as they grow in recovery. Later in the chapter, we will discuss specific sexual problems reported by recovering people.

Some Said Sex Was Different

Sometimes it was difficult for a couple to rate their sexual relationship as better or worse than before because their criteria had changed. Some couples reported decreased frequency but improved quality. They were no longer measuring sexual satisfaction by the number of times they made love.

A minister in recovery for several years from her sexual coaddiction was also dealing with her recently recognized sexual addiction. She responded: "It's both better and worse. It's better in that we don't use sex to cover up conflict. Worse in that it is less often. We need more intimacy."

Several addicts in recovery reported that their lovemaking was briefer. Some reported giving up fantasies that had prolonged lovemaking. Sexual activities that triggered addictive patterns were avoided. Instead of spending hours on lovemaking, many couples found their sex life curtailed. Understanding this can be confusing, especially to those who are not sure what normal sexuality is.

Lightening up on sex may also be an aspect of recovery. For coaddicts who have believed that sex is the most important sign of love, every sexual experience was full of symbolic meaning and the ultimate sign of love. But in recovery, couples learn that sex doesn't have to be so heavy, that it can be simply joyful and fun. As coaddicts change their core belief that sex is proof of love or security, they become less needy.

A couple's sexual relationship mirrors any changes that happen in the relationship, especially changes that involve loss. Giving up an addiction or codependent behavior is a significant loss. As a result, nearly half of our survey's respondents pointed to specific sexual problems since beginning recovery.

Problems Originating Primarily with the Addict

Feelings of Shame and Guilt

During active addiction, many addicts were able to rationalize their behaviors by telling themselves, *My spouse doesn't suspect anything, and what she (or he) doesn't know can't hurt her (or him).* Stripped of his or her defense mechanisms, an addict's sexual relationship with the spouse may suffer. In recovery for eight months, a thirty-six-year-old man who had been sexual with other men told us: "Sex is worse now, more uncomfortable. My hang-ups are still there, plus more guilt about not meeting my partner's needs."

Loss of Interest, Problems with Performance

Some men had less interest in sex and/or difficulties with sexual performance. Three respondents mentioned premature ejaculation as a new concern. Others mentioned related problems: "I have greatly reduced interest in sex and am sometimes unable to perform." . . . "I have periods of low interest in sex due to fears of old behaviors or rejection by my wife." A fifty-year-old woman married twenty-eight years wrote:

> *Sexual recovery has lessened my husband's desire for sex. When I spoke to his counselor about how I could work through this as his wife, he assured me my husband has to work through his own sexuality. I was glad to know this is all a part of getting well. Now sex is better, though decreased in frequency.*

Addicts in our survey were asked specifically about new problems that have arisen in recovery. Impotence and loss of desire are, of course, problems not exclusive to recovering people. Possible causes include various medical and hormonal problems, side effects from medication, stress, and marital and other emotional problems. Any of these factors may have contributed to sexual problems among our survey's respondents; however, there are particular reasons why men in early recovery from sexual addiction or chemical dependency might experience these difficulties.

For addicts, the preoccupation with sex is the beginning of the addictive cycle. "We tuned out with fantasy and masturbation. We plugged in by drinking in the pictures, the images, and pursuing the objects of our fantasies."[1] For many addicts, the distinction between fantasy and reality was blurred. Obsessive thoughts were soon transformed into compulsive behaviors. An addict told us:

> *When I masturbated to the image of someone I was attracted to, my brain didn't know the difference between fantasy and reality. If I saw her later, I would really think we had something going and it would make it that much easier to put the moves on her. In recovery, I had to eliminate fantasy as much as possible and certainly not reinforce it with masturbation.*

In recovery, addicts have to let go of the images and learn to make love without the lubricant of fantasy. They need to be present with their partner. For some addicts, this resulted in decreased sexual intensity, problems with getting or maintaining erection, premature ejaculation, or a general decline in sexual interest. Fantasy partners are easy to please; real partners require communication skills, risk-taking, patience, practice, and intimacy.

Some addicts have made a clear distinction between sex with their spouse, which they perceived as normal, and other sexual behavior. Others recognize that some marital sexual activities have been unhealthy for them, or that they trigger fantasies that lead to problem behavior. One challenge of sexual recovery is to define which sexual activities with the spouse are healthy and which are part of the addiction. During this process, which may take a while, marital sex can be scary. Six months into recovery and married for three years, a young couple reported:

HUSBAND: *I ejaculate before she's ready.*

WIFE: *He can't always hold back until I have orgasm. I sometimes lack interest, even though I enjoy sex. His letting me decide when to have sex is a problem; I feel he is not interested enough to initiate.*

In this couple, the wife was blaming herself for her husband's lack of desire. She needs to check this out with him. She might say to him, "When you don't initiate, I feel undesirable. Is this true?" She might learn that her husband's intention is to treat her more respectfully, giving her an equal voice in sexual decisions. Or his hesitation may be because he's concerned about his own performance. Having an open dialogue will give each a better understanding of the other. This couple also illustrates in more than one way how sexual recovery problems affect both partners.

A couple in their sixties with many years of recovery in AA wrote that their sex life was poor after a year in recovery from sexual addiction:

> HUSBAND: *I'm getting older. I don't use booze any longer. Booze helped me in sexual relations. Now I'm not aroused as easily.*
>
> WIFE: *We rarely have sex. He does not seem to be interested in trying to do anything about having sex at this point. If he did, I would be interested.*

Alcohol and other drugs can make people less inhibited. For some sex addicts, their ritual sexual behavior may have begun with chemical use. If the older man quoted above had inhibitions about sex, he may have found that once he stopped drinking he was less comfortable with his sexuality.

Recovering sex addicts who are not chemically dependent may find, nonetheless, that they are better off avoiding alcohol when they are in potentially slippery situations. A married middle-aged salesperson, who often took clients to lunch, told us that being in a restaurant with an attractive woman reminded him of the days when such meetings were preludes to affairs. Although not alcoholic, he realized that drinking was a gateway to inappropriate sexual behavior, so he did not mix alcohol and women. Part of his personal relapse prevention plan was to keep business strictly business.

Chronic alcohol use adversely affects the balance of sex hormones in men. Alcoholic men often have enlarged breasts, small testicles, a decreased level of male sex hormones, decreased sexual desire, and problems with impotence. Alcohol is aptly said to increase the desire but decrease the ability. People in their sixties and seventies often have sexual problems. These may result from health problems, such as diabetes or heart disease, or from medications that affect sexual desire or potency. The aging process itself may cause some changes in sexual functioning.

A retired professional man, sixty-six, and his wife agreed their once good sexual relationship had become a problem. They wrote:

HUSBAND: *Before, it was nearly "normal." She was somewhat inhibited. I probably used her as a sex object, at least some of the time. I began to have periods of impotence starting two to three years before recovery. Then I became quite impotent and have now slightly recovered. I seem to be a "sexual anorexic." She is troubled with vaginismus. We are virtually celibate. I feel that this is not natural, but both of us seem to be comfortable with it.*

WIFE: *There is not much of a sexual relationship because of lack of desire or capability.*

Sex and Aging

In 1984, Consumers Union reported on a survey of over four thousand men and women over fifty who were asked about their sexual attitudes and activities. As men got older, they required more time between orgasms before being able to get an erection again. Fifty percent of the men said that it took longer for them to get an erection, and many said that when fully erect they were not as rigid as before and lost their erections more frequently during sex. Many older men no longer experienced spontaneous erection from psychological stimuli alone; they required touching or a combination of touching and psychological stimuli. In addition, as they got older, fewer women and men reported orgasm each time they had intercourse and more lost interest in sex.

Despite these progressive declines, many older people were still sexually active and enjoying a wide variety of sexual activities, even some women and men in their eighties.[2]

Aging also causes changes in women's sexual functioning. After menopause, the body's production of the female hormone estrogen gradually decreases. Estrogen deficiency causes not only hot flashes, but also vaginal dryness and irritation, which can result in painful intercourse. Dryness is often not adequately relieved by use of a simple lubricant. The wife whose husband reported she was experiencing vaginismus (an involuntary contraction of the vaginal muscles that prevents penetration) may well have been experiencing pain as a result of the physiological changes of menopause.

Fortunately for most older women, a lack of estrogen is easily corrected. More physicians are recommending estrogen replacement therapy. This consists of taking pills or applying an estrogen vaginal cream several times a week. Older women no longer need to accept discomfort with sexual intercourse.

Yet many older men and women do not realize that sexual interest and activity commonly decrease with age. What is a normal part of aging may be erroneously interpreted as evidence of a significant problem in the relationship.

Unrealistic Expectations

An administrator in her thirties and in recovery from sexual addiction for nine months wrote:

> *My inability to communicate my needs to my husband continues to be a problem. I want him to learn to read me like other lovers I've had. I want him to respond the way others have. I feel much is missing.*

For many addicts, extramarital sex was more exciting than marital sex. There was drama, intrigue, and secrecy. Fear of getting caught may have added to the rush. To recreate the excitement of the forbidden, addicts may have tried to spice up marital sex by asking their spouses to participate in a variety of activities. This may have succeeded on occasion, but more often than not addicts were not able to sustain the high. This may have been because they realized their partner was uncomfortable with a particular activity and felt ashamed or guilty. Some spouses refused what they considered the addict's outrageous requests. They may have participated in watching pornography or in having sex with another couple only to find that their partner wanted them to do even more of what went against their own values.

Addicts who were involved in affairs may have understood that the conditions that made them so exciting—the newness, the secrecy, the intrigue, and the freedom from mundane concerns—could never be duplicated at home. For other addicts, the addictive sexual rituals—cruising, exhibitionism and voyeurism, telephone sex, and anonymous encounters—were so far removed from their daily routines that they truly felt they were leading two separate lives and had no desire to involve their spouse. Whatever their pattern, many addicts found that sex at home did not come close in excitement to sex elsewhere. One of the challenges for addicts in recovery, then, is how to be satisfied with sex with their committed partner. This can be a lengthy process, first requiring grieving the loss of the addiction, then developing a new attitude about sex with their spouse.

A thirty-year-old health care professional wrote:

> *Sex with my lovers was more exciting than with my husband, but I know that a lot of that had to do with the element of maybe being found out. Sex with my husband is not as exciting, but it's comfortable. Even though I know that sex outside can be more exciting, I've focused on the consequences of that and I really don't want to have those repeated.*

A man married for thirty years with a history of multiple homosexual relationships found marital sex disappointing. He wrote:

> *Homosexual sex created greater highs. My wife and I lack spontaneity. I expect my spouse to know what pleases me most and am disappointed when this is not anticipated as another man might. Now, the homosexual highs have been traded for average activity with my spouse.*

This husband's beliefs – that men know better how to please men sexually – suggests a basic homosexual orientation. His unrealistic expectation that sex with his wife can ever equal sex with his male partners may lead to ongoing disappointment and conflict. The particular problems of married homosexual or bisexual men will be discussed more in Chapter Ten.

Coaddicts, too, often have unrealistic expectations about sex. They sometimes cannot ask for what they want. They may not even know. Instead, they may complain about their spouse's lack of sensitivity. They need to work on improved communication and on willingness to ask for what they want sexually.

Problems Originating Primarily with the Coaddict

Loss of Interest Because Of
Anger, Betrayal, and Lack of Trust

A young couple married three years and in recovery for a year rated their sexual relationship as slightly worse than before. They wrote:

> HUSBAND: *There is a cloud over us due to my having only recently dropped the bomb that I haven't been faithful. Ignorance was bliss. My attraction for her persists while her ardor has grown cold.*

> WIFE: *He is still a lot more interested in sex than I am, and I completely equate sex with intimacy. Because I don't trust him, I distance myself from him when he becomes sexual.*

This wife had trouble trusting her husband because he had been so dishonest in the past and in so many ways. It was natural for her to feel sexually distant from her husband when she did not trust him.

A counselor married twelve years recalls:

> *Our only problem was the long period of celibacy at the beginning, when I felt repulsed by him physically and did not trust him. This has gradually improved.*

Sex, Lies, and Forgiveness

Memories of Addict's Behavior Interfering With Current Sexual Relationship

Most addicts can remember the first few weeks after their addictive sexual behavior was revealed to their spouse. Most addicts were relieved that the truth had come out and that they no longer had to deal with the fear of being found out. Yet many were angry over having to give up behaviors that had brought them pleasure—and pain. Their partner usually felt overwhelmed by the truth, but also felt validated that he or she was not crazy for suspecting the partner's sexual behaviors. Coaddicts felt a full range of emotions—anger, rage, sadness, and depression—before accepting the situation and hoping for a new beginning in a troubled relationship.

After learning of their partner's sexual behaviors, most coaddicts wanted nothing to do sexually with their partner. They were raw from the hurt and betrayal and recoiled from the slightest touch. A wife reported, "The other woman's presence was constantly in bed with us." Another woman wrote, "I can't get the pictures of him and his partners out of my mind. Oral sex brings on those thoughts and visions the most." When coaddicts were finally ready to resume being sexual, they may have needed to negotiate changes in what they allowed. Many may have been uncomfortable with some sexual practices and wondered what their partner had done with others. Paradoxically, some coaddicts wanted more sex with their partner as a way of being reassured that they were still loved. Fearing abandonment, some coaddicts tried to hold on in the only way they knew how—sexually.

Establishing boundaries about specific sexual behaviors is part of the challenge of recovery. Coaddicts need to understand their own sexual needs and desires, and learn how to communicate them.

Coaddict's Problems Are Bared As The Addict's Behavior Changes

If coaddicts believed that sex is the most important sign of love, they were affirmed each time their partner was sexual with them. The more sex they got, the more they believed they were loved. No wonder they were shaken to the core when their partner was sexual with others! They truly believed that this meant they were loved

110

less than the others. Changing this core belief is very difficult, and even in recovery, coaddicts may use the level of sex in their relationship as a barometer of its health. A woman wrote: "I get angry if he doesn't want me. After all, he wanted them!"

The belief that sex is the most important way of showing love can cause problems for a couple if one member has lost sexual desire. A man told us: "She believes that sex cures all. Her attitude is if we had more sex we would feel better."

Recovering coaddicts are challenged not to control their partner or try to fix him or her. Women wrote: "I have drifting thoughts during lovemaking. I wonder if he has fantasies." . . . "I'm still not able to say no." . . . "There are times when I feel his needs are from his disease and I have to say NO. It is very hard for me to do so without fear." When coaddicts are no longer preoccupied with someone else's thoughts or behavior, they may become aware of the need to look at their own issues. A nurse in COSA for several months and married for ten years wrote:

> *My problem is my discomfort about being made love to. It was always there, but before I could just make love to him. Now, he's concerned more with sharing, wanting to be there for me, and that has made me face my issues.*

As couples heal their sexual relationship, each person may have different sexual needs. Reaching a solution requires open communication and sharing of feelings.

Fear of AIDS and Reaction to Condom Use

Before the 1980s, health considerations were not a major factor in decisions about sexual behavior. Some couples were concerned about unwanted pregnancies and sexually transmitted diseases, but it was not until the AIDS epidemic that people began to talk about being sexual in life-or-death terms. AIDS infection is now a major concern for those who have not been monogamous.

In our survey, several respondents mentioned their concern about AIDS. One man's HIV infection was causing him sexual problems. His wife explained, "His fear of me catching the HIV virus has made him impotent." Because the wife was at risk of catching the disease from her husband, they chose not to have intercourse. She added:

> *We don't have sex. He is HIV-positive. We do have intimacy, though. It's okay and we're happy without the sex, although we both miss it terribly at times. But we talk about it and work our programs. We talk about it when we miss it, say that it's sad. We hold each other and spend time together.*

Another couple in their forties married for twenty-three years were also dealing with the husband's HIV infection. They wrote:

> HUSBAND: *I have been exposed to AIDS, but I am not sick with it. I told my wife after I had her blood tested and found it was negative.*

> WIFE: *I got as much information about AIDS as I could from his doctor after she secretly used my thyroid blood test to test me for HIV for his knowledge, but didn't pass the info on to me! I've just finally gotten strong enough to insist that when we do begin having sex again he'll have to use condoms.*

In the past, many coaddicts were unable to refuse their spouse sex, even if they knew they were at risk of catching various sexually transmitted diseases. None of those diseases, however, was potentially fatal. On the other hand, most people who are infected with the HIV virus eventually become ill with AIDS, and AIDS is usually fatal. Most people who understand this would not consider having unprotected sexual relations with an HIV-infected partner.

Another man who had been sexual with other men reported, "She is concerned that there will always be a risk for AIDS." Although he was not infected, he and his wife were avoiding intercourse. They could be reassured by a negative HIV test and continued monogamy. When both members of a couple have had a negative HIV test six to twelve months after the last extramarital sexual encounter, there is usually no further risk of contracting AIDS from previous sexual encounters.

Several couples who were concerned about AIDS were using condoms. Two wives stated that condom use presented a problem for them. One explained why this was a problem and how she handled it. She wrote:

> *I talked to my counselor about how totally outraged I was to have to use a condom with my husband. She responded that I could learn to use one with him or I could learn without him (after a divorce, when I'd be single), but that I probably ought to get over my revulsion about condoms.*

To this woman, condoms were the visible evidence of past betrayal. This woman was angry at having to change her sexual routine because of her husband's past infidelities.

Problems Both Partners Have

Wondering About What Constitutes Healthy Sex

Until the Kinsey Report was published in 1948, sex was surrounded by great secrecy and no one really knew what others did behind closed doors. Today, there is an abundance of books that claim to teach us how to live sexually fulfilling lives. But despite this information, many of us still don't really know what healthy sexuality is.

As we learn more about our addictive patterns, we may become analytic instead of simply enjoying ourselves. We may feel less spontaneous and enjoy sex less. One addict in early recovery reported: "Nothing is safe or okay. If I have sex or get excited, I'm afraid I'll get out of control." With time, he will develop a clearer understanding of what is healthy for him and what is addictive. Several women wrote about their concern over a definition of healthy sexuality. "Sometimes we have lust for each other. Being sexual is not appropriate at such times." . . . "We're both still unsure what 'healthy' sex is between us." . . . "We are trying to find out what a 'normal' relationship is all about."

Answers to what "normal" and "healthy" are will come from mutual exploration and discussion with our spouse, counseling, reading, and talking with other people. Gradually, we will learn what feels comfortable for us.

The authors have found that healthy sexuality is not exploitive of others, is life-enhancing rather than destructive, takes place within the context of a caring relationship, has a spiritual component, and can be fun and enjoyable.

Less Intense Sex

Before recovery, coaddicts tended to confuse sexual intensity with intimacy. For them, fear and uncertainty may have actually enhanced the sexual experience. But for addicts in recovery, sex may have become less intense. A thirty-four-year-old woman wrote: "Often, sex is more awkward and it is never as intense as it was before recovery. But it is a lot more real, maybe more intimate, and it is more consistent." In recovery four years, a forty-five-year-old nurse and her husband explained:

> WIFE: *Sex with my husband used to be very exciting. I expected that when he stopped having affairs, the sex would be even better. Instead, it is less intense. It took me a while to realize that the intensity I used to feel was all mixed up with the craziness of my life. When I'd spent all day obsessing about my husband, worrying whether he still loved me, it was very exciting and reassuring to have him make love to me. Now, I no longer feel that panic and uncertainty. Our lovemaking is less intense, but more intimate.*

> HUSBAND: *My wife complains that our sex is less intense. I'm aware that my high level of sexual energy was a part of my acting out. Now, I can't give her all that sexual energy.*

Changing Balance in the Relationship

As addicts change the way they express themselves sexually, the overall relationship is affected. While some addicts may become less interested in sex, others may find extra sexual energy to expend with their spouse since they are no longer engaging in other sexual pursuits. As addicts adjust their sexuality in recovery, some coaddicts may begin to pay attention to their own sexual needs and desires. Others may lose sexual desire as a result of the loss of trust or as they explore incest or other family-of-origin issues. An addict in recovery for a year related:

> *Before beginning her recovery, my wife never denied me sex. Now she's beginning to assert herself, and I find that I'm afraid to say no to her because maybe she won't give it to me for two weeks after that.*

A couple in their thirties wrote:

> HUSBAND: *There is a lack of sexual drive on my part and increased sexual drive on her part.*
>
> WIFE: *He says no a lot, and now I try to initiate sometimes and he turns me down. I find it very hard to initiate and be turned down.*

With fragile self-esteem and no experience at getting turned down for sex, this woman felt rejected by her husband. To adjust to a new balance in their sexual relationship, she might say to him, "When you turn me down, I feel rejected." He might then be able to voice his fears and concerns about his decreased sexual drive, which probably have nothing to do with her.

How Are They Working It Out?

We asked in our survey how couples are working on sexual problems in their relationship. They listed several approaches, including

- open communication.
- professional counseling or psychotherapy.
- changing sexual practices.
- educating themselves about healthy sexuality.
- an abstinence period.

Open Communication

Here is what several respondents said about open communication: "We talk and express our care and love for each other with patience." . . . "Sometimes we fight; other times we are okay and work it out." . . . "When we are able to talk about sex and take the pressure off, it helps a lot." A thirty-nine-year-old sexually addicted woman wrote, "We admit the lust and are not sexual unless intimate first." This couple no longer used sex as a shortcut to intimacy. Instead, they were able to reserve a sexual connection for those times when they already felt good about each other.

Several couples were using specific techniques to improve their communication. They wrote: "Regularly we 'dialogue' on a topic and explore how we feel." . . . "We talk openly and try to change with the help of the therapist." Other couples were trying new ways of relating, such as using "I" statements instead of "you" statements. For example, when we tell our spouse, "I feel hurt when you walk by me without even saying hello," we are likely to get a less defensive response than when we say, "You always ignore me! You make me feel you just don't care!"

If a problem persists because of a couple's unwillingness to compromise, marriage counseling may help the couple explore how motivated they really are to change.

A couple with several years of recovery were at an impasse over the wife's desire for more sex. He wrote, "We argue about it, we don't talk." According to her, "I tell him I have different wants and needs and would he please be more aggressive." The wife, who has never attended S-Anon or COSA, may benefit from meetings where she will hear how others have dealt with similar issues. These meetings may also help her understand her role in the conflict.

Professional Counseling or Psychotherapy

Many couples have variations of the same argument over and over again. For them, it's like being forced to watch the same movie dozens of times. It may be time to try a different ending.

In a scene from the Woody Allen film *Annie Hall*, a husband and wife are separately discussing sex with their therapists. Each is asked, "How often do you sleep together?"

"Hardly ever. Three times a week," he says.

"Constantly. Three times a week," she says.

The same reality can be interpreted differently by two people. Disagreements about the frequency of sexual relations are common. A therapist can help a couple understand whether an argument is truly about sex or about something else. A woman may want sex daily, her husband weekly. She may believe she simply has a stronger sex drive. He may see her as predatory. In therapy, she may understand her core belief about sex. It could be that when her husband makes love to her, she feels validated and whole; when he turns her down, she feels unloved and rejected. Her real need is probably not for daily sex, but for daily evidence of her husband's love. When the couple understands this, they can work together on other ways for the husband to show he cares, by buying her flowers or telephoning her at work to say he loves her, for example.

For this woman's husband, a sexually assertive woman may bring back memories of childhood incest. The more demanding his wife appears, the less interested he becomes. He probably feels threatened by his wife's sexual needs. He may need to work through any incest experiences in order to become more comfortable. In the meantime, if she understands his feelings, she may be willing to be less assertive.

Changing Sexual Practices

Open communication about each person's needs may lead a couple to change their sexual routine. Some sexual practices may have to be modified or eliminated for a time if they were a part of the addict's behavior. For example, a man who was sexual with other men may find that receiving oral sex triggers fantasies that could interfere with his recovery. The spouse of a sex addict may also want to make some changes. This may include choosing to wear different clothes, use different language, watch different television shows and movies, and limit or expand his or her sexual repertoire. Here again, continuing dialogue is essential.

Educating Themselves About Healthy Sexuality

A thirty-five-year-old recovering coaddict wrote, "My husband and I are trying to find out what healthy sexuality is all about." Many couples truly do not know. Only after beginning their recovery did many couples recognize that what their parents taught them about sexuality was often off the mark. How do we find out what healthy sexuality is?

Some of us may have difficulty speaking about sex because we don't know the right words. A good way of acquiring a working vocabulary about sexuality is to read some of the books listed in the recommended reading list on page 277. By giving information about common sexual practices and attitudes, these books can give us a feel for what is typical among American couples. (Because some of this material may trigger addicts' sexual addiction, they may need to be careful about what they read.)

A sex therapist is another good source of information about healthy sexuality. Again, it is important to go to a therapist who is familiar with sexual addiction.

Discussion within the safety of a Twelve Step couples' group can also yield valuable information. At one couples' meeting the authors attended, the topic of the evening was, "What does sex mean to me?" Another evening's topic was, "What is healthy sexuality?" For many people, these meetings were the first time they had heard other men and women speak openly about sex.

An Abstinence Period

A period of abstinence for recovering sex addicts is strongly recommended by inpatient treatment programs and some therapists. Abstinence is defined as no sex with another person and no masturbation. Almost three-quarters of our survey's respondents had had at least one such period. Most said it had been recommended by a therapist, their self-help group, or one member of the couple had asked for it. Several couples in our survey did not decide on a formal abstinence period, but found themselves abstaining from sex because of other problems in their relationship. Two couples were avoiding intercourse because of the husband's infection with the HIV virus. Another couple had not been sexual with each other for years because of the husband's extramarital sexual activities and his wife's conflicts over her own sexuality.

We believe that couples who make the decision jointly to abstain will benefit more than couples in which the decision has been made unilaterally. Recovery is a time when there needs to be a lot of discussion. Before deciding on an abstinence period, answering the following questions can be helpful.

- What do we hope to accomplish by being abstinent?
- How long should it last?
- How will we decide to end our abstinence?
- What can we do to support and nurture each other during this time?
- How can we show affection without being sexual?
- How can we help each other in not sabotaging our abstinence contract?

Benefits of Not Being Sexual

A couple in their early thirties who were married for nine years wrote:

> HUSBAND: *Abstinence was ninety days long, beginning two months into recovery. It resulted in a better awareness of what sets off the acting out.*

> WIFE: *We had a celibacy period on the recommendation of the therapist, who said it was a part of recovery. It was good for me. I was able to take a break from sex. I was initially relieved—I didn't want to perform or take care of him sexually. It gave me time to look at our sex life, examine what it really was. I was able to listen for and recognize my own sexual desire for the first time in a long time. It felt really good.*

A sexually addicted businesswoman, married five years, wrote:

> *I feel that thirty days of abstinence, as recommended when I entered SA, was good for me. I had never been able to go more than four days without acting out in some form. I learned that I won't*

die without sex, and I learned how to be more relaxed, not putting pressure on my husband.

In several cases, one member of the couple initially asked for abstinence, but both benefited. A couple, both thirty-three years old and married four years, wrote:

HUSBAND: *My wife asked for a period of abstinence to sort out her experiences with childhood sexual abuse. We started nine months into recovery and so far have had three months of abstinence.*

WIFE: *I requested the abstinence period because I needed to feel I had some control over this part of my life and so I could feel safe enough to explore the issues about my incest. It has felt empowering for me to be able to set this limit, as I have never been able to before.*

Many of us have equated being intimate only with being sexual. We did not know how to be physical without it leading to sex, or how to be intimate without being physical. Time out from sex can be an opportunity to learn new ways to relate, as one couple who are both recovering sex addicts found out. They wrote:

HUSBAND: *We had two thirty-day celibacy periods in early recovery in order to withdraw from lust and to establish boundaries. It was good. I felt freedom and more intimacy.*

WIFE: *Our goal was to experience intimacy without the confusion of the old sexual patterns. I feel good about it. I gained perspective on our friendship and how we have used intercourse selfishly to alter my mood or his in the past.*

A couple who had been in recovery for five years recalled an extended abstinence period. In addition to being sexual with his wife several times daily for many years, the husband had had other partners. They wrote:

HUSBAND: *I had over a year of celibacy. It was the best thing I could have done for my recovery. It made all the difference in rebuilding my relationship with my wife.*

WIFE: *My husband suggested it and I was thrilled. I found out my husband loved me and that he didn't only want sex. I discovered how little I wanted sex. I found out how I used sex as a power play.*

Through an abstinence period, this woman got information about her own sexual needs and discovered how she had used sex to manipulate her husband. It also affirmed her as a person, not just a sex object. Other coaddicts wrote: "I learned that he really did love me and respect me." . . . "I realized my partner loves me with or without sex and that sex doesn't need to be such a big overshadowing cloud." . . . "My self-esteem increased. I realized I was more than just a sex object, and so was he. It brought us closer."

Not Everyone Always Benefits

In some cases, only one partner reported benefit from the abstinence period. The other was neutral or even unhappy about it. A couple in recovery more than two years wrote:

HUSBAND: *We had a nine-month celibacy period. It seemed to be what she wanted. Celibacy was not my plan. I can live without sex, but at times, the lack of it makes me disappointed, and at times I feel unforgiven.*

WIFE: *I asked for it because I thought we had too many problems and I needed some space. It gave me time to concentrate on my issues and to deal with my fear of abandonment.*

When the wife of a recovering sex addict realized she too was sexually addicted, she decided a period of abstinence would help her. She wrote:

I recognized my need to detox, so I stopped masturbating and I stopped having sex with my husband. But I didn't discuss it with him or tell him how long a time I needed. I just started putting him off. I know now it was because I was so sick. But it made him crazy. Finally, after about forty-five days, he said, "Maybe you don't want to talk about it, but I do!" And he told me his feelings about it. I realize now we should have discussed it at the beginning.

Several couples saw their abstinence period as a benefit only to the addict. One couple wrote:

HUSBAND: *I had forty-five days of celibacy early in recovery. I actually desired it. I was able to focus on myself, my addiction, and my progress. Sex with my wife was not there to distract this focus, but it was upsetting to my wife.*

WIFE: *I wish I had more of a part in the decision. So far, I haven't gained anything except the frustration of crawling into a bed with someone who doesn't want contact, and not knowing what to do.*

Not Always the Solution

Abstinence is not always the solution to a couple's sexual problems. When one person gets his or her way at the cost of the other person's needs, trouble is likely. Abstinence needs to be used in a balanced way in order to be beneficial.

An attorney, in recovery for several years, and his counselor wife reported problems. They wrote:

HUSBAND: *I asked for several periods of celibacy, from two to six months. The reason was guilt and anger—to punish her. I gained nothing. It wasn't done with the right motives.*

WIFE: *I hated it at first. I felt a lot of bad feelings, worthlessness about myself. I felt lost and drifting. Identity crisis stuff. Other times, I've felt relieved not to have to be close or "intimate" with him because the sex brought up many bad feelings I have about myself. But abstinence was painful too.*

This couple's experience underscores the need for a therapist to involve both spouses in a decision to abstain from sex and to have a clear-cut goal and plan of action. Abstinence should be presented positively as a time for healing and mutual exploration. A couple may have to be guided in specific types of nonsexual touching and other forms of nurturing. This can be a wonderful time for discovery.

Because men in our society are brought up to judge themselves by their sexual performance, a period of no sex may be very threatening to them. Men whose wives are sexually addicted may experience particular difficulty in coping with an abstinence period, and they may need help understanding the value of abstinence. A thirty-two-year-old woman, married seven years, recalled:

> *After dealing with all the problems of why I acted out sexually, there was a time when I really didn't want any kind of sexuality between my husband and me. We tried a celibacy period, but he felt it as rejection. His comment was, "You could have sex with all those other people and you can't have sex with me?" I couldn't seem to explain it to him. Now that we're going to a group that has opened up some topics that we had been unable to discuss, our sexuality has improved.*

A therapist who recommends abstinence without taking a thorough sexual history may be compounding an already existing problem. For example, a couple married many years wrote:

> HUSBAND: *We've been celibate for thirteen years. It's been part of the disease.*
>
> WIFE: *We are sexually dysfunctional and do not have intercourse. This was not a planned therapeutic celibacy. This is our ongoing problem.*

A fifty-year-old woman with several years' recovery from sexual addiction related:

> *We didn't have a celibacy period. When I first got into the program, they suggested not having sex for a while, but I decided that*

part of my problem behavior was that I didn't like having sex with my husband anyway, so it seemed to me that the logical thing for me to do was to work on having a sexual relationship with him. So, we began working on our sexual relationship and having sex more often, and several times I climaxed, which was very unusual for us.

Making the Best of Involuntary Abstinence

Even when a couple is abstinent under the worst possible conditions—when one member has a potentially fatal disease and abstinence must be indefinite—growth and happiness are possible. Married for three years, a forty-year-old woman wrote about how she was dealing with her husband's HIV infection:

We've been celibate seven months now because of his HIV infection. I realized that I can be happy and fulfilled without sex. I don't need to use it to prove I love someone. I can be loved for who I am—not my body.

How Would They Change Their Sexual Relationship?

Although an abstinence period helped many couples work on skills that later improved their sexual relationship, we were curious about what other changes couples could make to improve their sexual relationship. We asked, *What changes would make your sexual relationship better than it is now?*

More Intimacy

Most survey respondents had some ideas on how to improve their sexual relationship. These ideas dealt not with sexual repertoire but with improving intimacy, trust, and time together. A man wrote, "We both realize that the actual sexual act is nothing without intimacy and communication." A woman said, "With more trust and intimacy in the relationship, I'll feel more safe to open up sexually."

An administrator and his wife married twenty-two years wrote:

HUSBAND: *It's important to me that my partner allow me to feel emotionally part of her life and not keep me at a distance emotionally. I also need to understand by her actions that I am the most important person in her life. Otherwise, having sex with her is akin to having sex with someone I don't know, which is what I did a lot of when acting out.*

WIFE: *The walls blocking emotional intimacy need to fall so we can truly give ourselves to each other.*

Personal Growth

A number of respondents believed that as they recovered individually their sexual relationship as a couple would improve. Addicts wished for: "Greater acceptance on both our parts." . . . "More recovery and less addictive need on my part." . . . "Sex as relationship healing and bonding, not to complete me or drug me." . . . "An increased trust between us and a realization that we are committed to each other."

Coaddicts also wrote of their need for personal growth. They wrote: "I need to become comfortable with being a good person who is also a sexual person. Much of it is in my own self-esteem and willingness to open myself and trust." . . . "More spontaneity. Greater self-esteem on both partners' part."

Several people wished they could erase the past. Others expressed the desire to talk more openly about sex.

In our obsession with our addiction or our partner, many of us grew out of touch with our own feelings. In recovery, we need first to identify our feelings and then share them. Many of us have repressed or suppressed our feelings for so long that we can no longer identify them. An important task in our individual recovery is to reconnect with these feelings.

We need to learn to make changes in our thinking and behavior, although these changes may come more slowly than we would like. One woman wrote:

He still uses some crude language from his acting-out days. I have asked him to stop it. It's not happening overnight.

Sexual Changes

Several respondents noted specific sexual areas that could be improved. Among the coaddicts wishes were: "Him initiating more. Me pressuring less. Him focusing on my body more." . . . "For him to slow down and give me more pleasure." . . . "Me getting aroused more and anticipating sex."

Some addicts wished for: "Greater frequency." . . . "More healthy variety, for her to initiate, more talking during sex, and not always the same time and same place." . . . "To have my wife initiate sex on occasion. To know she has climaxed."

A homemaker married for seven years would have liked to initiate sex. She wrote:

> *I would initiate if we had more time to make love and if I felt freer (less inhibited, less fear of rejection). My husband is uncomfortable when I lead. I feel controlled and have difficulty facing my fear of rejection by pursuing more often. But I'm trying.*

A man who wrote that his sexual relationship had gradually worsened during his more than two years in recovery believed that things would improve if he could eliminate sex completely. His wife agreed that their sexual relationship lacked spontaneity and intimacy, but they hoped to improve in those areas. Sex had been a battleground for this couple. Couple counseling might help them resolve the problem in a more constructive manner.

For some addicts, being abstinent feels safer than being sexual. They may envy the recovering alcoholic, who has only to put the plug in the jug. Being sexually active means making frequent choices about what is and what is not okay.

Conclusion

Most couples in our survey reported having some sexual problems during recovery. Most said they were working on them, either by themselves or with the support of Twelve Step groups and/or a therapist. Although some couples appeared to be at an impasse, the majority were optimistic about the future. These were for the most part people who were committed to the preservation of their relationship and were actively working on their problems.

In comparing their sexual relationship before and during recovery, most respondents noted an improvement, especially in increased intimacy. With individual recovery came the willingness to risk being open and vulnerable, to begin to let down defenses. Some respondents wrote that they were establishing new boundaries. Coming from addiction and coaddiction, our boundaries were often blurry or nonexistent. But as we progress in recovery, we learn more about what we want for ourselves. We determine which behaviors are healthy for us and what we are willing to accept from our partner. Setting limits and establishing boundaries is the subject of the next chapter.

CHAPTER SEVEN

Setting Limits And Establishing Boundaries

Anita had it all. She had a beautiful home in a presti-
gious suburban neighborhood. Her husband Donald was
on the staff of the university hospital and was warmly
regarded by his colleagues and well liked by the nurses.
Her two children were attractive and well behaved. She
was the program chairperson of the medical society aux-
iliary and was being groomed for the vice-presidency
next year.

Because Donald had a busy clinical practice and was
on the faculty of the medical school, he was absent from
home more than Anita would have liked. He assured his
wife that things would ease up once he finished some
important research work. But the success of that project
led to an invitation by a pharmaceutical company to
travel and report to other physicians on the results of his
trials with a new drug produced by the company.
Donald chose to have an attractive young research associate accompany him on his travels. The wife of one of
Donald's colleagues spilled the beans about Donald's
affair with the research associate and Anita found herself
plunged into a dark hole. She ricocheted from rage to
depression. She rehearsed for days how she would confront her husband when he returned.

But when Donald arrived home bringing Anita a beautiful blouse he had bought on his trip, her resolve melted away. *He really does love me, she told herself, and if I confront him it will just make the other woman look all the more appealing. I can't nag him — I'll just have to show him how lucky he is to have me for a wife.* Instead of expressing her anger and pain, she murmured pleasantries about the children's weekend activities, fixed her husband a drink, and listened to what she knew was an altered account of his trip. She dutifully had sex with him while fighting images of her husband in the arms of another woman. Two hours after he had drifted off to sleep, Anita lay in the dark silently sobbing.

Several weeks later, Donald began talking about Gretchen, a medical resident who had begun a rotation in his clinic. In order to assess the competition, Anita suggested that they invite his new colleague to dinner. When Gretchen walked in, Anita's worst fears were confirmed. As she watched Donald greet this stunning brunette, it was clear he was involved in yet another affair. As the months went on, Gretchen became more a part of their lives. The children loved her youthful enthusiasm and would sometimes spend Saturday afternoons at the park or zoo with her. Anita felt she was losing her mind. When she finally summoned the courage to confront Donald, he indignantly told her that nothing was going on and suggested Anita talk to a psychiatrist about her wild imagination. By then, Anita was experiencing frequent headaches, insomnia, and anxiety attacks; she agreed with Donald that she needed medical attention. She visited a woman doctor who asked the right questions and Anita began tearfully telling the story of years of not trusting her own instincts and of not being able to ask for what she wanted in her marriage.

Anita was a woman who was unable to set boundaries. Because of her fear of losing Donald, she accepted the unacceptable — her

husband's ongoing involvement with other women and his asser-
tion that she was the one with a problem. But staying silent, acting
as if nothing was wrong, and taking no position on a major issue
in her most important relationship were exacting their toll. Anita
was paying a heavy price in terms of her emotional and physical
health.

What prevented Anita from taking action about a situation that
was becoming increasingly intolerable? She had grown up in a
household similar to her present one. Her father, a busy physician,
was rarely at home. Her mother worked diligently to smooth his
path and raise a perfect family. Anita never heard an argument between her parents, although she could sense her mother's unhappiness at her father's frequent absences. Anita longed for affection
from her father, who rarely had time for his children. She convinced herself that she could win her father's attention by being the
"perfect" daughter. Since she was unable to attain perfection — or to
get much attention from her father — she came to believe that she
was not worthy of love. Her marriage to Donald gave her another
chance. This time she would do it right and get the love and attention she craved. The thought of losing Donald was intolerable to
Anita. She was willing to put up with just about anything rather
than risk failing once again to get love from the most important man
in her life.

Why Some People Lack Boundaries

Many codependents are like Anita. They are unable to set appropriate limits in their life because they don't really believe they
deserve any better. Their core beliefs, learned in their family of origin, tell them they are not worthwhile people. Because they believe
they are not lovable and do not love themselves, they try to earn the
love of others through their actions. On some level, they believe
they do not have the right to be happy. Their fear of abandonment
leads them to accept intolerable or abusive relationships. Many of
them learn to trade sex for affection. This is particularly true for
those who have experienced covert or overt sexual abuse. They confuse affection with abuse; sex and love become inextricably connected for them.

Why do these people stay in abusive situations? First, in order to leave, they must be aware of their choices, something they do not always realize they have. In recovery from addiction and coaddiction, people learn about their choices. They learn that only when they feel good about themselves can they make decisions about which of their partner's behaviors—and which of their own—are acceptable and unacceptable. They can then make a realistic plan of action in case unacceptable behaviors occur. Generally, people need to be in recovery for a while before they are in a position to establish boundaries.

This was recognized in retrospect by the wife of a man who had told her he was being sexual with other men. She told us:

> *During the time I was seeing a counselor, AIDS was beginning to become known and my counselor asked about it. I told my husband if he refused to practice safe sex, I would not sleep with him. The counselor and I decided that this was a very reasonable thing to say. Now, I realize I could have said, "I will not sleep with you, period." But my counselor was not an addiction counselor and he was trying to get me to accept my husband's bisexuality. When I told my husband this, he got angry.*

Before recovery, many coaddicts recognized their partner's unacceptable behaviors and tried unsuccessfully to force change. They may have threatened to leave if the behavior continued. Some may actually have left for a while, but were unable to take effective action because they were paralyzed by their fear of abandonment. They also feared the consequences if they were to stand their ground. Their threats to leave were not expressions of what was intolerable so much as they were ultimatums—a means of manipulating their partner into changing.

Ultimatums differ from boundaries. The goal of an ultimatum is to get other people to make changes they do not want to make; the goal of a boundary is to prevent us from finding ourselves in an intolerable situation. When we establish a boundary, we define what situations we are unwilling to live with and what we will do should the situation occur.

One task in early recovery is to recognize those situations where we need to set boundaries. We asked our survey respondents about their boundaries.

Boundary Agreement
Of all respondents, 70 percent believed they had an agreement with their spouse on what behaviors were not acceptable. Of the forty-nine couples for whom we received responses from both members, one-third disagreed about whether or not there had been an agreement.

Among the sexual activities within the relationship that some people wrote were no longer acceptable were: "The language that came with the acting out." . . . "Forced, angry, violent intercourse that could lead to an unchosen pregnancy." . . . "Sex when one of us doesn't want to." . . . "Oral sex, anal sex, and fantasizing during sex. Lusting and losing awareness of the other during sex." . . . "No sexy lingerie. No role-playing. No R-rated movies to warm us up for sex."

Some behaviors were considered more serious than others. For example, one man formerly had anonymous sex with men in pornographic bookstores. He and his wife wrote:

> HUSBAND: *We have agreed on no sexual contact with some other person, though less serious behaviors are not considered healthy either.*

> WIFE: *Our agreement is no sexual contact with others outside the marriage. Occasional "slippery" behavior is tolerated, like going into a bookstore.*

In early recovery, it is common for some coaddicts to have an extensive list of unacceptable behaviors for their spouse, ranging from affairs to looking at other men or women. Does looking at other men or women really need to be a boundary? Coaddicts need to ask themselves, *Am I unwilling to live with my husband if he should crane his neck at a pretty girl? Do I intend to leave my wife if she comments on a younger man's physique?* As addicts and coaddicts grow in their recovery, they recognize that people need to recover at their own pace. As both become healthier, both will learn what they can and cannot live with.

Addict/Coaddict Boundaries

Among survey respondents, 81 percent of coaddicts and 48 percent of addicts said that they had thought about what behaviors they would be unwilling to tolerate in their spouse. The only limit 16 percent of addicts had on their spouse was sex outside the marriage, even though that was what they, not the spouse, had been doing. If we subtract these respondents from the group of addicts who claimed to have limits for their spouse's behaviors, then only 32 percent of addicts had limits on their spouse's coaddictive behaviors.

Because some addicts did not yet understand how the whole family can be caught up in one member's addiction, they were unable to identify how their own boundaries could be crossed. On the other hand, when spouses of sex addicts were dealing with their own addictions, addicts listed their relapse as an obvious boundary. "No more alcohol," wrote a sex addict whose wife was a recovering alcoholic. Another sex addict whose wife had used cocaine considered her continued drug use unacceptable.

Only two addicts mentioned that they have set limits on their spouse's codependent behaviors. One man in recovery for three years found intolerable, "Excessive discussions (beyond two hours) where she outlines my faults and tries to fix me." The other man wrote, "Physical or emotional abuse not balanced with love and caring."

Most coaddicts had no difficulty defining behaviors that they would find intolerable in their partner. They listed as unacceptable any sexual behaviors that were part of their partner's addiction, such as affairs, pornography, exhibitionism, and masturbation. Some coaddicts paid attention to their own feelings as they described their limits. They wrote: "I will not participate in activities that hurt me or scare me." . . . "I won't have sex if I am angry or feeling any extreme feelings that I might want to escape from through sex." . . . "To be treated with respect, as a valid human being."

Some respondents mentioned honesty. One wrote, "My only limit right now is that we have to have honesty in our relationship." Only one coaddict listed "quitting the program" as unacceptable. Yet many said they would feel very threatened and upset if their spouse should leave their Twelve Step programs.

Dealing with Boundary Violations

Enforcing boundaries is more difficult than defining them. Sixty percent of addicts compared with 82 percent of coaddicts had a plan for dealing with boundary violations. Again, more coaddicts than addicts gave thought to this issue. The most common consequence mentioned was considering ending the relationship. Coaddicts wrote: "If he went back to that lifestyle, I would leave him. He has said he would not live with someone who wasn't in recovery also." . . . "I would leave my husband if he cheated on me or picked up a drink. I will continue to work with him on his anger."

A gay man living in a monogamous committed relationship with another man said, "I told him that if he is sexual with another man because he is out of control and has not taken the steps to prevent it, then we would separate."

Some respondents recognized that they might have difficulty standing their ground. In recovery over a year, a housewife said, "If boundaries are continually being crossed, I hope I have the guts to leave."

Sometimes a person's determination to leave a relationship is tempered by fear of his or her spouse's reaction. A woman who wrote she would divorce her husband if he had another affair added, "If he slips with an affair, I believe he would kill himself."

Respondents' second most common consequence of boundary violation was to talk about it openly or seek counseling. A middle-aged college student told us she would pray for God's help to communicate her fears and anger. She believed her husband would be ashamed, angry, and guilty, and she hoped he would not be suicidal. A counselor in recovery for several years said her husband's being sexual with other men would cross her boundaries. She said she would react by calling in reinforcements – elders/pastors from their church, seeking counseling, and restating boundaries. If her husband did become sexual with other men again, she hoped he would want continued recovery more than his addiction. She admitted, though, that there are no guarantees.

Despite concern about AIDS, surprisingly few respondents mentioned not having marital sex if their spouse became sexual with other partners. Apparently, divorce or separation was considered more likely than continuing to live together without sexual contact. Implicit in the thinking of many people was the notion that different boundary violations would result in different consequences. A young helping professional wrote: "If he has another affair, I'll divorce him. If he quits the program, I would urge counseling. If he lies, I would ask for counseling or divorce if he doesn't stop." After more than a year of counseling and Twelve Step involvement, she was able to articulate specific consequences for each potential boundary violation.

Conclusion

Boundaries can range from rigid solid walls that isolate us to totally permeable boundaries that force us to dance to the tune of anyone who happens to play. When we believe that these extremes are our only two options for setting boundaries, we are engaging in black-and-white thinking. In recovery, we learn the world is made up of many shades of gray.

Because of this black-and-white approach, some of us believed our only options were to put up with everything or to leave. "I didn't realize I could say no without saying good-bye," said one respondent. Since the thought of ending the relationship was intolerable, many of us accepted the unacceptable.

Many of us also feared expressing our feelings. We stuffed them and then exploded over some minor transgression. In recovery, we learn to recognize what is and what is not acceptable, and become willing to state this clearly in our relationships. We can deal with problems as they come up. We do not have to wait until we feel we have no other option but to end the relationship.

Some people are confused about what it means to develop

boundaries. For example, one woman believed her sexual boundaries changed from day to day because one day she wanted to have sex with her husband and the next day she did not. Actually, she had established a healthy boundary about having sex only when she felt like it and was respecting her feelings. Her boundary was not changing; rather, her feelings about having sex were changing, as do most people's. Redefining her boundary as "I will respect my feelings about having sex" helped her realize she was doing well.

Setting boundaries means taking responsibility for ourselves. Many of us had let others make decisions for us; we were reactors rather than actors. In recovery, we reclaim the power we have repeatedly given away. We learn to trust our feelings and let others know what is acceptable and unacceptable to us.

Learning to establish boundaries is a process. A woman whose husband was sexual with a number of men felt paralyzed the first year after she learned of his behavior. A year later, when they were sexual with each other, she insisted that they use condoms for her protection. After an additional year, she stopped being sexual with him. She ultimately divorced him when he was unwilling to stop his sexual activities outside the marriage. Her ability to recognize and act on her boundaries increased with her time in recovery and with her improved self-esteem.

Because addictions are not curable, no one can guarantee a relapse or minor slip will not happen. But the likelihood will decrease if we have a definite relapse prevention plan and a clear understanding of the consequences should a relapse occur. The next chapter will discuss in detail sobriety, relapse, and relapse prevention.

CHAPTER EIGHT

Sobriety and Relapse

Curtis believed his recovery program was good. He had more than five years of sobriety in Alcoholics Anonymous. He told his sponsor he felt he was one of those lucky people for whom the obsession to drink had been removed at the very first meeting. His sexual sobriety was another story. Despite over a year of attending a Twelve Step program for sex addicts, he had not been able to put together ninety days of freedom from what he called his bottom-line behavior, cruising the red-light districts and soliciting prostitutes.

Just prior to completion of his student teaching assignment, Curtis was arrested for soliciting an undercover policewoman he thought was a prostitute. Six weeks before, he had pawned his prized stereo equipment in order to pay a prostitute who had threatened to blackmail him.

"I don't understand what comes over me," he tearfully told his support group.

Curtis did not realize that he had been making a series of relapse-prone decisions and engaging in a number of risky behaviors that led to him driving into the red-light district where he stopped and solicited the policewoman.

The early concepts of sobriety and relapse in alcoholism were simple. *Sobriety* was not taking the first drink and *relapse* was drinking. Now, addiction professionals understand that drinking is the last step in the relapse process, not the first. Relapse is a much more complex process than addiction professionals initially believed. It is even more complicated in behavioral addictions. How do people with eating disorders make decisions about food? How do sex addicts determine what is healthy sexual behavior and what is addictive? And how do codependents or coaddicts define sobriety and relapse for themselves? This chapter will help answer these questions.

Sobriety for the Addict

For sex addicts, establishing a definition of sobriety is essential for relapse prevention. According to Carnes, "If neither the group nor the professionals involved have carefully and systematically helped the addict to think through and create a personal definition of sobriety, then relapse is almost inevitable."[1]

The importance of avoiding behaviors that are preludes to relapse cannot be overstated. Some of the everyday behaviors that addicts list as part of their relapse definition may be considered normal for most people, but they may be dangerous for addicts because they initiate the relapse process.

An example given by a five-year Sexaholics Anonymous (SA) member illustrates this point. Before getting into the program, he had been involved in a number of extramarital affairs. When he began to look at his behavior, he realized he was consciously making choices that invariably led to his cheating. The process began with him feeling resentful about a situation at home and not discussing it with his wife. Next came euphoric recall of the last affair. Then, he would flirt with someone, engage in conversation with her to elicit personal information, and ask for her telephone number. He would save the number for later, then use it, meet her for lunch, talk to her about his marital problems, obsess about having sex with her, set up the tryst, and then follow through with the date. At some point in the process, he could not turn back.

Various Definitions

Every one of the addicts in our survey was able to define what relapse was for them. The responses reflected the definition of sobriety in the particular Twelve Step program to which they belonged. Members of Sexual Compulsives Anonymous developed a sexual recovery plan and defined sexual sobriety for themselves. Members of SA defined relapse as, "Sex with self or anyone other than my spouse," or "Masturbation or sex except with spouse." Sex and Love Addicts Anonymous (SLAA) members defined relapse as "bottom-line acting out" or "a return to bottom-line behaviors." Sex Addicts Anonymous (SAA) members listed the specific behaviors that to them represented a relapse: "Masturbation, attending peep shows, strip shows, pornographic movies, and having sex with someone other than my wife." . . . "Going to adult bookstores and having sex with another man." . . . "Affairs, going to prostitutes." . . . "Fantasy, masturbation, indecent liberties—touching, however slight or discreet, to get a buzz or to entice. Affairs and adultery are out of the question, as is bestiality and incest." . . . "Extramarital affairs, or trying to convince my husband to swing or to watch pornography."

All addictions consist of two components—a *thinking* disorder (denial, blaming others, obsessive thinking about the drug or activity) and a *behavior* disorder (compulsive use of the substance or behavior). These two elements reinforce each other. For the recovering addict, slips into addictive thinking can lead to slips into addictive behavior.

A relapse prevention plan must address the addict's thinking and behavior disorder. Many addicts in our survey were aware of this and included certain thoughts as part of their definition of relapse. They wrote: "Desire to have an affair." . . . "When sobriety loses its priority." . . . "To become out of control with lust." . . . "To return to the former thinking, behavior, and secrecy. To become closed off from my spouse and to engage in deceitful actions." . . . "Fantasizing about others to achieve orgasm." . . . "An internal decision not to keep coming to meetings, regardless of whether I am slipping or not. This inevitably leads to masturbation, fantasy, and a breakdown in my spirituality."

A forty-seven-year-old businessman envisioned his relapse prevention plan as follows:

> *For me, sobriety is like standing on the roof of a very tall building. Having another affair would be like falling off. If I were to have lunch with an attractive associate in a cozy, dimly lit restaurant, and if I steered our conversation around to her marriage problems and mine, I would be getting awfully close to the edge of the roof. I feel safer standing closer to the center. So, I avoid situations that get me close to the edge. I don't drink at business lunches, so I don't cloud my judgment. I keep business meetings professional. I particularly avoid talking about any personal or marriage problems.*
>
> *If I'm attracted to a woman, I make a deliberate decision not to pursue a personal friendship with her. I know that the farther I allow a "slippery" situation to proceed, the more powerless I become in stopping it. I've learned that I have to set my boundary at a place where I still have the choice. I've learned to stay away from the edge of the roof.*

One respondent listed "perpetual boundary bumping" as part of his definition of relapse. A married thirty-three-year-old woman who had had multiple affairs told us:

> *My bottom line is no sex with anyone but my husband. Also, there are certain people and places and situations that trigger me. I don't do any social activity with men. I don't go to movies with men. I don't go to lunch with men. I won't go to a male co-worker's house.*

Another recovering woman had a history of sadomasochistic sexual activities as well as compulsive masturbation with unhealthy, violent fantasies. She said:

> *I no longer have sex with myself with these sick fantasies. My counselor thinks I should masturbate. She feels that it's nurturing to myself. I don't do it right now, though, because every time I start to do it these sick fantasies come up and I really don't want to act out. I also won't have affairs with anybody else. I want to be monogamous.*

The complexities of defining sobriety and relapse for sex addicts can lead to some confusion. A saleswoman two months in recovery from sexual addiction wrote, "To me there's a gray area between going beyond my boundaries (i.e., not calling or seeing certain guys) and a relapse." Although she recognized that certain behaviors were dangerous for her, she did not want to call them actual relapses. To her, a relapse was actually falling off the roof. Getting close to the edge was simply taking a risk.

Recovery from sexual addiction is more like recovery from an eating disorder than from chemical dependency. Unlike an alcoholic who can never drink alcohol, all people need to eat and all are sexual beings. This means that instead of deciding whether or not to partake, sex addicts have to decide which sexual activities fit into their recovery plan. They also need to examine their motivations when engaging in a particular behavior. For example, one addict listed "having sex to avoid feelings" as part of his relapse definition. Another wrote, "acting out sexually to escape." For one woman addict in our survey, a relapse was "when I have sex to change the way I feel." These respondents recognized that the same behaviors can be healthy or addictive.

How Coaddicts Saw Addicts' Relapse

Although Twelve Step programs teach us to concentrate on our own recovery and to let others be, it is inevitable in a marriage that our partner will be affected by our recovery. For example, a woman's affair obviously has an impact on her husband. He must decide whether to continue in the marriage and whether he is willing to be sexual with her.

Nearly all coaddicts surveyed were able to define what they considered relapses for their partners. Often, they had a list very similar to the addict's: "Having an affair, obsessive masturbation, use of pornography, voyeurism." . . . "Viewing pornography. Visiting bookstores, massage parlors, voyeurism, exhibitionism, being sexual with someone else, compulsively masturbating." . . . "Flirting openly and obsessing." . . . "Even without breaking sobriety, he can go on a 'dry drunk' by visiting strip bars, renting

X-rated videos, or cruising. That to me is still out of control and is a relapse."

Some coaddicts had highly specific definitions of a relapse: "Spending more than an hour obsessing sexually." . . . "Obsessing about another woman for longer than thirty seconds. Infidelity, compulsively masturbating. Buying a pornographic magazine." . . . "When he fantasizes about other women or looks longer than three seconds." Interestingly, no addicts listed the same time constraints in their own definition of relapse.

Several coaddicts were aware of the role of thoughts and feelings as preludes to relapse and included these in their definitions. They wrote:

> . . . *Presence of old thought patterns and behaviors that focus on encounters with other women. This may include obsessing, flirting, meeting. Of course, total relapse would be actually acting out sexually.*

> . . . *Masturbating to pornographic images or fantasies; going to peep shows, massage parlors, hookers; engaging in any activity that produces a sense of shame and that he feels compelled to do rather than chooses to do.*

> . . . *When he tries to do something for me that I have not asked to be done (rescuing). When he feels lonely, very angry, and has an alcoholic slip. Then, he will act out in some other way, such as masturbating at a porno movie.*

There can be a connection between drinking or other drug use and sexual relapse. Often, one can lead to the other. For the recovering alcoholic/sex addict, prevention of sexual relapse must include maintaining alcohol sobriety. The last quote above also illustrates the progression from "stinking thinking"—anger in this case—to an actual relapse.

Recovering coaddicts sometimes encounter skepticism when they tell others that their spouse is not continuing his or her old behaviors. They are asked, "She lied to you before. How do you know she's not lying now?" or "He slept around before. How do you know he's being faithful now?" "We just *know*," they answer. Before recovery, coaddicts may not have known because they did not trust their intuition. In recovery, they learn to pay attention to their feelings. Instead of blaming themselves, they consider other possible explanations for their spouse's behavior. In our survey, several coaddicts realized that behavior changes could be a sign of relapse. One wrote, "If my spouse had a relapse, he would start treating me very critically and sarcastically and he would become unavailable to me emotionally."

Relapse Prevention

All but a handful of addicts in our survey were attending Twelve Step meetings. The programs provide them with tools for relapse prevention. These include the meetings themselves, working through the Steps of the program, reading the literature, praying and meditating, calling members on the phone, consulting a sponsor, and sponsoring others. Most addicts used some combination of these tools to stay sexually sober. Others indicated they were also involved in individual, couple, or group therapy.

Honesty is one of the foundations of the Twelve Steps and is the key to maintaining sexual sobriety. This was recognized by several respondents, whose relapse prevention plan included seeking spiritual help, going to meetings and sharing, talking with others, keeping a sponsor, and maintaining honesty.

To prevent relapse, addicts must first understand their personal relapse course. Because denial may prevent them from recognizing what is happening to them, it is helpful to have ongoing feedback from others. This is where the Twelve Step group and the sponsor can be of great help. Once addicts can identify their own relapse warning signs, they must then make concrete plans for interrupting the sequence of events that can lead to relapse. They must practice each new response until it becomes a habit. The relapse prevention plan must include contacting a sponsor or group member. And addicts need to understand that a slip does not have to lead to a full-blown relapse.

A comprehensive relapse prevention plan has both negative elements (things to avoid) and positive elements (activities to do and people with whom to interact). For the alcoholic, simply stopping drinking is unlikely to bring about long-term alcohol sobriety. Unless the use of alcohol as a solution to problems is replaced by a more constructive approach, the urge to drink is eventually likely to become too strong to resist. The program of AA provides the recovering alcoholic with a new set of friends committed to sobriety, increased self-esteem, guidelines for problem solving and living without alcohol, and the connection with other people and a Higher Power. The recovering sex addict needs a similar support system and a relapse prevention plan that includes far more than just a list of behaviors and places to avoid.

Myths About Relapse
Stopping an addictive behavior once is easier than staying stopped. Ask anyone who has quit smoking only to begin again. The average smoker who wants to quit tries four times before staying stopped. Ninety percent of people who lose weight gain it back.

In their book *Willpower's Not Enough*, Arnold Washton and Donna Boundy list some myths about relapse.[2] These include:

• Relapse is a sign of recovery failure.
• Relapse is a sign of poor motivation.
• Relapse starts the instant you "use."
• Relapse is unpredictable, and therefore unavoidable: It hits you out of the blue.
• Relapse applies only to your drug [or behavior] of choice.
• A relapse cancels out all progress made up to that point.
• If a relapse isn't the end of recovery, then it's okay to have one.

These myths contribute to the high incidence of relapse. The fact is, even highly motivated recovering people have relapses. A temporary setback does not cancel out the recovery that preceded it. A relapse does not occur out of the blue; it is preceded by warning signs and opportunities to prevent it. Indulging in any behavior that triggers addictive thinking can lead to a relapse. And the use of *any* mood-altering drug or activity can lower one's resistance to relapse.

For addicts who have relapsed, it is a golden opportunity to learn more about what triggers the chain of events that leads to relapse. By reviewing in detail the feelings and events that preceded the relapse, addicts can revise their relapse prevention plan to make another slip less likely.

Slightly more than half of the addicts surveyed said they had had one or more relapses. For 21 percent, relapse was masturbation; 31 percent had engaged in other behaviors. These other behaviors, all described by men, included: "Sex with another woman." . . . "Fantasy, looking at pornography at an adult bookstore, contact with other men or oral sex with them." . . . "I stole a woman's panties from a laundromat." . . . "I had an affair with an old classmate." . . . "I drank and acted out." . . . "Anonymous liaisons." . . . "Emotional involvement with others, poor boundaries, and multiple sex partners in gay bathhouses and bookstores."

An administrator who had been sexual in a wide variety of ways wrote:

> *I lost my Higher Power connection over a two-week period. I was struck with the desire to act out and completely gave in and compulsively drove to a bookstore and lost my sobriety. I was tempted strongly to binge, but remembered my desire for sexual sobriety and made a call and came back to the meetings. I recognized more how powerless I was and really dug into the program and haven't let up since.*

This man was able to return to the program rather than continue his downward spiral. He was able to understand the link between the loss of his spirituality and the loss of his sobriety. Many addicts who relapse may find themselves thinking, *I blew it. I might as well eat the whole cake and have a whole series of sexual partners.* One of the lessons of relapse prevention planning is that a single relapse does not have to lead to a binge.

A bisexual man in our survey went to a public rest room and had sex with another man. Since then, he has learned to avoid public parks, public rest rooms, and gymnasiums. His wife told us:

With his last experience over a year ago, it was a mutual under-standing that we would separate for a while, and maybe for al-ways. He came and told me what had happened. He moved to his own place. While he worked out his difficulties, I wondered whether we would ever continue together. I was ready to say, "If divorce is going to happen, now is as good a time as ever."

And yet part of me believed in the concept of forgiveness and repen-tance. If he came to honestly believe he wanted to live a straight married life, then I had no other choice except to forgive and ac-cept. And when he made that decision, we got back together.

Breaking the News

Of the addicts who had relapsed, three-quarters told their spouse, with varying results. None divorced, but some temporarily separated. Because our surveys were sent only to recovering cou-ples who were still together, we have no information about couples whose marriages ended because of relapse.

One man told his wife about his relapse and went into inpatient treatment. She participated in family week. They subsequently rated the quality of their marriage as excellent. Another man had an affair with an old friend one month into recovery. He told his group, his wife, and a therapist. The wife said that the episode trig-gered her codependent behavior. She wrote:

We had crazy discussions where I demanded impossible promises and reassurances. I recognized it as a relapse for me, but I couldn't seem to get out of the crazy cycle at the time. I beat myself up about it, then called my sponsor and tried to learn from it. I talked about it with my husband and shared how I felt.

Because she knew of more than one slip, she still did not trust her husband, but said their chances of remaining together were very good.

Other addicts who told their spouse reported a less positive out-come. For example, a man who had a variety of compulsive sexual behaviors, including affairs and molestation, relapsed and went to inpatient treatment. Regarding his wife's reaction, he wrote:

> *It was very difficult for her. It was painful for me to fail in such a public manner—once in the hospital, all those strangers knowing and all. We just muddled through.*

He rated the odds of their remaining together, however, as excellent. They were actively working on their couple relationship in a support group for couples.

Several addicts who had masturbation slips told only their support group. A man whose relapse consisted of another affair told his group and his wife. He and his wife wrote:

> HUSBAND: *I felt shame and remorse. She is still angry. I am trying to understand why I did what I did, looking at the way I felt at the time.*
>
> WIFE: *I treat him terribly. I get depressed. I blame him. He is beginning to understand that behind my anger is hurt and behind the hurt there is love.*
>
> *I haven't gotten over the pain of this last betrayal. Having taken the blame for previous affairs (which I shouldn't have), I feel these affairs were a direct rebellion against me. He knew that adultery would hurt me more than anything else he could do. He recognizes that he is full of anger and resentment toward his father— redirected at me.*
>
> *I am also so angry with the other women. If they weren't so damn available to have sex with married men, these affairs wouldn't be so prevalent.*

Summary

In addition to having a concrete list of behaviors to avoid, addicts need a plan of action for handling setbacks if they occur. If addicts can stop the process while they still have choices, a minor slip does not need to end up as a relapse. A solid support system is both good insurance against a slip and a way of getting help if a setback occurs.

Using the telephone to check in with program people even when addicts feel good is like a "fire drill" for dealing with setbacks. It helps if addicts take daily inventory of their thinking and behavior and daily examine their motives. Friends in the support network can also be helpful in letting them know when they are getting into relapse-prone thinking and behaviors, such as isolating themselves and feeling angry or resentful.

Finally, recovery is more than just monitoring negative behavior. Addicts need to learn to nurture themselves in healthy ways.

Sobriety for the Coaddict

Just as defining sobriety for the sexual addict requires an examination of the pattern of sexual acting out, so defining sobriety for the coaddict requires taking a look at behavior patterns.

The essence of codependency is looking outward for self-worth. It is a pattern of personality traits that *precedes* addiction and coaddiction and predisposes people to one behavior or the other. Codependency develops before adulthood as a result of people's experience in their family of origin. We believe that all addicts and coaddicts start out as codependents – as shame-based people who believe they are fundamentally defective and unlovable. Consequently, they developed additional beliefs to help them deal with their pain. For example, if they found that being sexual eased their pain, they may have become addicted to sex. If they equated sex with love, they became a coaddict – addicted to their partner, who was often a sex addict.

Instead of putting themselves first, coaddicts became obsessed with pleasing their partner to keep them from leaving. Using whatever means they had at their disposal, coaddicts attempted to control and manipulate their partner. Coaddicts who became involved with a sex addict understood at some level how important sex was for their partner, so coaddicts often used it to control them. Coaddicts may have become sexual superstars or withheld sex to punish their partner.

Coaddicts may have spent hours obsessing about what they should or should not say or do. Crying, pleading, shaming and blaming their partner, or giving them the silent treatment may all have become part of their arsenal of dysfunctional behaviors. They tended to accept the unacceptable. Because of low self-esteem, coaddicts became, paradoxically, self-centered, seeing in their partner's words and behaviors a reflection of their own inadequacy or accomplishment—coaddicts failed to appreciate that their partner was dancing to his or her own tune, not to theirs.

Coaddicts are vulnerable to developing addictions of their own, and many do. They may use alcohol or prescription medications to calm their nerves, spend money compulsively, or develop eating disorders. Those who are overly responsible may become the neighborhood supermom or superdad, neglecting their own needs as they organize car pools, lead the local Boy Scout troop, and chair the PTA at school. Coaddicts totally lose themselves in others, and they try to look good doing it. They may throw themselves into work, keeping so busy that they do not have time to feel their feelings.

How Coaddicts Defined Relapse

In our survey, several coaddicts defined relapse in terms of sexual behaviors. They wrote: "Worrying over him having sex with others. Saying yes to any sexual behavior when I mean no." . . . "Having sex for him instead of me." A secretary in recovery for over a year said:

> *When I give in to his desire for sex even if I don't feel like it; when I berate him for the past and I just go crazy; when I do something sexual that I'm uncomfortable with—that's a relapse.*

A psychotherapist in his thirties wrote:

> *Relapse of my coaddiction would be accepting flimsy excuses for weekend trips or late nights out. It would also include participating in pornographic movie watching or other sexual activities that are against my values.*

Others emphasized controlling and manipulative behaviors: "To be manipulative, hiding my feelings." . . . "Trying to control his life instead of mine." . . . "Exhibiting old behavior such as controlling, projecting, needless worry."

Obsession was also a frequently mentioned symptom of relapse. One woman wrote:

> *It would be relapse for me if I started obsessing about the future or "terrible crisis thinking." Or if I let myself get depressed and rely on my husband to make me happy. Or if I interrogate my husband on his problems and motives.*

Other coaddicts answered what relapse would be for them: "Ruminating on problems, not living in the present." . . . "Anxiety attacks. Compulsive checking on him and obsessing about him." . . . "Obsessing about my husband when he is late. Worrying about him when one of us is out of town." . . . "Obsession about his doubtful actions and trying to control the situation."

Putting the spouse's needs first was mentioned by several coaddicts. Two wrote:

> . . . *A relapse of my coaddiction would be to care more about him than I do myself—to take care of his feelings before mine.*

> . . . *My relapse would be going back to letting him do anything he wants and accepting it as always. Or going back to the fear of losing him if I insist on my needs and he learns about my needs.*

Related to putting the spouse's needs first is assuming the victim role, which so many coaddicts played before recovery. One woman said her relapse would be: "Taking verbal abuse. Expecting him to know my needs. Hiding my feelings." A woman married to a sex addict for thirty-five years wrote:

> *A relapse for me is when I fall back into a self-pity trap to the point where I cannot do things for myself or make my life worthwhile for myself. Or when I think like a victim.*

Another symptom of coaddict relapse is jealousy and checking up on the addict. Survey respondents wrote: "Going through papers of his." . . . "Snooping in her personal belongings. Overreacting to situations." . . . "Trying to find out what he is doing, where he has been, and who he sees each day. Not attending my own Twelve Step meetings."

Most recovering people would agree that boundary erosion constitutes a major coaddictive relapse. Tolerating behaviors that were previously defined as unacceptable was defined as a relapse by several coaddicts. They wrote: "Accepting my husband back if he started having affairs again." . . . "Tolerating the acting out."

The general theme from our survey respondents was that relapse for the recovering coaddict consists of once again putting the primary focus on their partner instead of on themselves. One woman wrote:

> *To fall into controlling him. Being a savior to his victim, a mother to his child. To let my anger overwhelm me and to use it as a weapon against him; to lose sight of any of the good things; and to blame him for problems of mine that he's not to blame for. To dump him because every time things for me start to look secure I have to shake it up a little.*

How Addicts Saw Coaddicts' Relapse

Just as we asked coaddicts how they saw relapse for their partner, we asked the addicts, *What is your definition of a relapse for your partner's coaddiction?*

Whereas most coaddicts had no difficulty defining a relapse for the addict, only 58 percent of the addicts in our survey were able to define a coaddictive relapse. The others replied: "I don't have one for her." . . . "Her decision, not mine." There are probably two reasons for this difference. One is that the addict is traditionally the "identified patient" or "the one with the problem." Attention is focused on their behavior, recovery, relapses. Most treatment programs support this focus as they typically devote four weeks to treating the addict and one week to working with the family. Even during that week, much of the time is spent talking about addiction. The result is that the coaddict's thinking about the addict's recovery tends to be much clearer than the addict's thinking about the coaddict's recovery.

A second reason for the addict's confusion about coaddiction is that, as we have seen, recovery and relapse for the coaddict is often more difficult to define. Even when addicts recognize that their partner has problems, too, they are not clear about what those problems are.

In our survey, when coaddicts were also addicted, it was easier for their spouse to define relapse: "If she drinks again." . . . "A relapse in her primary addiction of food. I can't define a codependent relapse." . . . "Affairs with others." . . . "To go back to her obsessive masturbation and lusting for others."

A little more than half of all addicts in our survey were able to give a definition of coaddictive relapse. We have separated their definitions into five categories:

1. *Sexual behavior:* "Having sex with me when she's unwilling."
2. *Obsessing:* "Obsessing about my addiction."
3. *Ignoring his or her own needs, focusing on the addict:* "Governing her life based on my reaction to things she does or situations in our lives." . . . "Attempting to fix me. Wanting to spend hours discussing all the things that are wrong with me." . . . "Allowing her to 'take care' of me in unhealthy ways." . . . "Her depending on me to change her mood or fix her."
4. *Controlling behaviors:* "When my partner presses for a change in my actions or reactions." . . . "Trying to control me through sex." . . . "Her using my guilt, shame, and self-hate to control me."
5. *Blaming and shaming:* "Blaming her bad life on me. Depression." . . . "Return to behavior in which she was continually using me as a scapegoat." . . . "Demeaning behavior and comments." . . . "Extremely controlling or shaming behaviors."

Relapse Prevention

The same tools that can help addicts stay sexually sober can help coaddicts avoid relapse. Here are the methods one woman used: "Read daily, go to meetings, meditate, go to church, think about God, focus on myself, and listen openly to my husband without judging."

Another woman wrote:

> *I attend Twelve Step programs, do a daily maintenance program, and talk with my sponsor as much as I can. In general, I take care of myself and try to stay out of my partner's life when it is none of my business. I try not to manage, manipulate, or control.*

Some coaddicts said they were trying to understand themselves. They wrote: "I am clinging to my new supports, trying to keep the focus on *me* for the first time and live my own life." . . . "Stay in AA and NA, keep working on communication, keep processing the past when it surfaces—these are the things I need to do to understand myself." . . . "Exploring my own values, wants, needs, and feelings, and expressing them more. And paying attention to my own intuition."

Overall, most coaddicts were aware that to avoid a coaddictive relapse they need to maintain the focus on themselves and not on their partner. They were learning that the best gift they can give their relationship is their emotional and spiritual health.

Dealing with Codependent Relapse

According to our survey, coaddictive relapse is more common than sexual addiction relapse—72 percent of coaddicts (compared with 52 percent of addicts) said they had relapsed.

The types of relapses fall into several categories, including

- manipulating their spouse with sex.
- trying to control things over which they have no control.
- slipping into low self-esteem.
- trying to fix their spouse.

155

- returning to the victim role.
- neglecting their feelings.

Manipulating Their Spouse with Sex
A homemaker married fifteen years wrote:

> *I allowed myself to be used sexually to prevent him from acting out. It felt like I'd destroyed what progress I'd made. I got very scared and called my sponsor and my counselor. I immediately tried to get in touch with what happened and why. I tried to talk it out and not allow it to eat me up. It was a real blow, but the group really understood and helped me.*
>
> *I also talked to my husband about two days later. I was able to express what it did to me. He was able to tell me his side, and both of us understood each other a little better afterward.*

Because of the addict's addiction, it is not surprising that many coaddicts tried to control their spouse through sex. In recovery, it is easy to fall back into the same behaviors.

Trying to Control Things Over
Which They Have No Control
This is another common relapse behavior. One woman wrote:

> *My codependency has recently emerged in dealing with my family and in work-related conflicts. I became obsessed and controlling and tried to solve problems I had no power to solve. I talked with my husband and program friends. My spouse was very supportive. He really helped me on this one and I communicated my gratitude.*

Letting go of worry, projection, and control is difficult. When coaddicts slip, they can try to recognize it, work through the feelings, discuss them with others, and work on changing their attitudes. Still, worrying about their spouse's addictive behaviors is hard for many coaddicts to avoid. One woman wrote:

I snooped at his Couples Survey. I wondered if he was where he said he would be in his recovery. I acknowledged the slip and apologized to him. He accepted my apology.

Slipping into Low Self-Esteem

One of the primary symptoms of coaddiction is low self-esteem. Some respondents reported slipping back into such feelings. A chemical dependency counselor who is a recovering alcoholic wrote:

I often feel bad about myself, get into bad self-talk, self-abuse, and neglect due to how he interacts — or fails to interact — with me. And because of his lusting after other women. I'm only beginning to see the depth and breadth of my codependency. My style is usually self-abusive. I'm now staying conscious of my self-talk and realizing that I have choices to think and see differently.

I have shared this with my spouse. We still don't deal with it too well, but now we can apologize and accept apologies. We can see better what's happening and separate from our enmeshment.

For coaddicts, improving their self-esteem is one of the most important recovery goals. They need to stop the steady stream of negative self-talk, a change that is not easy.

Trying to Fix Their Spouse

Many coaddicts have had the experience reported by a forty-year-old psychotherapist. She said, "When reading *Bradshaw on the Family,* I kept wanting [my husband] to read the parts I had highlighted."

How many coaddicts can resist pointing out to their partner a description in a self-help book that fits them to a tee — especially when the advice seems to have been written specifically for them? It is to this wife's credit that she recognized her behavior as a slip.

In recovery, coaddicts find out that others have to learn for themselves, and that their well-meaning advice may not be helpful.

Sex, Lies, and Forgiveness

Returning to the Victim Role

A key ingredient of recovery for coaddicts is leaving this role and learning that, no matter how bad their situation, they always have choices. A fifty-five-year-old housewife wrote:

> It is like an emotional blackout. I get angry, depressed, hopeless, or helpless. I'm back to the victim role. I try to get out of it as fast as I can by talking to my sponsor, reading, and attending meetings or letting myself feel bad. If nothing works, I see a counselor. I try to tell myself this will happen from time to time and it's okay. I try to get out of it as soon as I can.
>
> I do tell my spouse. We seem to go our separate ways a little more at these times, but we are also getting better about talking about what is going on during this time. It helps.

Neglecting Their Feelings

For coaddicts, another recovery goal is to begin to experience feelings and to pay attention to them. A twenty-seven-year-old woman in S-Anon almost a year wrote:

> I had stuffed feelings, then, realizing I was not feeling right, discussed that. Once I realized it, I began to talk it out. I told my spouse and we talked.

In S-Anon for several months, a self-employed thirty-five-year-old woman wrote:

> I was not honest about how I was feeling because I was scared how he would react. I admitted it to my spouse. We were able to talk about it and it was good.

Conclusion

To prevent a coaddictive relapse, coaddicts must first define what such a relapse is. Coaddicts must monitor their thinking and actions so that they recognize a slip when it occurs. Next, coaddicts need to get help for it—by talking with their group, sponsor, or therapist.

When they get back on track, it is helpful to look at the circumstances that led to the relapse, so they understand why it happened. In this way, coaddicts may be able to prevent a recurrence. Sharing with their spouse is also helpful most of the time. However, if coaddicts repeatedly relapse in a sensitive area such as trust, it may be better to share with their group.

Discussing addiction and recovery with other family members is another challenge faced by recovering couples. This difficult task is described in the next chapter.

CHAPTER NINE

Sexual Addiction And The Family

Eight years after their divorce, Paul was still angry at Anne, which made unpleasant their frequent interactions regarding their children. Paul's and Anne's marriage had foundered on the twin addictions of workaholism and sex addiction. As Paul, an attorney, had become more and more involved with his work, Anne turned to other men for companionship and affection. Eventually, there was nothing left of their relationship and they parted ways. Shortly after Anne asked Paul for a divorce, he learned from a friend of her latest affair. Angry and embittered, he petitioned for custody of their children, calling her an "unfit mother." Following a prolonged and expensive court battle, Anne was awarded custody.

As the children got older, they became aware of the hostility their father felt toward their mother, but could not understand why. They saw Anne as a loving mother who was kind to everyone, including their father. Three years into her recovery from sexual addiction, Anne decided to talk with her sixteen-year-old son Brian about her addiction and recovery. After lengthy participation in a "program of rigorous honesty," Anne no longer felt comfortable misrepresenting to her children why she was attending meetings twice weekly and receiving telephone calls from people the kids had never met.

With great trepidation, Anne explained to Brian that she was recovering from an addictive illness that had manifested itself as an unhealthy need to receive attention and validation from men. As she explained, Brian became agitated and exclaimed, "No wonder Dad is so angry with you! He has a right to be! You did a terrible thing to him!" He was not interested in any further explanations about the changes Anne had made in her life. Anne felt she had lost her son.

After several days had passed, however, Brian began asking Anne for additional information. Gradually, their relationship was restored. Brian also felt increased empathy for his father after years of being critical of Paul's animosity toward Anne. Now, Brian was able to understand why his father felt the way he did, although he would have preferred his father forgiving his former wife.

Why Telling Family Members Is Hard

Telling family members about recovery can be scary. It took Anne three years to gather the courage to talk about it with her son. Many of us were brought up with family rules that stressed secrecy: "Don't wash the family's dirty laundry in public." . . . "What would the neighbors think?" . . . "Don't tell Grandma—it would only upset her." We made great efforts to keep up appearances, no matter how much we were hurting inside. Many families keep secrets from each other. For example, one parent may have had an affair, and if the children knew, they may have kept quiet for fear of causing pain to the other parent. Or if we were sexually abused in childhood, we may have been repeatedly warned not to tell anyone.

Even in recovery, it seems more natural to keep secrets than to tell the truth. The more we value another person's opinion, the more difficult it is to tell them something about which we are ashamed.

Talking about sex with others is difficult. Women friends who share their deepest feelings with each other may never mention their sexual concerns. Men almost never discuss sexual problems with other men. Even physicians generally have to initiate discussions about sexuality in order to learn if their patients are having any problems in this area. The fact is, our society does not accept sexual concerns as an appropriate subject for discussion—except in a joking or boastful way.

There is another reason why recovering people may find it difficult to discuss sexual addiction with others: Some people prefer to look at problematic sexual behavior as a moral issue and think addicts should be punished. When the behavior is not illegal—for instance, multiple affairs—addicts might not be seen as having a problem at all. Instead, they might hear, "I wish *I* had that problem, you lucky dog!"

A man who had had a series of affairs shared his problem with an old friend. The friend, who himself had been unfaithful to his wife on numerous occasions, was incredulous. He said, "I would never let my marriage interfere with my social life! You're just letting your wife lay a guilt trip on you! Who's the boss in your family, anyway?" That closed down further conversation about the topic.

Addicts need to be discerning in deciding with whom to share their stories. If their behavior has made the front page of the newspaper, however, they do not have a choice.

In this chapter, we will focus on talking with children, parents, and other family members. Deciding when and what to reveal to family members is very much an individual decision. It depends on the length of time in recovery, the relationship with the family member, whether they live in the same household, and each person's assessment of whether or not the knowledge will hurt or help the other person and his or her relationship with them.

What They Told Family Members

A young business owner and his wife, three months into recovery, wrote:

HUSBAND: *I feel real nervous. I don't like to let others close to me. Maybe I'm delaying my recovery because of my fear of disclosure.*

WIFE: *I feel very uncomfortable. I tried to talk to my mother about it last week, but didn't. But I did let her know that I have been overwhelmed by work, been depressed, but doing a little better.*

*Mom was very understanding. I didn't have the heart to tell her
that her favorite son-in-law is a sex addict.*

In early recovery, many people find it hard to change their life-
long habit of keeping secrets. Shame tends to keep them isolated.
In our survey, several addicts told us they were uncomfortable sharing with their family because of shame, embarrassment, or fear. Doing a Fifth Step helps overcome the shame by showing people that
they can be loved and accepted even when their character defects
and past behavior are revealed.

Some addicts, however, were reluctant to talk with family members other than their spouse even after years of recovery. An alcoholic and sex addict with four years of sexual recovery said, "I am
fearful about telling my parents or siblings. It still creates shame for
me to talk to someone outside of recovery about my addiction." He
told his family nothing other than that he is in a recovery program.
They think it is just Alcoholics Anonymous (AA) that he attends.
Unless the addict believes that telling the truth will cause more pain
than gain, being honest is preferable. As a father of young adult
children put it, "I had to tell my children. The secret was destroying
me."

Several coaddicts decided not to speak to their families because
of fear it would damage their relationship with the addict. A
businesswoman in recovery for nine months said, "I want to tell my
family about my sexual addiction, but my husband feels very
strongly about not sharing it with his family." In recovery thirteen
months, a coaddict wrote:

> *I don't feel comfortable at all. I have told one family member on my
> side. I am considering talking with my parents, but I'm afraid my
> husband will be rejected by my mother.*

A retired counselor with grown children chose to tell them nothing. She said:

> *He is their stepfather, but they have never lived with us. We don't
> want the grandchildren to know about this. As much as I know*

> *about the addiction, I don't think they would understand, and I
> don't want to take a chance on alienating them from "Grandpa."*

A woman sex addict who anticipated a negative reaction from her
family decided to share with them only under certain circumstances. She wrote: "If they have a crisis, if their lives become unmanageable due to sexual addiction, then I will tell them about my
addiction. But not until then."
Several people had decided not to tell their families anything. A
homemaker had talked with her brothers and sisters, but planned
to say nothing to her parents. She wrote:

> *My parents would react with total rejection of us. Shame is the
> only way my parents deal with what they see as mistakes or prob-
> lems. Mistakes or problems are never forgiven or forgotten.*

This woman had decided in advance that her family members
would react negatively and that telling them would hurt her relationship with them. Her decision may have been best for her, although some people have been surprised by how supportive family
members were when they were told. The decision to talk about the
addiction to others is best reached jointly by the couple. In deciding
to tell others, we really need to examine our motives. We need to
ask ourselves, *Will sharing foster our recovery or are we more interested
in blaming or shaming?* For example, a woman who reveals her husband's affairs to a mother-in-law may be more interested in revenge. A man who points his finger at his father in blame may
destroy an already shaky relationship. It often takes some time in
recovery before we can search our souls for how best to proceed.
The decision to tell a family member should be made only after talking about it with our partner, members of our recovery group, and
our therapist, if we are seeing one.
In recovery six months, an accountant wrote: "It's none of my
family's business about my spouse's sexual addiction. I want to tell
them about my recovery, but it's difficult to do without the sex
topic." Her dilemma is shared by others who want to tell friends

and family about their own recovery but find it difficult to do so without revealing their spouse's addiction. People have to decide for themselves how best to do this. Some coaddicts have found that giving details about the addictive behavior is unnecessary. Instead, they talk about how addiction has affected them and how they are now taking care of themselves.

Telling Children

Telling children gives them information they might be able to use in their own lives, either to avoid problems or to recognize their own addictions and seek help. Addiction can be passed down from one generation to the next. Often, by the time adults become aware of their own behaviors, their children have problems of their own.

We can begin to break the cycle by being honest with our children, telling them whatever is appropriate for their age. As openness replaces secrecy, children will feel okay about expressing their feelings and asking questions. A middle-aged woman in recovery one year understood this. She wrote: "All of our five children know. I believe if we are going to break the chain of addiction, everybody in the family must know and work on their own healing."

Some people who were reluctant to tell children compromised by telling them only about their recovery from other addictions. A man who attended several Sex and Love Addicts Anonymous (SLAA) meetings per week wrote: "My children know only of my Twelve Step involvement through Overeaters Anonymous (OA), AA, and Al-Anon. They know I have no alcoholism, but that the AA meetings provide growth." His wife wrote: "I answer any and all questions as they occur. I don't lie, but I don't dump on them either."

Children may wonder why their parents attend AA and Al-Anon in the absence of family alcoholism, but may never ask about a topic if they sense it is off limits.

In recovery for four years, an older woman whose husband had a history of exhibitionism said:

> We feel our children would be shocked about the arrests and the nature of the addiction. Of course, we are both very open about be-

ing recovering alcoholics, but this is socially acceptable these days.
He does not want his sister to know about the sexual addiction.

The belief that chemical dependency is more socially acceptable than sexual addiction is a common one. Those who are not dealing with multiple addictions do not have the option of sharing only about their other programs and are therefore more likely to tell their children about the sexual addiction. A couple in recovery four years talked about their motivation for telling their pre-teenaged children. They said:

HUSBAND: *One of the greatest hopes we have for breaking the cycle is our honesty with the kids. We talk about "you are only as sick as your secrets," yet many sexaholics seem to think that that doesn't apply to their own family. I don't buy it. Our honesty with our kids has given us freedom and hope for the future. They generally know my story and some of the consequences of my addiction. They know of our involvement in a Twelve Step program and our concern for our family's dysfunction. We talk openly about sex and sex education issues.*

WIFE: *I think that honesty is the best policy—it gives me the freedom to be the real me and not have to pretend with my children. We told them what was appropriate according to their ages and what they could understand. As they get older, we'll tell them more. They have handled it very well, and they hopefully know that they can talk to us about it and that we'll be honest.*

Parents Who Told Their Children

Several respondents felt that sharing with children was important for their own recovery and their children's. An attorney in recovery four years wrote, "I feel good about telling my children. No more secrets. The addiction must stop with me." A professional couple in recovery only a few months agreed. The husband said, "I have told the children because I felt they needed to look at themselves with the knowledge of my addiction." His wife added, "It's a necessary step in learning to be honest."

A fifty-two-year-old man who was working up the courage to tell his adult daughters wrote:

My goal is to first disclose to my children, then I plan to disclose my addiction to my mother. I agree with my therapist that the less I live in secret, the less power my addiction will have over me, and the greater my quality of recovery.

His wife, who completed the survey some time after her husband, told us what actually happened. She said:

We talked individually with each girl and their two husbands recently. I was fearful, but God helped my husband and the girls were understanding. My husband was already ten months into recovery before telling them, which helped.

People who are unwilling to share with their children often assume that the children did not know what was going on. In fact, children often knew. They may have overheard telephone calls, arguments, and conversations, but kept the information to themselves. Even if they didn't know the details, they may have sensed the stress and tension between their parents. Telling older children about the addiction and recovery can validate their feelings. Furthermore, it gives them permission to talk about what they may have felt and experienced during their parents' acting out.

Most of our survey respondents had told their children something about the addiction and recovery. A couple with three daughters in their twenties wrote about what happened when they shared information with their daughters after several months of recovery. According to the mother:

We told them the whole story—from his childhood of daily masturbation and interest in males to his visiting bookstores and bathhouses and watching porno films. They said they forgave him for his lack of interest in their life (he asked them to forgive him). The oldest daughter had never heard of sex addiction. They were very loving and wrote a beautiful letter of support to get well. The middle daughter had the same acceptance. Both of their husbands were a wonderful help and support to them after we left and as the girls digested the news.

The youngest daughter was also understanding and said that for the first time she felt like she was beginning to know her dad and wanted to get close to him. She started walking every other night with Dad and gave him a birthday gift of a bicycle. The day after we talked with her, she said she felt "sick" about it and cried. She doesn't cry easily. They are all supporting him and are glad for his recovery.

Another couple also reported a positive outcome of sharing with their older children. They wrote:

HUSBAND: *I told my twenty-six-year-old daughter everything. My daughter cried, then hugged me and said she loved me. I only told my thirty-year-old son that I am a sex addict but did not go into detail. He was nonjudgmental.*

WIFE: *My husband and I told our daughter about his acting out and arrest for exhibitionism. We also told her about his treatment and SA attendance and about my S-Anon and our Recovering Couples Anonymous involvement. When she has a question about it, she asks me and I encourage her to ask her dad, which she does. She says she still loves him and seems as close to him as before. She seems glad that we're trying to recover.*

Addicts who go through formal treatment for sexual addiction sometimes tell their children sooner than they might otherwise. This was the experience of a banker with three older children aged eighteen to twenty-two. The couple wrote:

HUSBAND: *In treatment during family week, I took responsibility for my sexually addictive behaviors in the presence of my children. It was a shaming, then liberating experience for me. They reacted initially with anger, then with hurt, and now, I pray, with understanding.*

WIFE: *All three children went to family week during my husband's treatment and are now very familiar with sexual addiction and coaddiction. At first, they were totally torn apart and very, very angry. Probably because of their ages, they realize they need to look at what their issues are from being in a dysfunctional family. It was very difficult for me at first, but it is also a great relief to get the truth out in the open.*

When their teenaged daughter went into inpatient treatment for an eating disorder, one couple decided to reveal to her her mother's sexual addiction. The father recalled:

They were treating her eating disorder along the lines of an addiction, with a Twelve Step program. We chose that opportunity to tell her about it, thinking that maybe it might assist her in her recovery, but it didn't. She instantly went into a big shame attack, and was really upset because we announced it to everybody in the group. She gets very embarrassed by everything. We were trying to demonstrate that you didn't have to have a lot of shame about it, that it was really okay to air your secrets and get into recovery. It didn't work. I'm not sure we'd do it the same way again.

After telling her, we felt we had to come home and tell our son about it, so we told him and he basically never has really dealt with it. He asked a few questions, but I think he reserved his questions for his sister, because she asked us more about it.

Parents Who Told Some Children but Not Others

Two months into recovery, a sex addict told her story to her fifteen-year-old daughter but said nothing to her seventeen-year-old son. The father said nothing to either child. In the survey she sent to us, the mother wrote that she was worried her daughter would talk to her grandparents. A physician and his wife told their fifteen-year-old son about the addiction and recovery program, but said nothing to their younger son, aged twelve.

Unless one of the children is too young, it is generally not a good idea to share information with one child but not another. The pattern of keeping secrets is perpetuated when one child is told not to share information with a sibling or other relatives. Relationships between siblings can also suffer because some children have information that others do not.

If the child with the information chooses to tell a sibling, the sibling who was told by his or her brother or sister is likely to feel left out. This child may wonder why he or she was not told directly and may also receive partial or inaccurate facts. Not knowing whether or not he or she is supposed to have this information, this child may not feel free to ask for clarification. As a result, the child may pretend not to know and struggle alone with the news. Or the child may react by intensifying his or her own acting-out behaviors. It is best for parents to talk with all their children, either together or individually.

Finally, let us address the mother's concern that her fifteen-year-old daughter will talk about the addiction to her grandparents. In early recovery, many people still feel shameful and are unwilling to say anything to relatives and friends. Many recovering addicts wait a year or more before sharing with anyone outside the program. There is no urgency for this addict to tell her parents. However, it is a burden on her daughter to swear her to secrecy. Telling her children implies trust that they will do with the information what they must for their own recovery, even if it means sharing that information with people who are outside the family.

Parents Who Told Young Children

The mother of two young children found it necessary to give her six-year-old daughter some information. She wrote:

> *We handle the SA telephone line in our state, so my older daughter has heard the message on the machine referring to sexual addiction. Because we didn't want her wondering, we've told her that our meetings are to help us not use sex to feel like we're okay people. She's been exposed to drug information at school, so we told her sometimes people use sex to get high and hide feelings just like they do with drugs and alcohol, and that we're trying to learn not to do that.*

> *She expressed gratitude for our honesty, said she had been won-*
> *dering why we went to separate meetings when they were about*
> *sex, and generally seemed to appreciate the opportunity to have*
> *her questions and concerns addressed.*

Another approach was taken by a couple who told their nine-year-old son. They wrote:

> HUSBAND: *I told my son that I have a sexual problem that has hurt*
> *the family by my inattention, resentment, and abandonment. I*
> *also told him that porno shops are a problem for me and that I can't*
> *safely go in there. I try to right wrongs as they come up.*
>
> WIFE: *We've told our son quite a lot — what he could understand.*
> *We don't believe secrets are healthy.*

Both parents grew up in families where it was not okay to talk about feelings. Both had difficulty sharing their feelings with others, something they were now learning to do. Their honesty helped their son feel free to share his own feelings with his parents and others.

A homemaker in recovery seven months wrote:

> *I told my ten-year-old son that Daddy has an addiction but that*
> *he's trying hard to recover. My addiction has only been spoken of*
> *in terms of wanting to be a good mom and wife and needing the*
> *help of my group and my doctor (therapist). He was very worried*
> *that Daddy was addicted to drugs and was relieved when it wasn't*
> *that.*

Parents Whose Children Responded Negatively

Sometimes children need time to understand and accept what they have been told about sexual addiction and recovery. They may respond negatively or withdraw, but this does not necessarily mean it was a mistake to tell them. Rather, it may be the first phase of a more honest and open relationship.

A middle-aged couple who separated because of the husband's sexual addiction had three children who were in their early twenties. The husband, in recovery three months, said he had not told his children, but his wife had. She wrote:

> *I have told the children that their dad attends SA. They hate him. They hate me for still seeing him. They refuse to recognize their own codependency issues. They do not accept the sexual addiction—they think it is a cop-out.*

A salesman with four children in their twenties, including a daughter he had molested, described the negative results of talking with them. He wrote:

> *My daughter never wants to see me or talk with me. She won't let me see my two grandchildren. It's very painful. My sons reacted with anger, resentment—but understanding. They are much more receptive, but more healing is needed.*

After only a month or two in recovery, a couple shared some information with their two daughters, aged nineteen and seventeen. The father reported both girls were very upset. The mother wrote: "One child is trying to accept. The other daughter has anger and resentment and is acting out sexually and drinking."

It is not unusual for children to be angry and upset when given information about sexual addiction. They may go through a grieving process when told their parents have problems. But it is unlikely that the daughter's resentment, drinking, and sexual acting out are a consequence of learning about her parent's addiction. Instead, they may be the consequences of growing up in a family affected by sexual addiction. When adults share with their children, they are planting seeds. In a year or two, the seeds may sprout—the daughter may remember what she was told and may get help for her own behavior years earlier than she would have if she had not heard about sexual addiction.

Parents Who Told Their Children Nothing

In recovery over two years, the father of a twelve-year-old told us, "My daughter is not living with us and therefore does not know. I do not feel any gain would come from telling her." This child was not exposed to the daily stresses of active addiction nor to mysterious calls and frequent parental absences that may occur during recovery, so there may be less urgency to talk to her. Nonetheless, if he has any regular contact with his daughter, it is likely that on some level she is aware that there are problems and she may have noticed some changes in her father as his recovery progresses. Telling children as they get older will most likely promote a closer and more honest relationship and might give them useful information for their own lives.

Some couples were advised by others not to tell their children. For example, the mother of three children, ages twelve, ten, and seven wrote:

> We told them nothing, only that we are going to a counselor to have a better marriage. We were told not to tell them yet—they are too young. Their reaction? They get tired of us always going to meetings.

While there are different opinions about what is appropriate to tell young children, the authors believe that children as young as eight or ten are likely to be aware of what is going on in the home and deserve some explanation about the nature of the problem and of the meetings that their parents so frequently attend. Evasiveness with children is likely to continue the legacy of secrecy, which promotes addiction.

Children Will Learn from Parents' Recovery

In early recovery, we focus on our own thoughts, feelings, and behaviors. As we progress, we start looking at our family history. We often begin by casting a critical look at our family of origin. Some therapists help clients construct a genogram, a diagram of several generations. Here, we may discover a multigenerational pattern of addictive behaviors or mental illness. Later, we recognize that the pattern did not stop with us—while we were active in our own addiction or coaddiction, our children may have been developing codependent and addictive behaviors of their own. It is difficult for us to watch our children go through their own struggles without wanting to jump in and fix them. But we have to remind ourselves that our children have their own Higher Power and that the example of our own recovery may help them get into recovery.

Telling Other Family Members
Telling parents about sexual addiction and recovery is often more difficult and occurs later than telling children. Many of us still have unresolved issues with our parents. We may not have dealt with our own abuse—physical, sexual, or emotional. Talking with our parents about our addiction also means talking with them about our own childhood experiences. They may often deny our reality and not validate our feelings.

Talking with our parents can be stressful and may threaten our initial tenuous sobriety. But as we progress, we will be more ready to face the demons of our childhood—the painful feelings we may have buried long ago. Dealing with family of origin issues is often best begun a year or two into recovery. We may become aware of these issues earlier, but a decision to address them directly with our parents should not be made lightly.

Some of us, after careful consideration of the likely consequences, may decide it is best to say nothing to our parents—our relationship with our parents may be so toxic that we need to avoid contact with them rather than attempt reconciliation. Others of us may have parents who are old, in poor health, and in no condition to review the past. Some of us may decide to share our own experience with our parents but not confront them on their role in engendering our addiction or codependency. Still others may have parents who are supportive, open to discussion, and willing to talk about the patterns of addiction in the family. Those of us who have taken the risk and received a supportive response have often found that the relationship with our parents has greatly improved.

When we were growing up, many of us were unable to talk about our feelings with brothers and sisters. Reviewing the past with siblings who may also have been abused can help validate our perceptions about what was happening in the family. This can be valuable, especially if this reality was denied by our parents. Usually, sexual abuse involves a conspiracy of silence. If we were molested, it is highly likely that our siblings were too. Talking with them about family secrets may open the door to their getting help. But we must be prepared for the possibility of rejection and continued denial. Even though we grew up in the same family, siblings' reality may be very different from ours.

Many people have been greeted with disbelief as they tried to describe to a brother or sister how they remember being treated by their parents. Even if siblings' experiences were similar to their own, not everyone is ready for help at the same time.

With Positive Results

Nearly three-quarters of our survey respondents gave their siblings or parents some information about their addiction and recovery. Most people who told family members reported it was a positive experience. One couple stated:

HUSBAND: *Two years into recovery, I told my mother. She was understanding and shared her suspicions about an uncle in the family who molested a child.*

WIFE: *At first I didn't tell my family, but after my spouse went into treatment for chemical abuse, I told my parents first and then my brother and sister. One of my sisters does not know yet. I sent my parents a tape of* Out of the Shadows *and tried to answer any questions they had. They were concerned and didn't fully understand. Unequivocally, I received their love and full support, as did my spouse.*

Other parents were willing to listen, but not to share, as a thirty-three-year-old man learned. He wrote:

I told my father. He admired my courage and was willing to listen but was unwilling to share from his own life. I know that he also saw prostitutes during his marriage to my mother.

A young woman who told her family was glad she did. She wrote:

I told them everything—from being molested as a child by my brother to finding out about my coaddiction and my course of recovery. They listened openly. They were surprised about the molestation and felt badly that I kept it inside all those years. I have told everyone in my family. It makes me feel close to them. They did not judge us. They accept both my husband and me and are happy to see us working on our problems.

Some people also learned they were not the only ones in their family struggling with the consequences of sexual addiction. They wrote: "My father was silent. My mother eventually told me that my grandfather was a sex addict." . . . "My husband told his parents and discovered that his father was also a possible sex addict. His mother told him that his father was molested as a child."

For some, telling family members was also a way of making amends. A seventy-year-old man wrote:

My parents are dead. I told all to my sister, whom I had molested. My sister told me of her outrage that I had violated her trust, told me she still loves me, and said she is glad that I am engaged in a recovery program.

Many of us who have identified addiction and codependency in our parents and siblings hope that by sharing our own stories we can encourage them to make changes in themselves. Occasionally, this happens. In recovery three years, a counselor reported:

My father, a practicing alcoholic, is totally unavailable for a relationship. My mother's in denial and is also an active alcoholic. I told my sister I had coaddictive issues—we are both incest survivors. She has the same problems and was receptive and grateful for the info.

Sex, Lies, and Forgiveness

A recovering sex addict wrote, "I shared totally with a brother when he shared his own problem with sex. That bond has grown very strong." Other families reacted with denial or disbelief. When a businesswoman recovering for nine months from sexual addiction told her mother, her mother said she believed nothing was wrong with her daughter. A man who was hospitalized because of his sexual acting out wrote:

> *My parents found out about my acting out when I was placed in a hospital. They reacted with denial and rationalization. They never mentioned it. They preferred to call it a "nervous problem" or "defect in brain chemistry."*

Some families did not want any further information. A woman in recovery over four years described her family's reaction:

> *I have told my sister my partner was a sex addict. She does not understand much but is very supportive of me. I told my dad the same. His reaction was, "Ho hum, you can become addicted to anything. Hang in there with him."*

The "Don't Talk" rule is strong in dysfunctional families. Some recovering people who had told their family found concern that others would find out. A man with over three years in recovery spoke about his family. He wrote:

> *They admired my courage and offered support. Some of my younger siblings and my wife's family wished that I wouldn't talk to others, thus "exposing" the family.*

Although some people attempted to educate their family about sexual addiction, others chose to share only generalities: "My family knows that we have sought marriage counseling for compulsive behavior. That's all." . . . "I told my mom and dad that I have a sex problem and that it affects my marriage. They were supportive and accepting."

With Negative Results

Very few people who chose to talk with family members reported a bad experience. Several women said they did not tell their family for fear the family would turn against the spouse. This happened to one woman who wrote: "I told my two sisters everything and they are bothered by it, but they are trying to understand. They are angry at my spouse." A homemaker who revealed everything to her relatives reported, "Most of them want me to leave my husband."

A man who told his brothers and sisters that he was a recovering sex addict found most of them to be supportive. However, his wife reported: "One of his brothers, a recovering alcoholic, never contacted us again after my husband told him. Honesty may have cost us the loss of a relationship."

Some survey respondents reported losing friendships as a result of talking about their addiction. "I'm finding that people I thought were friends really weren't. They seemed threatened at my calling my behavior an addiction, because they were doing the same thing too—cheating on their wives," wrote a man who had had multiple affairs.

Family Patterns Revealed

Of survey respondents who had talked to family members, over half of the addicts and a third of the coaddicts obtained new information. Here is some of what addicts said they learned:

- "I found out about sexual abuse within my family of origin."
- "My father masturbates frequently and my parents engaged in partner swapping when I was young. I was molested by a boarder at age three."
- "Telling them about my addiction confirmed and expanded my knowledge of my father's extramarital affairs."
- "My mother informed me of an affair my father had. Cousins have told me of uncles' incestuous behavior and grandfather's sexually abusive and incestuous behavior."
- "Sex addiction goes back many generations on both sides of my family."

- "Not only do my brother and I have a problem, but another brother, a sister, and perhaps my father also have it."
- "I learned that my father molested my sister."
- "I discovered that my mother and brother are sex addicts."
- "The family tree is filled with birds of addiction—chemical, eating, sexual, codependency."

Sexual coaddicts often also have a history of sexual addiction in their family. Here is some of what coaddicts said they learned:

- "My brother touched my sisters in inappropriate sexual ways. I confirmed with my sisters that he had at least one affair."
- "My mother told me that my grandfather was a sex addict."
- "I learned about a grandfather who was probably a sex addict and heard some behaviors about my father that sounded like behaviors of a person who is sexually addicted."
- "My sister is an incest survivor, grandmother also."

The Next Generation

We asked survey respondents if any behavior of their children suggested addiction or coaddiction. Nearly half of the respondents had no children or the children were too young to judge. Of those with older children, 56 percent of addicts and 70 percent of coaddicts believed at least one child showed signs of addiction or coaddiction. (Of course, the results of this question are only speculative.)

A woman wrote that her husband's oldest son molested his younger brother several years ago and is now in prison. Another woman wrote:

> *Our oldest son has said he can see the pattern in himself toward television movies on the sex channels and porno magazines. He actually broke his television to stop himself.*

Several parents recognized that their children were already involved with sex addicts. The mother of four children, nineteen to twenty-seven years old, said, "One daughter is living with an active sex addict and the other is married to a sex addict, but they don't realize it." A mother of four children who are in their thirties wrote:

> *Our oldest daughter thought she was a sex addict because she used sex to manipulate men. However, I know of no acting out she has done. One son is drawn to alcohol and one is a workaholic — so much so that he is bored with life unless he is working much too hard. Basically, I think we've raised codependents. One daughter is divorced from a sex addict and is working on getting her life together.*

Diagnosing Sexual Addiction
And Coaddiction in Adolescents

Since our survey results are based on respondents' opinions, we cannot say for certain that the young people described are really addicted. Diagnosing sexual addiction and coaddiction in teenagers is a great deal more difficult than it is in adults. Behaviors considered addictive in adults are often part of an adolescent's development. These include excessive preoccupation with sex and dating, frequent masturbation, and need for peer approval. Looking at teenagers' motivation and the effects of their behavior may help determine if the behavior is addictive. Does the adolescent masturbate because he or she is "horny" (a normal phenomenon in teenagers) or because he or she is angry? If the behavior is out of control and used to alter his or her mood, then addiction may follow.

If the behaviors are causing an adolescent problems, the parents should seek professional help for the adolescent from a therapist who understands sexual addiction. The therapist can then take a detailed sexual history to distinguish between "normal" and sexually addictive behavior. The history should question the adolescent's relationships, masturbation, use of pornography, exhibitionism, and other behaviors. For example, if a sixteen-year-old masturbates several times daily, has already had several sexual relationships, and has a history of being molested or molesting others, sexual addiction is most likely present.

Although it may be difficult at the time to determine whether early interest in sex is healthy or addictive, many adult sex addicts can look back to their early teens and recognize the beginnings of their addiction. Rather than progressing through the typical teenage stages of sexual exploration and moving on to more meaningful relationships, addicts get stuck in adolescence. Addictive behaviors that begin around age ten to twelve typically accelerate between thirteen and seventeen. Young sex addicts may get into a diet/binge cycle, where after a period of intense sexual acting out they try to restrain themselves for a while.

Still, differentiating "normal" from addictive romantic and sexual behaviors in adolescents remains a challenge to concerned adults, and they should not try to diagnose their child without the help of a therapist who understands sexual addiction and coaddiction.

Conclusion

One goal of recovery is to improve our relationship with our family — our family of origin and the family we have made with our spouse. One way to do this is to discuss our feelings with our children — and if possible, with parents and siblings. Deciding how much, when, and with whom to share information about our addiction or coaddiction is a major challenge.

In general, the authors believe that sharing with family members enhances recovery and improves relationships. It is also an effective way to obtain more information about the addictive patterns in the family.

Early on, as we struggle with our own shame, guilt, and embarrassment, it may suffice to tell our children we are getting help for some problems. Later, as we feel better about ourselves, we can become more specific. When talking with our children, we need to take into consideration how much to tell them. A sponsor or therapist can help us find the right way to talk with our children.

In the next chapter, we will look at the specific problems faced by couples when the sex addict is gay or bisexual.

CHAPTER TEN

Gay or Bisexual Husbands

Mark and Elena were good friends for five years. They met during a college class they took together. Initially, their relationship was not romantic. In fact, they spent a lot of time together talking about their other relationships. They became very comfortable with each other and would spend hours in the college cafeteria talking about their hopes for the future. Mark's goal was to be like his older brother, who owned a successful restaurant, had a good marriage, and two young children. For Elena, it was to lose fifty pounds, find a nice Catholic man with whom she could settle down, and have children much like her mother.

As the years went by, the two stayed in touch and began to consider the possibility of marriage. Each had a good job. Elena had slimmed down somewhat, but Mark had a problem that might get in the way of a happy marriage. He was being sexual with other young men, acting on homosexual impulses he had hoped were a passing fancy in high school and college.

Although Elena knew about Mark's secret life, she believed that once they were married, it would no longer be a problem. She joyfully planned a big wedding and prepared to live happily ever after. Mark talked of his doubts to his priest, but was reassured that once he had taken the marriage vows, all would be well. Mark assured Elena that he planned to be faithful. The newlyweds found an apartment in Greenwich Village and began their life together.

For five years, all was fine. But when Elena became pregnant with their first child, Mark found himself turned off by his wife's expanding body. One night after work, he stopped for a drink at a bar frequented by gay clientele, got drunk, and was picked up by an older man who took him to his nearby apartment. After having sex with him, Mark returned home after midnight to a fretful wife. He was feeling intense shame.

The next morning, he tearfully confessed to Elena and promised it would never happen again. Although hurt, Elena was able to stuff her feelings and believe in Mark's sincere pledge. The excitement of his sexual escapade, however, continued to haunt Mark, and he eventually could not resist seeking another clandestine adventure. He began a pattern of illicit behavior that added to his feelings of worthlessness.

With time, Mark became increasingly ambivalent about his wife and family. At times, he considered Elena his best friend and his soul mate; other times, he felt trapped. Increasingly, she became the target of his unprovoked anger. He would look at her and see his jailer—the person blocking his freedom of sexual expression. His parenting, too, became inconsistent. He would look at his children and marvel at the wonderful human beings they were, but he would become depressed when he thought about the tremendous long-term financial and emotional commitments they represented. He would often yell at them for some minor infraction.

When Mark was away from his family, he could temporarily forget about his ambivalence. He spent more and more time with men friends. He withdrew emotionally from Elena as he increased the frequency of his homosexual encounters. Sensing the emotional distance between them, Elena withdrew sexually. Mark felt relieved, particularly because he knew he was practicing unsafe sex with his male partners.

During this entire period, Mark and Elena were teaching a course at the local community college on communication for marriage partners. Aware of the disparity between his public image and private life, Mark promised himself to cut down on his extramarital sexual activity. He could see that his own marriage was falling apart; he felt guilty about the times he yelled and shamed his children for no reason; and he could not imagine life without Elena and the children. Despite his resolve, he pursued more sexual encounters with men. Whenever Mark read another article in the paper about AIDS, he would vow to avoid unsafe sex. But once the sexual ritual began, he would forget about the risk of infection. Mark's life was becoming increasingly unmanageable.

Homosexuality among married people is a complex issue, and much more common than generally recognized. Kinsey et al. reported that 10.6 percent of married men ages twenty-one to twenty-five were having sex with other men, thereafter dropping gradually to about 2 percent at age forty-five,[1] figures they believed were underestimated.

In addition to our survey, we interviewed men who believed they could have the best of both worlds and others who saw their sexual encounters with men as part of their sexual addiction. Some had had isolated sexual encounters with men but considered themselves primarily heterosexual. One man we talked to said he didn't feel he was being unfaithful to his wife of many years. He said, "She can't give me what I can get from another man." Another couple who married in the seventies saw the husband's gay encounters as part of the sexual revolution. "If that's what he wants, who am I to stop him?" his wife told us.

The threat of AIDS has invited a reevaluation of sexual behavior. Some of the married homosexual and bisexual men we interviewed have been unable to stop unsafe sex despite their desire to stop;

others have recognized the sexually addictive components of their behavior and have sought help through counseling and Twelve Step programs for sexual addiction.

Not all gay or bisexual men in relationships with women behave in a manner warranting concern about sexual addiction, nor do all married gay or bisexual men feel a need to act on their homosexual feelings. And of those who do, many are not compulsive. But when life becomes unmanageable, using the addiction model may lead to solutions for the couple. But how can people separate feelings that seem to be an integral part of their sexual identity from unhealthy patterns of acting on those feelings? Some people are naturally drawn to persons of the same sex. Homosexuality is recognized as one way to express one's sexuality. It is only the inability to accept one's sexual orientation that is considered a disorder by the American Psychiatric Association, which up until 1973 considered same-sex activity between adults to be deviant.

Sexual Identity

Although many people think of sexuality as an either/or proposition—one is either gay or straight—it has been long recognized that attraction to the same sex occurs on a continuum. In 1948, Kinsey constructed a seven-point heterosexual/homosexual rating scale,[2] which rated men as

- exclusively heterosexual.
- predominantly heterosexual, only incidentally homosexual.
- predominantly heterosexual but more than incidentally homosexual.
- equally heterosexual and homosexual.
- predominantly homosexual.
- exclusively homosexual.

Bisexual men are sexually aroused by both men and women. Kinsey's classification for each person was based on both psychological reactions and actual experience. Some men, for instance, had strong homosexual arousal but little or no actual homosexual behavior.

It is important to make the distinction, as Kinsey did, between sexual identity and sexual behavior. *Sexual identity* refers to the way we look at ourselves, as well as the way others view and label our sexuality. Sexual identity encompasses our sexual orientation, which is our inner feeling of being sexually attracted to other men, women, or both. What we do about our sexual feelings constitutes our *sexual behavior.* We have more choices about our sexual behavior than we do about our sexual identity. Although most sexologists now believe it is impossible to change our sexual identity, a person can learn to make choices about sexual behaviors.

Sexual identity is different from gender identity. *Gender identity* is our feeling about being a man or a woman. Gay men, like heterosexual men, view themselves as men. In contrast, *transsexuals* consider themselves to be males in the body of a female or vice versa.

Why Do Gay and Bisexual Men Marry?

Gay and bisexual men marry for several reasons. They may fall in love with someone of the opposite sex or want to have a family. They may hope that a sexually fulfilling marriage will eradicate any interest in same-sex sexual relations. Some marry to provide a socially accepted cover for continuing same-sex contacts. Still others may not even recognize they are attracted to people of the same sex until some time after they have been married. A predominantly gay man may say, "The physical contact with my wife is nice, close, warm, and caring, but that's because I love her, not because I'm attracted to her." Sooner or later the desire to be sexual with others of the same sex surfaces, which may result in a marital crisis.

How Stable Are Their Marriages?

Before the AIDS epidemic, some couples, after working through the crisis of the husband's disclosure of his sexual identity, came to an agreement that allowed him to have homosexual encounters. Couples agreed to definite "rules of engagement"—the time allowed for these activities, the extent of emotional involvement the husband could have with other men, the primacy of the marriage relationship, and the husband's responsibilities toward wife and children. Some couples agreed that the wife was also free to have other relationships, and some wives did indeed seek out others.

Published studies showed, however, that the most stable marriages involving gay or bisexual men appeared to be those in which the wives were sexually exclusive with their husbands and the husbands were free to be sexual with other men, whether or not they acted on this freedom.

In her study of thirty-three women who had been married to bisexual men, Jean Gochros found that the wife's satisfaction with the marriage depended not on the degree of a husband's homosexuality, but rather . . .

> . . . his degree of *heterosexuality*—or at least his ability to find heterosexual satisfaction, his love for his wife, and his ability to show empathy and regard for a wife's needs, rights, and feelings.
>
> Those marriages that seemed to flower rather than wither were marked by that ability. The husband retained a primary commitment to the wife both emotionally and sexually, no matter how homosexually active he might be. The wife felt listened to, heard, understood, loved, and treated fairly. Communication was increased. Displays of emotion—even overreactions, unanticipated reactions, and conflicts about homosexuality—were both tolerated, understood, and given empathic help. The sexual relationship was maintained and was usually good.[3]

Not many marriages in Gochros's study contained these characteristics. In fact, over two-thirds of her sample had already divorced their husband and only a few of the rest had a stable marriage.

This study was done before the AIDS epidemic. Many women are now less willing to remain married to men who continue to be sexual with other men. Women who in the past reluctantly agreed to their husband's ongoing homosexual encounters now risk a life-threatening illness.

As a result, having sex with both their wife and other men is no longer an option for many gay and bisexual married men. Those men who have disclosed their same-sex preference to their spouse have often found themselves forced to choose between the marriage and their homosexual activities. Some choose to divorce and enter into same-sex relationships. Others have identified their homosexual activities as compulsive, themselves as sexually addicted, and have determined to cease gay activities with the help of Twelve Step programs.

Who We Interviewed

In this chapter, we will look at these couples' experiences in Twelve Step programs. We will focus primarily on those couples who have decided to remain married. Twenty-eight people in our written survey (sixteen couples, since both husband and wife did not always respond) fit this category. We were able to interview three of these couples at greater length by telephone. In addition, we interviewed by telephone eight other couples (sixteen persons) who were committed to making a go of their marriage, and a woman recently divorced from a bisexual man. All told, we received information from forty-five persons from twenty-five marriages in which the husband had been sexual with other men. Two couples and the divorced woman were not in Twelve Step programs; their experiences will be contrasted with those of the couples in recovery. Finally, we also interviewed a monogamous homosexual couple who both identified themselves as recovering sex addicts. We were unable to find any couples where the woman was bisexual. Perhaps bisexual women are less likely to remain married than are bisexual men.

It must be emphasized that the men in our survey viewed their homosexual activities as addictive. Sexual addiction in homosexual men is a highly controversial subject. Some sociologists and sexologists have opposed the whole concept of sexual addiction, suggesting it is being used by some who would suppress the sexual behavior of a repressed group. Before the advent of the AIDS epidemic, the opportunity for gay men to have multiple anonymous sexual encounters was asserted by some gays to be part of an acceptable homosexual lifestyle.

But times have changed. Many in the gay community acknowledge that some behavior by homosexual men is compulsive. Some men who continue to have unsafe sex with strangers, despite the risk of contracting a life-threatening illness, have recognized that their behavior is out of control.

Among the twenty-two couples in Twelve Step programs, the husbands ranged in age from twenty-four to fifty-seven, the wives twenty-one to fifty-five. Most were over thirty years old. Sixty percent were both in first marriages. For an additional 23 percent, it was the first marriage for one of the pair. Five couples had no children; the other seventeen couples had an average of three children.

Ten husbands and seven wives reported some recollection of sexual abuse in childhood. Sixty percent of the men reported no sexual encounters with other men since joining Twelve Step programs for sex addicts. Other men reported activities ranging from a single relapse in early recovery to an ongoing inability to maintain sexual fidelity.

Four of twenty-one men said they were also chemically dependent; three identified themselves as workaholics; and five said they were also compulsive overeaters. Five of seventeen wives reported they were chemically dependent; four were workaholics; and four were compulsive overeaters.

When asked how likely it was they would be together in five years, 68 percent of the couples thought it was likely or very likely; 12 percent thought it was unlikely. The remainder were uncertain.

Sexual Identity, Sexual Behaviors, and Sexual Addiction

Where a man's sexual identity lies along the heterosexual-homosexual continuum is one of the key determinants of his ability to achieve happiness as a monogamous heterosexual. The more strongly gay he feels, the less likely he is to be satisfied with his marriage. Possible exceptions are sex addicts who work an active recovery program and believe that their gay sexual activities represent their "addict," and their straight side their healthy side.

We asked each member of the twenty-two couples who were active in Twelve Step recovery groups how they viewed the husband's bisexuality.

Men Who Said Their Gay Side Is Their Addict
A fifty-year-old man who led an active gay lifestyle several times during his life has been monogamously heterosexual for the last seven years, with satisfactory but infrequent sexual relations with his wife. He told us:

> *I guess I'd classify myself in two ways—physiologically I'm bisexual, but my true orientation, my preference, is heterosexual. I think I fit Patrick Carnes's description in* Out of the Shadows *of men whose addiction is acting out homosexually. When I discovered that, it just seemed to fit exactly.*

> *It's been a long time since I've had a fantasy about men. It will come up once in a while. The only area that is still a problem, and I guess it will be a problem forever, is being stimulated visually by men.*

Having identified their gay side as their "addict," several men chose not to label it further, but to regard it as a part of their life they wished to avoid. A young couple who married after the husband was in recovery explained:

> HUSBAND: *I don't consider myself homosexual or bisexual—my acting out with men was a manifestation of my sexual addiction.*

> WIFE: *I view him basically as heterosexual. The sex with men was something necessary for him to go through to know that he wasn't gay. I would say that probably every man has gone through something like that.*

This husband had had multiple homosexual encounters before and during a previous marriage, often in conjunction with cocaine use. He and his present wife rated their current sexual relationship as very good.

When asked whether he believed his homosexual activities were part of his personality or part of his addiction, a forty-year-old man replied:

I don't want to answer that question because it's taken me a lot of years to get away from that. I am not gay, straight, or bi. I am an addict. I've had sex any place, any way. I've also had sex with female prostitutes when male prostitutes weren't available. I do not believe I can ever successfully have sex with a man again. If I were alcoholic, it would be exactly like taking another drink of alcohol.

What was important to him was not so much a sexual label as the understanding that he had an addictive disease. His wife said she believed he is bisexual. When asked about her husband's satisfaction with heterosexual monogamy, she stated:

Since I believe that his sexual acting out was a disease, then I don't think the word "satisfaction" has any place in the discussion. The most important thing is his recovery.

She seemed more concerned with her husband's sexual sobriety than with labeling his sexual identity. This couple both wrote that they believe their sexual relationship has greatly improved.

Men Who Said They Are Bisexual

Some husbands did not identify their gay side as their "addict." Rather, they saw it as an integral part of their identity, but had accepted it as something on which they could no longer act. A middle-aged former minister who lost his job because of his homosexual activities told us:

I identify myself as bisexual. I've never had any trouble being attracted to my wife. I don't look at my homosexual side as part of a disease.

I never involved myself too much in what you would call the masculine pursuits. As I look on the masculine/feminine scale, I'm somewhere in the middle. It's the acting-out part that is the addiction. Just because I'm attracted to men doesn't mean I'm going to have to do anything about it.

A person could be homosexual or bisexual and not be addicted. I see sexual preference and sexual identity as different issues from being sexually addicted. It took me a long time to recognize that I was sexually addicted.

Sexually sober for three years, this man and his wife reported a good sexual relationship. Her opinion of his sexual orientation was:

I think that except for our relationship, he's drawn primarily to men. I guess he would say he's primarily gay. I don't think too much about it. Since he has become sober, it doesn't have a lot of relevance to me.

Acknowledging a person's sexuality does not imply that he or she must act out the sexual feelings. Heterosexual married men may be attracted to other women, but usually choose not to act on that attraction. Because the former minister was no longer acting on his homosexual feelings, his wife was less concerned about what his primary sexual orientation was. The husband recognized it was the compulsive acting out that made his life unmanageable, and he elected to stop the behaviors, not to try to alter his sexual identity.

Bisexual married men who make such a choice acknowledge they have feelings that they best not act on. As adults, people have choices about what to do with their feelings. When they do not have a choice about a particular feeling, but rather are compelled to act on it, despite adverse consequences to themselves or others, then they may be in the grip of an addiction or a compulsion.

A forty-one-year-old man in Sexaholics Anonymous (SA) for three years was another person who believed he had a bisexual identity but considered his homosexual behaviors as an addiction. He wrote:

I am married, but I've also had homosexual affairs, so I guess I'm bisexual. My acting out was very compulsive. The gay side of me is always there, and just coping with that fact is sometimes overwhelming.

I have to acknowledge and accept it, but that doesn't mean I need to dwell on it. Because I don't spend so much time cruising or fantasizing or acting out, I have more time to devote to worthwhile projects. These projects have helped build my self-esteem, which in turn makes it so I don't feel I have to resort to sexual acting out as often.

This man did not find the going easy. He added:

A year ago I had a slip and was kicked out of the house for two months. It's been a rough road, and I don't have any guarantees. If I get into certain places—public parks, public rest rooms, gymnasiums—I'm hopeless.

Acknowledging the addictive nature of his activities, he attended meetings regularly and called a good friend in the program when he needed help. He learned to avoid situations that were likely to lead to acting out. Meanwhile, he told us his sexual relationship with his wife was good.

Asked whether she believed her husband's homosexual activity was free choice or compulsive, his wife said:

I always believed it was free choice, and I sometimes still do. Even though we talked about the word "addiction," part of me still believes we do have a choice not to participate in things that lead into the addiction. For example, cruising. You just don't cruise, because you know what comes next. If you choose to cruise, then you're also choosing to do what comes after that.

His wife recognized that being addicted does not absolve her husband of responsibility. People who are addicted to alcohol and cannot stop after the first drink have a responsibility to stay out of places where they are likely to take the first drink. They may not have a choice about how many drinks they take, but they do have a choice whether or not to walk into a bar. Similarly, if sex addicts recognize that they are unable to stop themselves from picking up a sex partner when cruising a park or public rest room, then they have a responsibility to avoid those locations, especially when they feel vulnerable. A basic element of relapse prevention is for addicts to clearly understand those situations that are likely to lead them toward addictive behavior, and to avoid those situations while they can still choose.

Men Who Said They Are Primarily Gay

Some respondents recognized their desire for sex with other men as part of a broader gay identity. Nonetheless, they made the decision to separate their identity from their gay behavior, and to commit to sexual fidelity. A thirty-six-year-old man said he considered himself primarily gay, but learned in therapy to fantasize about his wife instead of about men. Regardless of his sexual preference, he continued to regard himself as a sex addict in need of a program. He said:

> *I believe that the bottom line for sex addicts is that we have been gluttonous with our addiction. Our sexual preference doesn't really matter. If you love the other person emotionally and there's a reasonable amount of attraction, which there is with my wife, it can work. Rather than getting hung up on sexual preference, the real issue is, Am I willing to rule out fantasizing about other people, cruising, picking up people, and wanting to be titillated all the time?*

Because his wife was unable to forgive him, he and his wife had not had sexual relations since he began his recovery from sexual addiction and his marriage was on the verge of ending.

Another man who had a strong gay sexual identity had difficulty staying away from gay encounters. He told us:

> *I consider myself sexually predominantly homosexual, but relationally I seem to be strongly heterosexual. I like to be with my wife and family. In large measure, my gay experiences have been positive. I'm comfortable with the fact that I'm gay. Were I not married*

and didn't have a relationship already established, I would seek a gay relationship.

But the one thing that holds me back is that if I am gay because I was abused emotionally and physically by my dysfunctional alcoholic family, do I want to be gay? If I'm gay because I was pushed into it by circumstances, I want to be what normal is. If it was not a free choice, then I don't want it. I enjoy the lifestyle, I enjoy everything about it. But if I'm compromising who I really am, then I want to get out of it. I'm not really sure about this.

I really mean what I told my wife—that I love her and want to live the rest of my life with her. If she can tolerate my stumbling efforts to hang in there and be faithful to the marriage, I want to hang in there with her. I'm having a rough time being faithful. I don't think there's any way it could work if I'm active sexually the way I have been in the past. I have to completely break that pattern.

When asked how she views her husband's sexual identity, his wife replied:

He has relationships and sex totally intertwined. He doesn't know the difference between friendship and sex. If he could become able to have male friends just for male bonding, if he could experience male friendship without introducing sex into it, maybe it would help him be able to start seeing the difference.

This couple wrote that their sexual relationship had deteriorated. They exemplify the dilemma of the man with a strong homosexual identity and a strong commitment to his wife and family. The pain of his ambivalence and her efforts to understand and explain her husband's behavior are clear. He attended Sex Addicts Anonymous (SAA) and they both went to counseling in an attempt to keep the marriage together.

Whether or not the men we interviewed considered themselves primarily heterosexual with an addictive gay side, primarily gay, or bisexual, all were in agreement they were sex addicts who needed to be in a recovery program to learn how to make healthier choices about their sexual activities. They believed this to be true whether or not they would remain in their current relationships. Because they hoped to remain in a heterosexual relationship, their goal was to eliminate their gay behaviors, whether or not they could change their sexual orientation. They hoped that the strength of their commitment to their wife would help them achieve this goal.

Two Couples Who Do Not Perceive The Husband as a Sex Addict

The two wives whose husbands did not identify themselves as sexually addicted had different perceptions of their husbands' homosexuality. One wrote:

The counselor I saw after my husband told me about his homosexual affairs suggested that I look at my husband's sexual activity with other men not so much as unfaithfulness, which is what I wanted to call it, but as a kind of impulsiveness. It wasn't a planned sort of meeting with a particular person, but it came about on a whim, on the spur of the moment.

I didn't think it was compulsive. I felt that there was free choice involved, and I still feel that there's free choice. When I stop to think about it, it makes me angry, and I have a hard time talking with my husband about this without getting angry because I want to say to him, "You don't have to do this. You can make a decision not to." And I've said that to him, and he acknowledges that it's true, that he can make a decision not to.

I have a very hard time understanding or believing that men don't choose to be homosexual. It feels to me that if they chose to be bisexual and yet be faithful to the marriage, they could. But what they say is different than that. I just don't understand it.

The other woman wrote:

I don't think my husband's behavior is compulsive. I know some other guys who screw around a whole lot more than he does. In fact, they risk their lives doing it. One of his friends picked up a

> *man on the street and got robbed at knife point. And on the way home afterwards, he picked up somebody else. That's pretty compulsive. I see none of that in my husband.*
>
> *But I also don't think he has a free choice about his sexual behavior. I see it as very much a part of who he is. I think it's always been a part of him. I can see that he's much happier and much calmer about himself now that he acknowledges it. A good friend of ours has commented more than once about how much more relaxed my husband is since he came out. There was a noticeable change in him.*

Because the first wife believed her husband had a free choice with regard to his homosexual behavior, she found it very difficult to accept. On the other hand, the second wife, while not seeing her husband's behavior as compulsive, nonetheless did not view it as free choice. Because she believed that homosexual experiences are essential to her husband's well-being, she was more comfortable accepting them. The first wife did not make a clear distinction between homosexual identity and homosexual behavior, nor did she consider the possibility that her husband might have a choice about his gay activities, but not about his gay identity.

Spouses of gay and bisexual men who are acknowledged sex addicts have it easier than spouses of gay and bisexual men who do not consider their extramarital homosexual activities to be compulsive. First, by viewing their husband's homosexual behavior as addictive rather than free choice, spouses of acknowledged sex addicts may find it easier to understand, especially if they themselves are in a recovery program. Second, men who view their own gay behavior as addictive generally desire to stop the behavior. Their goals—heterosexual monogamy—then become the same as those of their wife. With this understanding, additional episodes of homosexual acting out are viewed as relapses to be avoided or learned from, not behaviors the wife is expected to accept.

Women married to bisexual men with a strong gay sexual preference are often expected by their spouse to accept the ongoing extramarital homosexual activities. If these women accept this situation, the major stresses for them arise from possible unhappiness. In contrast, for women married to men who define themselves as sex addicts and attempt to become heterosexually monogamous, the major stresses appear to come from the husband's difficulty in adjusting to monogamy.

Another Opinion

Finally, a dissenting opinion about sexual identity and sexual addiction comes from one of the two husbands who did not view himself as sexually addicted. He wrote:

I think you can become addicted to anything—I think that sexual addiction is real. But I believe the sexual addiction program helps some gay people keep that side of themselves in line, so I think it's part of their internalized homophobia. I am not saying that everyone who is in the program is that way, but there are a lot of people who try to escape their sexuality in various ways. Some of them become priests. Some people who cannot accept their own homosexuality seek programs that say you can't act on it.

There is certainly validity to what he says. Sexual addiction programs, just like the priesthood, can help people avoid their sexuality. The other side of the coin, however, is that there are people whose sexual behavior is compulsive and is causing them significant problems with personal relationships, jobs, the law, and their health. Sexual addiction programs can help them change their behaviors. Whether these behaviors are heterosexual or homosexual is not the point; what matters is that the behaviors are causing distress. Bisexual men who have chosen to commit themselves to a heterosexual marriage but keep seeking quick encounters with men may wish to join a program that will help them stop that behavior.

Homosexual Couples

Most people join sexual addiction programs not to change their sexual identity, but to stop thoughts and behaviors that are causing them difficulty. Many strictly homosexual men who were unable on their own to avoid multiple sexual partners and the risk of AIDS have joined Twelve Step programs to learn how to live contentedly with one male partner or by themselves. These men were very clear that it was not their homosexual identity that was the problem, but rather the compulsive expression of their homosexuality. In SA for over two years, a thirty-year-old homosexual man in a committed, monogamous relationship with another man explained why he joined the fellowship. He said:

> *I was raised a Catholic, and a lot of people tried to tell me what God thought about me and what I should do. So I tried to do all the things they said. In my late twenties, I went to a Christian counseling program for people trying not to be gay. But what it did was escalate the shame, the hatred, and try to push the gayness down. But I couldn't push it down.*
>
> *I struggled with compulsive masturbation, buying porno magazines, going to adult bookstores, some massage parlors, and then it progressed to anonymous sex and picking up people. I was nearly hysterical about the possibility of dying of AIDS. I finally went to an AA meeting and told them I was struggling with something similar to chemical dependency but that it has to do with sex, and some people told me about SA. At that time, insecurity, low self-esteem, and shame were interfering with my ability to relate in healthy relationships.*
>
> *In coming to truly love and accept myself for who I am, I've been able to get recovery and to abstain from all those behaviors. I think God would rather love me as a gay man who's sexually sober and in recovery than as someone who's struggling with their homosexuality by acting out continually.*

This man recognized that his "disease" was not his homosexual orientation but rather the compulsive behaviors and their associated shame and low self-esteem. Through his involvement in a Twelve Step program, he was able to stop those behaviors, improve his self-esteem, and become involved in a healthier relationship. His partner, a thirty-one-year-old businessman, told us:

I had a relationship for three years with a man who was an alco-
holic. As things got worse in that relationship, I began to act out
more with compulsive masturbation and pornography, and several
times I went outside of the relationship and picked somebody up.
He did the same thing and the relationship broke up. That was my
low. I had been going to Al-Anon and began going to SAA. My
sobriety definition now is no sex with self and no sex outside a com-
mitted relationship. For a lot of men in the program, acting out
with a man is not recovery, but for me, sex with a man is my only
option. That's my orientation.

What led this man to SAA was not discomfort with his homosexuality, but his awareness that turning to compulsive sexual behaviors, both in and out of the relationship, was not an appropriate
solution to relationship problems.

How Much Did the Wife Know
At the Time of Marriage?
Most of the wives in our survey knew nothing of their husband's
homosexuality or bisexuality at the time of marriage. Sometimes,
this was because the husband was unaware of it himself. Other husbands did not mention it because they assumed it would not be a
problem, or hoped it would not be. In fact, some men hoped marriage would "cure" them of their homosexual behaviors. Still other
men chose to deceive their wife out of fear they would call off the
wedding if they knew. Most of the men believed at the time of marriage that they would be monogamous in the future. A man who
eventually lost his ministry after being arrested for soliciting men
in a public rest room said:

My attraction to men began in my teenage years. My wife didn't
know about my bisexuality when we got married. I thought mar-
riage would be the solution to the problem. I wasn't aware enough
of the problem at the time. I was able to stay monogamous for five
years.

Other men also became aware of their inclinations only after marriage. One couple wrote:

> HUSBAND: *The first time I identified it and said, "Oh, my God, I'm gay," was after I'd been married three years. I fell in love with a guy. I didn't think it was part of me until then; it was just something I did once in a while. But when I looked back I could see the basic attraction I would now identify as a homosexual orientation going back to pre-kindergarten.*
>
> WIFE: *We'd been married about two years when I got pregnant with our first child. When the doctor told him at the end of the pregnancy that we couldn't have sex for about six weeks, something triggered in him that said, "I can't do without it." That was when he started going out and acting out with men. He told me about it two years after that.*

At the time of marriage, some men clearly did not understand their sexual identity. Later, as their sexual attraction for other men surfaced, they found themselves caught between their love and commitment to their family and their emerging bisexual identity.

Other men were clearly aware of their sexual attraction to men at the time they married but believed they could control or suppress it. Although some wives were told before the marriage about prior homosexual behavior, they were usually assured it was a thing of the past.

A middle-aged professional man, now in a Twelve Step program for sex addicts, went for many years through alternating periods of living a gay and then a straight lifestyle. He recalled the events leading up to his first marriage:

> *I first identified my interest in males in high school. It was mostly fantasy and masturbation with friends, but I didn't see it as homosexual at the time; it just felt good. In college, I still dated women, but more and more I became restricted to sexual relationships with males. At age twenty-six, I believed I was gay. It was wonderful to be free of the conflict. I went to gay bars frequently, picking up*

and being picked up, and just reveled in that. My first major rela-
tionship was with a man, and it lasted five years.

About a year after the breakup of that relationship, I had some ma-
jor surgery, which really scared me. I had been searching most of
my life spiritually, and I really intensified the search at that time.
I found a charismatic church that provided me with a home, a fam-
ily, and a spiritual faith. I made the decision with the help of the
priest to cease my gay lifestyle.

It was at the church that I met my first wife. I felt good that I had
another choice, where there was social acceptance and openness.
I wanted to get back into mainstream society and have a wife and
family. So, in short order, I fell in love and was married six
months later.

At this point, his discomfort with his gay side became acute. He
feared he might be unable to abstain from sex with men. He added:

My faith was very strong, so I prayed ardently that I wouldn't act
on my gay side ever again. The week before I got married, I bar-
gained with God. I said, "If this ever happens again, I want You
to strike me dead." But it did happen. I started acting out in rest
rooms, just a few times, but I felt massive guilt afterwards, and
after the first time I confessed to my wife.

Although he had shared his past with his first wife, he was unable
to remain monogamous and the marriage eventually ended. He
then returned to the gay lifestyle. Years later, after further struggles, he met his present wife, who gave him a different perspective
about his bisexuality. He wrote:

My wife is a recovering alcoholic and both of us wanted to talk
about my bisexuality early in our relationship. I described it to her
as something I didn't really like—that I was driven to it and that
it was wonderful at the time, but that I hated myself afterward,
and that I didn't seem to be able to stop. She said, "That sounds
a lot like my alcoholism." And as she talked about how alcoholism

worked, I said, "She's describing my condition exactly." I was very
excited to consider that possibility.

This couple went for extensive counseling before they married. Both had been in recovery programs since marriage and were doing well.

How Was Bisexual Identity Disclosed to Spouse?

For most couples who did not discuss sexual identity before marriage, the eventual disclosure of homosexual activities caused a major crisis. Even if the wife had been aware of her husband's homosexual feelings, disclosure of actual sexual encounters with other men was often devastating. Many women felt anger, betrayal, and fear of abandonment. Yet a surprisingly large number of wives convinced themselves that they were overreacting or that the problem would disappear. They tended to deny evidence that the sexual activity was ongoing. The result of this was a series of disclosures, often spread out over several years, that continued until some final event—such as arrest or the fear of AIDS—led to the husband's involvement in a recovery program. Between the time of the first disclosure and the final crisis, the couple's marriage was typically troubled, their sexual relationship deteriorated, and their self-esteem plummeted.

A man who had multiple homosexual encounters in addition to twice-daily sex with his wife eventually admitted his homosexual affairs to her. Interviewed after six years of fidelity, the couple told us:

HUSBAND: *I was drunk one afternoon at a bar and I met this guy and went up to a hotel room with him. I was getting out of the shower afterward and tripped and hurt my knee.*

WIFE: *He came home limping and told me what had happened. I was absolutely furious. After I dropped him off at the emergency room, I sat in the car and cried. Then, I went into the emergency room and yelled at him. On the way home, he begged me not to leave him. And the craziest thing was, I never even thought of leaving him.*

He promised to stop, but then he told me he just couldn't. I became more and more depressed. I was crying and miserable. Eventually, I decided to see a psychiatrist.

A man who had had many years of anonymous sex with other men gave gonorrhea to his wife after twenty-four years of marriage. He then disclosed his sexual activities to her. His wife wrote:

He told me he had gonorrhea and that I had to make an appointment to get treated. I felt ashamed, unloved, violated, hurt, embarrassed. I was angry at him. My doctor gave me a shot and wanted me to go for counseling. I didn't go because my spouse was going, and after a few months, when his therapist told him he didn't have to return, I assumed he was "cured." This was foolish on my part. Then, when AIDS was in the news, I got scared and angry, but only mentioned it to him. I really didn't want to know he was acting out. After twenty-nine years of marriage, he got arrested.

The disclosure of a husband's bisexuality often results in lowered self-esteem for the wife. A forty-year-old homemaker described her reaction to her husband's disclosure:

I thought, How can I compete with other men? I have no rules to tell me what to do. Should I leave? I felt that he'd used me, that he was not honest with me before we got married. But I was grateful that he was being honest now. I was angry and wondered if he might be an incurable pervert. I felt I couldn't trust him.

Other wives had mixed feelings. An attorney whose husband confessed he had had sex with other men in adult bookstores wrote:

I felt he did it because I wasn't good enough. I was fat; I felt defective as a human being. His acting out confirmed for me that I was no good, worthless. I felt anger, fury, rage, sympathy, pity, compassion. When he acted out in bookstores, I felt that he must really have a problem that had nothing to do with me. He was so remorseful. I cried, tried to understand, and consoled him.

Effect of Bisexuality on the Marriage

For many couples, one of the early casualties was trust. This was especially true when disclosure followed many years of bisexual activity. A forty-two-year-old nurse told us:

Even if we could totally separate the sexuality issue, there's so much damage to the basic trust between us. I keep going back to how he lied to me twenty-three years ago when we got married. It wasn't a direct lie. It never occurred to me to ask the question, which is one of the things he said to me—"But you never directly asked me if I was homosexual." Well, no, but I also never directly asked him if he was in the Mafia or had ever been a CIA agent!

Most couples reported that the husband's gay activities lowered the self-esteem of each member of the couple. Husbands wrote that their dual existence caused them to pull back and be unable to share emotionally. They also wrote that they would lie and sneak around, so they felt guilty and lost respect for themselves. An administrator and his wife, both forty-five, wrote:

HUSBAND: *It degraded our relationship to the point that we lived entirely separate lives—lots of fighting, pain, isolation, and loneliness. It lowered my self-esteem tremendously.*

WIFE: *I blamed myself for his unhappiness. I didn't have any self-esteem. Everything was my fault. I believed everything I was told. I was very needy. I tried to please him so he would not be angry. I resented him and hated him at times. I tried to be cute and seductive, but it did not work. He had no interest in sex with me because he was acting out outside of the marriage. I could only assume I did something wrong.*

Withdrawal and anger were a recurrent theme among the couples we surveyed. Another marriage where the husband had anonymous sexual contact with men in adult bookstores was very stressed. The couple wrote:

HUSBAND: *I was not willing to learn to relate to a real woman; the addiction was easier. Each sexual release made sex with my wife seem unnecessary for a while. But my secret life built its own wall of fear and resentment. I felt cut off from God and deeply ill at ease.*

WIFE: *My coaddiction made me afraid to ask questions about the acting out. I was afraid to rock the boat, even when I was angry about his behavior. I shut down emotionally and sexually. His addiction made him extremely moody, critical, and secretive. He pushed me away. I felt undesirable—or why would he turn elsewhere? I found self-worth in my job instead of at home. I thought he didn't love me, or couldn't. I thought his addiction was my fault in some way, which lowered my self-esteem.*

If a wife recognizes her low self-esteem and gets help, she can learn she has choices, and can sometimes favorably affect her marriage. This was the lesson learned by a woman, now active in S-Anon, who knew for many years about her husband's homosexual activities. Eventually, he was arrested on a sex-related charge, lost his job, and got into a recovery program. She told us:

Although we had always had a good sexual relationship, I was developing a lot of difficulty in responding because I was angry and hurt. I fluctuated a lot between accepting the relationship and not. I went through a period of feeling trapped. I didn't feel I had a choice. It took me several years, but when I went into counseling it was the beginning of my detachment and learning to care for myself. I began to develop the feeling that I could manage alone, that I could take care of myself. But I had not, at the time he was arrested, got to where I was ready to say, "I'm ready to leave this relationship." But I think it would have come.

*As I look back on it now, I think if I would have been able to do
that at an earlier point—telling him we would either split up or
he would have to get help—he would have gone into recovery
sooner. But my own codependence actually allowed this to continue much longer than it otherwise would have.*

She believed that by not forcing her husband to make a decision,
she had enabled her husband's addictive behavior and prolonged
the time that he was able to avoid the consequences of what he was
doing.

Effect of Bisexuality on a Couple's Sexual Relationship

Most couples whose marriage is complicated by extramarital sex
have to deal with emotionally charged issues such as trust, betrayal,
deceit, resentment, anger, and low self-esteem. But when the sexual activity is homosexual, the problem for men is compounded by
the feeling that their need to be sexual with other men is part of their
identity and cannot be satisfied in their marriage beds. The strength
of this feeling is one of the key factors in determining whether the
marriage can survive.

Of the twenty-two recovering couples we surveyed, ten believed
their current sexual relationship was good or at least significantly
better than before recovery. Six couples rated their sexual relationship as poor or worse, and six couples were abstinent at the time
of the survey.

Before disclosure of the husband's homosexual activities, the couples wrote that their sexual relationship was generally good. Over
the years, however, it tended to deteriorate more than the sex life
of couples where the sexual addiction involved the opposite sex.

Why Sex Was Better Since Recovery

A middle-aged man who engaged in frequent sexual activity with
other men until he joined SA several years ago described what happened to his sexual relationship with his wife. He wrote:

HUSBAND: *I was always abusive to her. We had sex at least once
or twice a day from before we were married right until I got into*

SA. *She didn't want it and I always wanted it. She finally found it was easier to give in than to say no to me. I'd get angry or upset. When she was sick, I'd want sex. At inappropriate times—we'd be walking out the door to go to a party and she'd look good—I'd have to have sex with her.*

After I confessed to her about the men, the sex with her just got more. Apparently, she thought if she were only more sexual with me, I'd have less reason to go out. She never knew I was masturbating as well.

After several years in SA, we had over a year of abstinence, and during that period I believe I got true recovery. I understood that lust even permeated my marriage. For two years or so, the only time we had sex was when she requested it, which was maybe only once a month. We now have sex about once a week, at her request.

WIFE: *He was my only sexual partner. Before we got married, we spent hours in bed. And then it seemed once I got married, I didn't want it anymore. We had sex several times a day. I was always able to have an orgasm, but I don't think I ever enjoyed it. Physically, my body was responding, but I felt used. I didn't feel it was love, it was just animalistic. I don't remember if it changed after he told me about the men.*

I was very happy with the abstinence. And the sex now is a lot different than the way it used to be. I don't feel used any more; he's more loving. There's cuddling afterwards and he's just very much more considerate.

Why Sex Was Worse Since Recovery

For women who rely on their partner's approval for their self-esteem, knowledge of their husband's other life can be devastating to the way they feel about their own sexuality. A forty-six-year-old woman described what happened to her sexual relationship with her husband over the years. She wrote:

After he told me about the bisexuality, I turned kind of frigid. I felt shell-shocked; I just didn't respond to his advances any more.

> *He began getting the compulsive stuff taken care of with other men and stopped insisting on sex with me. After that, we had sex a couple of times a week, and I thought it was pretty normal.*
>
> *About three years ago, I experienced orgasm for the first time and started wanting sex. But as soon as I wanted more, he got scared, so it's been just a total flip-flop. Now, he isn't interested at all and we haven't had sex for months.*
>
> *Recently, I realized that all along I've been getting these vibes from my husband that made me feel very bad sexually. I was having to repress my sexuality. There's an unspoken wall between us.*
>
> *I don't want to be hurt any more, so I'm pulling my emotions back from him. In the last few months, whenever he would even touch me, I would pull back and he would get angry with me. He was taking it as a rejection, but I explained to him that it was coming from my fear that if I let down my guard once again I will be hurt.*

Some men also had sexual difficulties with their wife as a result of their acting out. A thirty-five-year-old man, married for three years, reported his sexual relationship to be worse than before recovery. He wrote, "I have so much guilt and shame about my acting out that I feel too guilty to have relations with my wife." As a result, his sexual drive diminished and they rarely had sex. His wife, in contrast, believed the quality of their sexual relationship had improved because her husband was more present for her when they made love, but she was disappointed at how infrequently they were sexual.

A businessman, thirty-six, married three years, rated his sexual relationship as worse since his disclosure because it was less frequent. He believed the reason was that his wife was still angry over his infidelity. His wife wrote:

> *Because he was worried about AIDS, he began wearing a condom any time we had intercourse, which was awful because it was a physical, visible reminder of where he had been. By that time, I'd had a tubal ligation, so there was no way I could pretend it was for contraception.*

A fifty-year-old accountant, married many years, related how his homosexual activities adversely affected his marital sexual relationship. He had been aware of his homosexual leanings at the time of marriage. He wrote:

> *When we got married, my wife's understanding, and my hope, was that our sexual behavior would be normal. If there was anything sexually that I wanted and she was unfamiliar with, I would explain it. Sometimes she was willing and sometimes not. The activities she was not willing to participate in, I just put aside and experienced those with other men.*
>
> *In the years before recovery, our sexual relationship was poor. This was because of my fear of transmitting disease, my preoccupation with other partners, and because I was too often spent when my spouse was interested. Just before I got into the program, I counted four times in a year that we'd made love. I was having sex with male partners as many as three times in one week.*
>
> *Since getting into the program, our sex life has lacked spontaneity and creativity. Homosexual sex created greater highs for me. I expect my spouse to know what pleases me most and am disappointed when she cannot intuit this as another man might. However, we have sex more frequently than before because I no longer practice high-risk activity with homosexual friends. I've tested negative for HIV, so I'm less worried about transmitting a disease to her.*

Whether a bisexual man can successfully make the transition to heterosexual monogamy depends also on his level of sexual arousal with his wife. If he finds that sex with men is much more exciting, then he is likely to have a difficult time giving it up.

Some Couples Were Abstinent

Two couples we surveyed were abstinent because the husband was HIV-positive and therefore could transmit the AIDS virus to his wife. One of these couples had apparently decided that the only really safe sex was no sex. For the second couple, the husband's positive HIV status added to an already troubled sexual relationship.

Abstinence was part of the recovery process for some other couples as well. A couple married seven years told us:

> HUSBAND: *Part of the reason I got into the program was because it got to the point where I could not get aroused unless I was fantasizing about a man. So I forced abstinence. I said I needed to really dry out. Looking back on it, I think she thought it was good for a month or two, but after a while she started feeling neglected. About a month ago we talked it out, and I had to face my fears. I realized that I was scared about stuff that went back to my childhood. I'm not just scared about having sex with her, I'm scared about proving that I'm a "man," and completing the sex act.*

> *Through talking with my sponsor, I realized that even though we were abstinent, I became sexually anorexic and was still in control. So I've told her that it's now up to her to make the first move. In the meantime, we hug and kiss.*

> WIFE: *I had sex very early, and between ages fifteen and twenty-two I had a lot of sex partners. Then, I moved to a religious community to try to get some "sexual sanctuary," and to leave my old friends and my old life behind. I went for a long time without having sex.*

> *When we first got married, we had a strong, pretty good sexual relationship, but it gradually deteriorated. After I had the kids, my energy level dropped and I was more tired. He continued to be interested in having sex with me, but I just couldn't keep up as much.*

> *When he told me about the other men, it actually made me want to have sex with him more. I tried harder. It was like I was desperate in wanting to hang onto him. It didn't work, of course. Later on, when he started in the program, he told me that he had been still going out.*

> *Once he got into the program, he strongly wanted a celibacy period. I thought that was a good idea at first, but then I started*

rebelling because I didn't feel I had a choice. I felt like it was his program, and I was feeling left out. Somebody in his group advised him to give me the choice to initiate any sexual relationship. That was a little over a month ago, and it made me feel better, but I haven't taken any steps yet to try to do anything. I've been so busy, I'm just exhausted.

This couple's story illustrates that sexual problems are not necessarily due only to the question of sexual identity. The wife's account suggested sexual conflicts and concerns existed for her long before they met. Their abstinence period had generally been a positive experience, allowing them time to work on nonsexual expressions of affection and childhood sexual issues.

At times, the damage appeared to be beyond repair. This was the case for a couple who had been married ten years. The husband had had multiple relationships with men. He has been in a Twelve Step program for over two years; she was not in a recovery program. They wrote:

HUSBAND: *Before I got into the program, we were sexually active about once every two or three weeks. I always fantasized about men while we were making love. Over two years ago, I got panicked about the possibility of giving her AIDS and killing the whole family, so I went to a counselor. I really felt that a heterosexual relationship was possible, especially about eighteen months into recovery.*

The counselor insisted I tell my wife everything, which I did. We have not had sex since—it's been over two years. I haven't put pressure on her to have intercourse, but I've put pressure on her to make out, to be loving and holding. That hasn't happened. I don't think she's capable of trusting me. I believe the only way I can make amends is to change my behavior and be patient, and I have been.

We're about to separate, and I will probably go back to being gay. But I'll stay in the program. I'm a sex addict. Unfortunately, there's no quick fix for happiness if I change my sexual preference.

WIFE: *Since he told me two years ago, we haven't had sex at all. He'd had hundreds of partners! The thing that really angered me — it was a double whammy — was that I was this close to dying, this close to having AIDS.* I kept thinking, How could you jeopardize my life and my child's life?

He is moving forward, but I'm remaining stagnant. I can't forgive. I've fantasized the steps of allowing him to make love to me, but my fears are that I will not perform, that I will not feel.

I don't think I can ever trust him, even though he's been sexually sober and is going to a lot of meetings. I still can't get out of my mind that I could have died. We're planning to separate by the end of the month.

This couple's story illustrates the importance of a recovery program for both members of the couple. No matter how healthy one or both partners may have been at the start of the marriage, the ravages of sexual addiction and coaddiction — deception and emotional distancing, infidelity and betrayal — leave deep wounds in both partners that need healing.

The Marriages that Survived

In her study of thirty-three wives of bisexual men, Gochros found in the marriages that survived that the sexual relationship was maintained and was usually good. She wrote: "Even when problems occurred, the husband was committed to helping the wife obtain sexual satisfaction within the marriage, found some degree of satisfaction himself (as opposed to merely 'servicing' his wife), and engaged in empathic problem solving rather than criticizing."[4]

Our survey cannot address this question directly because all but one of the twenty-two recovering couples were committed to survival of their marriage regardless of their sexual relationship. Nonetheless, what the couples told us supports Gochros's conclusions. Those persons who perceived their sexual relationship to be most unsatisfactory appeared to be having the greatest difficulty in their overall relationship. In Gochros's study, the bisexual men had the option of freely getting their homosexual needs met with other men. In our survey, the husbands had committed to getting all their sexual needs met within the marriage. For this reason, the men in our survey who most strongly identified themselves as homosexuals had the most troubled marriages.

Therapy Experiences

Unfortunately, this group of respondents often reported generally unproductive experiences with therapists. Gay and bisexual men had a particularly difficult time with therapy.

A forty-year-old man who had had multiple brief sexual encounters with other men went to five therapists hoping to change his sexual orientation. The first therapist tried aversion therapy by administering electric shocks if he became aroused while viewing pictures of gay sex. The only result was to introduce the man to pornography, which along with masturbation, then became a part of his sexual behavior. Talking with three other therapists resulted in only temporary periods of abstaining from sexual encounters with other men. The final therapist recognized the behavior as addictive and referred him to SA, which he was attending for several months at the time of the survey. During this period, he was not being sexual with other men, but reported he still had sexual feelings for other men and was pessimistic about the survival of his marriage.

When counseling spouses of gay and bisexual sex addicts, therapists often failed to understand the addictive nature of the marital relationships. For example, one wife reported being advised by her therapist to leave her husband. She wrote:

> After my husband told me about his affairs with other men, we went to our first psychologist. After seeing my husband three or four times, the psychologist wanted to see me. He didn't even bother to talk to me, he just flat out told me, "Lady, he's incurable. My advice is to take all the money you can grab and get out of this marriage as fast as you can." And I told him, "That's easy to say, but we really do love each other."

Giving advice like this to a coaddict is about as helpful as telling a drug addict to "just say no." Before recovery, coaddicts in relationships make decisions based on their fear of abandonment or their poor self-esteem. It would be much more helpful for a therapist to work with the coaddict on her self-esteem and sexuality, her expectations of a marriage relationship, and how they are being met. The goal would be to help her see that she truly does have choices.

Several people went to clergy for counseling and found little help. A couple in recovery for three years recalled their experience with their church, in which they had previously been active. They wrote:

HUSBAND: *When I brought my problem to the church, I was told I would not be able to participate in services for two years. I could not take communion, I could not speak. For a while I white-knuckled it, but then I resumed the compulsive cruising and masturbation and occasionally acting out in bathrooms and parks. But in my church they feel as if time cures things, so after a while they asked if I wanted to be reinstated and I said yes, so they did.*

I felt guilt-ridden about being reinstated because nothing had changed. I wasn't in the program, I didn't have any tools, I was still dysfunctional, I was still cruising, I was still compulsively masturbating. The church was supposed to help me but it didn't.

WIFE: *When my husband was working with our religious counselor, I was really alone because they never even thought about asking me to come and talk to them.*

I felt isolated, I felt disappointed, but I also recognized that in their minds they were simply dealing with my husband, and it was probably just ignorance on their part. They never recognized that it affected another person.

Many professional therapists increasingly recognize that the problems of one family member impact the entire family system. We hope that more clergy will include the family, especially when counseling on compulsive behaviors.

A psychotherapist who works with gay and bisexual married men described to us the logic he uses in helping his clients make choices. He wrote:

> *When each guy first gets into the group, we ask him to ask himself: Do I disclose to my wife? If I do, what price must I be willing to pay? If I don't, what price must I pay? If I do or don't disclose, do I act on my sexual attractions to men? If I do, what price do I pay? If I don't, what price do I pay? We look at the cost of the different options, not in terms of the right or wrong way, but the costs.*

A therapist with a nonjudgmental attitude can help a gay or bisexual client sort out his goals and identify his conflicts. The client will then be better able to recognize if his behavior is congruent with his beliefs and goals, or if it is compulsive and in conflict with what he wants for himself. If compulsivity is present, then referral to a Twelve Step program may be appropriate.

Was It More Difficult for Women to Accept Husbands' Infidelity with Other Men?

Gochros wrote, "On the positive side, dealing with a homosexual affair need not force a woman to doubt her own abilities as a woman, since she knows there are no added feminine wiles or 'techniques' that will help. It is not in her power to compete with her husband's male lover."[5] In other words, it is easier for her to accept that her husband was with a male rather than a female lover. This, however, was not true for most of the women we interviewed. Their reaction was expressed well by a bisexual man who told us:

> *When I told her, "I'm not messing around with other women, so you don't have to worry," her reaction was, "I can't compete because I'm not a man." And surprisingly, I've talked to thirty-some men who have told their wives and have had the identical conversation.*

Feeling sexually desired by their husbands is a normal expectation for women. It is also normal that they feel a blow to their feminine sexuality when they are told by their husbands that they want or need something sexually that women cannot give them. No matter how positive their self-esteem is, they are likely to feel devalued.

We asked the nine women whom we interviewed at length whether it made any difference that their husband was seeing other men rather than other women. Most thought that their husband's gay sex had been harder to deal with; one thought it was easier; and two believed it made no difference. Here are the words of one woman who thought it was more difficult for her because her husband had had sex with men:

> If it was another woman, I probably would have thought I just have to compete better. I could be sexier, wear different clothes, or do more. But how do you compete with a man? What they really want, you can't give them. Over the years, I found myself squelching my female side an awful lot and becoming more male. I found myself stopping wearing dresses and becoming more logical and less emotional. I even offered him anal sex.

Another woman agreed. She said:

> It was like a total renunciation of my womanhood. I used to love the pride I had within myself as a woman, being attractive to the man I chose to marry. Even though he says, "You're the only woman that I have really been attracted to, you're pretty," it doesn't help.

In contrast, two women not in recovery programs, who had accepted their husband's ongoing homosexual activities, believed it would be worse if the other sexual partners were women. One told us:

> If my husband had sex with another woman, I would be much more upset than I am now, because I would take that as a very personal affront. It would tell me that I'm inadequate. I know I can't give him what a man can, but if I can't give him what another woman can, then there must be something wrong with me.

Deciding What to Do with Gay and Bisexual Friends

For gay and bisexual married men in recovery, how do their gay and bisexual friends fit into their new life? How do male friends in general fit in? We asked several people this question. Some had found it necessary to avoid gay and bisexual people except those in recovery programs. One man wrote:

> *Just like people who stop drinking have to change friends, the same is true for a sex addict. I think being around a lot of gay people would make it very difficult for me. Although I have a few gay friends, there are lots of controls.*
>
> *Instead, I've developed good male relationships that are, of course, nonsexual. I've got lots of males to be intimate with, in other ways than sexual, to get some of my needs met.*

Others men saw it differently. One wrote:

> *I have several gay friends. There are a lot of gay people who don't act out. Most of the people I associate with are in a relationship. They're not acting out with a lot of people.*

Everyone needs friends. Because people are usually most comfortable with friends who are like them, it is natural for gay men to seek out other gay men for friendships. For those who want to change their behavior, it is probably wisest to make friends who are also recovering in Twelve Step programs or who are in a committed relationship.

A psychotherapist in the authors' city leads a weekly support group for gay and bisexual men who are in committed relationships with women. The group is not a Twelve Step meeting or a therapy group. He told us:

> *When I was seeing men in therapy, they would say, "There's no place for me to go. I can't go to a park, I can't go to a bookstore, I can't go to a bar to just talk. For one thing, when I get in there, people expect different behaviors of me, and I still don't feel like I*

have control over my own body. If I get into a male/male situation, it leads to sex. I haven't yet recognized that I can be gay without being sexual."

In the group, I try to provide a place where gay men can talk in a nonsexual atmosphere. For some of the men, the group is the first opportunity they've had to be gay without being genital. They learn they don't have to be sexual to be gay.

Wives' Support System
The biggest single problem for wives of bisexual men is isolation. One woman wrote:

If I had some friends I thought would understand, I would feel free to explain my situation. Right now, I don't have a lot of close friends because I isolated myself for years. It probably has a lot to do with my relationship with my husband. I do have some friends who are my children's friends' mothers, but I haven't felt so far that any of them would understand, and I think it would scare them to hear what I've gone through. Going to S-Anon meetings and being able to talk about my problems has been very helpful. Bisexuality is stigmatized in our society. It's so difficult to find people to talk to.

Friends who can listen without judging can be an enormous help to spouses of bisexual men. A good place to find such friends is S-Anon, Codependents of Sex Addicts (COSA), or other Twelve Step fellowships. These are also good places to find others who have been through some of the same experiences.

Advice for Readers
Several people we interviewed had suggestions for our readers. Here is what one bisexual recovering sex addict said:

I have been able to avoid acting out with other men through a combination of finding my own spirituality and the Twelve Step work. What has helped me the most has been my sponsor, with whom

I have regular contact and a real commitment. Thoroughly working the program has been very important.

Another addict said:

If a bisexual man was contemplating marriage, I would tell him to be honest with his fiancée. Honesty is the best policy. If they love each other, his bisexuality doesn't mean they shouldn't get married.

Here is what the wife of a bisexual recovering sex addict told us:

One thing that has helped me is to have my husband quit telling me details of his past sex life. I used to think that he had to come completely clean and tell me every detail of what he used to do, and it was like picking at a sore. It's better for him to tell that stuff to people in SA. Not hearing about it has helped me heal.

Another wife said:

First, talk to others. Don't try to carry the burden of getting well and keeping well all by yourself. Second, don't get involved in the question of whether you are sexual enough and whether you are fulfilling his sexual needs. Don't even pretend you have to try to fulfill his sexual needs, because you may not ever fulfill his bisexual needs. Third, you need to be honest with yourself. It's your job to take care of yourself emotionally, socially, spiritually, sexually, and physically. If there are things that are uncomfortable for you, it's okay to say so, and you don't have to say why.

I would also advise women to keep the door open for affection. If they're not going to participate in sexual activities, then they should hold hands and be able to give each other hugs. If they're going to totally shut down the relationship, then they don't have to worry about affection. But if what they're still working on is recovery, don't shut out affection.

Conclusion

People do not choose to be homosexual or bisexual any more than people choose to be heterosexual. Our sexual identity, which most psychologists believe is established in early childhood, is something most of us could not change even if we wanted to. What we do have a choice about is our sexual behavior. For example, heterosexuals who are married might continue to be attracted to others of the opposite sex, but if they are committed to monogamy, they choose not to act on the attraction.

Support and therapy groups for married gay and bisexual men can be of tremendous help to them in sorting out the role of their homosexual identity in their lives. They can be helped to see the costs of being sexual with other men while remaining in a relationship with a woman. If they determine the emotional and health costs to them and their spouse to be excessive, they can get peer and professional support in their decision to leave the marriage or to commit to a monogamous sexual relationship with the spouse while maintaining a gay or bisexual identity. If they choose the marriage, they can be helped to see that homosexual identity does not mandate homosexual activity.

CHAPTER ELEVEN

The Woman Addict And Her Partner

The first thing I can ever remember about sex was when I was ten years old and my older brother molested me. That started the shame and the guilt. Whenever I heard the word "sex," I was tense and frightened. Sex was not talked about in my house. My mother once gave me a book about sex and told me to read it, and if I had any questions, to read it again. During this time my dad was having affairs and Mom used to take me with her to look for Dad's car in front of other people's houses. More than once it was so obvious to me that my dad and some other lady we knew had something special. It just made me sick to watch them.

I started dating early and by tenth grade I was having sex with whichever guy I was going steady with. I always had two guys in my life, although I went to bed with only one of them. I thought that marriage would solve the problem, but within a year after I got married, I met a guy at work and just couldn't say no. My husband was working during the day and going to school at night, and I was just so lonely. I didn't even enjoy sex with this guy. To get over him, I got into another affair. This was someone I obsessed about day and night while the affair lasted.

After my first child was born, I got right into another affair—this time with my best friend's husband, although I kept telling myself, *This is not what I want to do.* For the first time, I thought I had a real problem. But when I returned to work, I got into yet another affair, this one with a married man. By then, I was so confused that I asked my husband for a separation. At the same time, I lost my job because I was so obsessed that I wasn't working well. My husband thought I had ended the affair, but when he found out I was still seeing the other man, he immediately filed for divorce.

Over the next few months, I went from one guy to another. They were truly one-night stands; I simply could not say no. In the end, I married the man I'd had the last major affair with, who in the meantime had divorced his wife. I was determined not to have any more affairs, and for five years I didn't, although I did a lot of flirting, teasing, and fantasizing. Eventually, I met a guy at work I was very attracted to, and I got into a long affair with him. I felt a tremendous amount of shame and guilt over all the lying and conniving I had to do to be with him, so to get over it, I got into another affair, even though I hated the sex with him.

I couldn't understand what I was doing. Sex with my husband was so wonderful. I enjoyed it and felt like he loved me and he cared, not just for sex, but for me. I kept saying to myself, *I've got everything I want. What is wrong with me?* But I couldn't stop.

Years later, when my daughter got into treatment for drug use, I went to family week where I heard about the importance of not having secrets in the family. That was when I told my husband everything. The result was that I went into treatment for my sexual addiction and joined SA.

—Lorna

Approximately 25 percent of people in sexual addiction recovery programs are women. In our survey, twelve women (16 percent of all addicts) said they were sexually addicted; nine of them were married to sex addicts and were dealing with sexual coaddiction issues as well. To obtain more information about women sex addicts and their husbands, we interviewed an additional twelve women, as well as nine of their husbands. We talked with a male member of S-Anon who recently separated from his wife after learning of her affairs. One-quarter of the women sex addicts were also chemically dependent, as were half of their husbands. The twenty-four women averaged thirty-six years of age, the men thirty-eight.

This chapter will discuss the problems particular to women sex addicts, to men married to them, and to couples in which both are recovering from sexual addiction.

Sex Addiction Is Not Only a Man's Problem

Fifty years ago, alcoholism was considered to be a man's problem. Women were rarely seen drinking in public. Because of the shame attached to women's drinking, families often colluded in their effort to hide Mom's problem from the rest of the world. Today about one-quarter of the membership of AA is female, and alcoholism is widely understood to be a major problem for women.

Today, admitting sexual addiction is more shameful for women than for men. The most common expression of women's sexual addiction—sexual encounters with many partners—is a behavior that society encourages in men but condemns in women. Women are more shamed about their sexual addiction than men, so they keep it to themselves. Women often will not tell even their closest friends. A woman who had multiple affairs reported: "For eight years, I had a support group of women. We met regularly and were very close and we did a lot of things together. But I couldn't talk to them about my addiction. I was just too ashamed."

Shame can also affect how willing women are to share at Twelve Step meetings. A woman who had heard other women speak openly at a sexual dependency treatment center contrasted her treatment group with what she had observed at women's Sex and Love Addicts Anonymous (SLAA) meetings. She wrote:

> At those meetings, I was unable to get a sense of what made them sex addicts. When you get with a group of women, you hear the relationship addiction. There was only one woman one time who

had a father and brothers who used pornography, and she said that she'd been under a lot of stress and that she began to use pornography and to masturbate. That was the only time I really heard anybody refer to what was actually going on with them sexually. What I'm finding is that women are a lot less willing to come out with the sexual acting out.

The Nature of Sexual Addiction in Women

For over half the women addicts we surveyed and interviewed, extramarital affairs had been a problem either in the present marriage, a previous marriage, or both. One woman had been a prostitute and a topless dancer before getting into her current relationship. Several women had not had sex with others, but felt they had devoted an excessive amount of time and energy to fantasizing, obsessing about men and other women, flirting with men, masturbating excessively, or a combination of these. A thirty-two-year-old woman in Sex Addicts Anonymous (SAA) told of multiple affairs. She wrote:

I was involved with my husband, with somebody out of town, and also with somebody in town. I was lying to them all. The person from out of town called me one night and said, "I'm just so afraid you're going to be running around on me." I said, "Why?" He said, "Well, you're doing it to your husband now, why wouldn't you do it to me?" I said, "You can trust me."

Toward the end, I was noticing I'd be with one person and thinking about another, and I'd be telling myself, I can't be doing this; it's not right, it's getting out of hand. *I seemed to be two different people.*

Desire for Power

Several women reported that power was the driving force behind their sexual addiction. A woman who had multiple affairs during both her marriages told us:

With the affairs, by the time we got down to the sex part, I just wanted to get it over with. I was never orgasmic with any of the other people. I was looking to get even, to get revenge. It was a real power thing to be seductive. When I was a teenager, my girlfriends would say you can't have sex unless you're in love, that it has to be special. But the men would talk about getting it however they could, and they'd say whatever it took to get sex. I used to say to myself, I can be like any man. If a man can do that, so can I.

Recalling the women she met during her treatment, a woman who had affairs in her first marriage and fantasized a great deal in her second marriage commented:

Women addicts seem to be more focused on the attention, the feedback, not so much the sex. In fact, the orgasm seemed to be totally optional for most of the women, unless they were into masturbation. It seemed to be the power of getting the man, getting the attention, the chase, and the capture.

Fantasy

In describing their affairs, most of the women did not mention the sexual element. A thirty-three-year-old therapist told us:

Sure, the sex with those men was exciting, but it wasn't the act of intercourse. The actual sex act for me was a very very small part. The excitement was in the intrigue. I'd spend a lot of time being flirtatious and seductive, orchestrating encounters, planning and thinking how it would be, where it would be, and how I could make it happen. A lot of it was in my head.

Attraction to Other Women

Men sometimes reported that their sexual addiction crossed gender lines. The same is true for women. The women we interviewed all considered themselves heterosexual, but several said they had also been attracted to other women. A thirty-four-year-old businesswoman recalled:

The only way I knew how to be close to people was to have sex with them. I had sex with lots of men, and then I decided I wanted to get close to women, so I had sex with them. I discovered I wasn't bisexual, so I stopped that behavior. Now, I have some good friends who are women.

Even now, when I'm really frightened in my relationship and am feeling too close, I start obsessing, usually about gay women. It's not that I obsess about being sexual with them, and I don't really want to act on it, but I just feel attracted to them and I want to be close to them.

A twenty-eight-year-old member of Sexaholics Anonymous (SA) and S-Anon related:

When I am really going with my addiction and there are fears about my relationship or about recovery, I will start having lesbian fantasies. But I've never acted on them, and lesbian fantasies are not a part of my lovemaking.

"Acting In"

Sexual dysfunction can run the gamut from excessive sexual involvement to a determination not to be at all sexual. These opposites have been termed *acting out* and *acting in*. In both, there is an unhealthy preoccupation with sex. An analogy can be drawn with eating disorders, which range from compulsive overeating to anorexia nervosa. In both conditions, there is preoccupation with food. In her sexual relations, a young woman exhibited both extremes at different times of her life. She said:

From age sixteen to twenty-six, I had many sex partners, usually one-night stands who I never saw again. I used a lot of alcohol and drugs during that time, and I married a man who was an alcoholic.

Our sexual relationship was terrific before we got married, but a few months after the wedding I started shutting down, and for the last eight years I haven't been interested in sex—with my husband or with other men. Shortly before my husband joined AA, I started going to Al-Anon and they told me to stop drinking, which I did. I think I understand now what my problem is—it's my fear of intimacy. I want to be close. I want to connect with everybody, and I want to belong. When I'm with a stranger, I can do that by showing them something about me, and I was choosing to show them my sexual side. But when I was married, and he started getting to know me better, I had to somehow keep him away. Since I couldn't stop how much he knew, I could stop him seeing me sexually.

A loss of all desire for sex once a caring partner is present can be a symptom of childhood sexual abuse, even if memory of the molestation has been repressed. In *Aching for Love: The Sexual Drama of the Adult Child*, a study of one hundred women who were adult children of alcoholics, Mary Ann Klausner and Bobbie Hasselbring wrote:

"Splitting," in which we're either sexual or affectionate, but not both, is a common adaptation for many of us who have experienced some type of abuse or serious neglect in childhood. Unable to combine sex with affection because it stirs painful incest memories, we may opt for one or the other. In our study, the women said they either had nonsexual relationships with men or women they genuinely valued or loved, or engaged in frequent sex with strangers—which allowed them to avoid partner intimacy.[1]

Several women in our survey reported losing sexual interest in their partner after marriage, when they were convinced of their spouse's commitment and faced the possibility of experiencing real intimacy. Some therapists believe that for incest survivors to take on the additional label of sex addict can be detrimental rather than beneficial, and can add to their shame. Some women, however, find that acknowledging their sexual addiction gives them a framework in which to understand themselves.

Men's Behaviors Versus Women's Behaviors
Based on her observations at Twelve Step meetings, a woman sex addict drew some conclusions about how sexually addicted men and women differ. She wrote:

Women may have a lesser tendency to get involved with really compulsive masturbation. I hear so many men's stories in meetings about how compulsive masturbation is the hardest thing to give up. I don't often hear that in women's stories. But I still feel that if you get underneath the symptoms, the main issues are the same.

A therapist who was previously involved with pornography, prostitution, sadomasochism, and multiple affairs said:

I would say only a small percent of the women I've met in SA are truly sex addicts. The rest are love addicts, codependents. I'm working with a girl who's a real sex addict, just like me. She's had abortions; she's slept with every Tom, Dick, and Harry; she's lost her job; and her husband is getting ready to divorce her and take the kids. This woman's life depends upon what we do in this group. These other women are talking about the married man with whom they've had a ten-year affair and how much they love him. Those women are different. But I think true women sex addicts aren't that different from men. I can match stories with any guy I've met so far.

Women are much less likely than men to be arrested for exhibitionism, voyeurism, and rape. This is a reflection of how women are raised in our culture. But another part of the difference is that the law views the same behavior in women differently than in men. For example, when a woman exposes herself and a man observes her, the man will likely be arrested for voyeurism, not the woman for exhibitionism.

The Relationship Between
Sexual Addiction and Coaddiction

Several women who were married to recovering sex addicts had identified their own sexual addiction only after first recognizing their coaddiction. This was particularly true of women who had not had affairs, at least not in the current marriage. Because they did not break their marriage vows, it took them a while in recovery from coaddiction before they could identify their addictive sexual behaviors.

A twenty-eight-year-old woman, married eight years to a man who is now in SA, realized she was a sex addict only after two years in S-Anon. She felt stuck in the recovery process and began to look more closely at her own sexual behavior. What she learned led her to SA. She wrote:

I never had an actual affair, but I had emotional affairs constantly. I was inappropriate with people—I talked about my personal sexual life, trying to shock them. I made sure people knew I was very highly sexual.

I was always pursuing my husband sexually. That's what I thought love was. I can also remember numbing out with sex. If I had a hard day at the office, I wanted to have sex—any excuse in the world.

I was able in S-Anon to get away with it for a long time. I said I watched pornography because he wanted to. Well, he did want to, but I definitely enjoyed it myself. I watched it when he wasn't at home, and then the minute he came home I would seduce him.

I used to call men on the phone, men I barely knew, and talk about intimate details. I would act drunk, although I wasn't, so it was acceptable. But the minute these men would want to see me, I would tell them I couldn't.

Once, I got an obscene phone call in the middle of the night and I thought it was an old boyfriend of mine, Joe, with whom I used to have telephone liaisons while my husband was at work. I talked to him for over an hour. The next morning, I called Joe and said, "It was nice to hear from you last night." He told me it wasn't him! That obscene caller really lucked out.

Yes, my life was unmanageable. I would stay up until three or four in the morning on the phone. I wasn't getting enough sleep and my work performance was showing it. I wasn't present for my husband; I was so involved with the telephone.

My addiction and coaddiction are so intertwined, I don't know which is my basic disease. When my codependency is totally out of control, when I'm feeling frightened or insecure, that's when my addiction kicks in, to cover the pain of the coaddiction. Then, when my husband confronts me about my acting out, my coaddict comes back.

A useful way to look at the difference between sex addicts and coaddicts is to examine the goal of their behavior. The goal of the coaddict is to influence another person—to win them over, manipulate them, or keep them in the relationship. The goal of the addict is to get the good feeling of the connection—the thrill of the chase and conquest, the sense of power over the other person, or the sexual high. The same behavior can be in service of different goals. If "the sex was always to keep the guy," as one woman said, this would be coaddictive behavior, no matter how many sexual partners were involved or the nature of the sexual activity.

Women sex addicts and coaddicts have a great deal in common. Both were probably victimized in childhood in some manner and developed a set of shame-based core beliefs that included, *I am not a worthwhile person, No one would love me if they really knew me,* and *I cannot rely on other people.* In adulthood, these women take a path that leads either to sexual addiction or coaddiction. Charlotte Kasl, in her book, *Women, Sex, and Addiction,* concludes, "The essential difference between the two paths is that the potential addict denies her neediness and seeks power, while the potential codependent [coaddict] denies her anger and searches for security."[2]

Sex addicts acknowledge their anger and seek power over men; coaddicts recognize their fearfulness and seek the security of a relationship. Some women behave like addicts some of the time and like coaddicts at others. Sex addicts married to sex addicts may flip from the addict to the coaddict role, depending on what is going on in the relationship.

How Addicts See Their Coaddiction
Underlying all addiction and coaddiction is codependency—the need to get validation from others because we do not believe we are

worthwhile people. Because codependency plays itself out in relationships, and women are generally more concerned about relationships than men, women tend to be more aware of their codependency. Men who are married to women sex addicts, and are sexually addicted themselves, are less likely to be aware of their coaddiction and therefore are less likely to attend S-Anon or Codependents of Sex Addicts (COSA). Thirty-six percent of our survey respondents said they had a sexually addicted parent; many said that they had been adversely affected as children by sexual addiction in their family and could benefit from working on family-of-origin issues, also.

A male sex addict who attended S-Anon regularly told us:

Probably 98 percent of the people in SA could use S-Anon. I think that behind all the sexual acting out is codependency. It took me a while to realize this. First, I thought it came from fear; then, I thought it came from pride. It wasn't until I got to S-Anon that I really saw how the codependency fit in.

The majority of women sex addicts we surveyed or interviewed were aware that their behavior was influenced by their coaddiction or codependency, but only a minority of the sexually addicted husbands had this understanding. Among the male sex addicts in our survey whose wives were not sexually addicted, only 12 percent identified themselves as coaddicts.

Recovering in a Relationship
Versus Recovering as a Single Person

As recovering people, all of us have the same basic tasks—to stop the behaviors that had made our life unmanageable, to develop healthier ways of dealing with life's problems, to learn how to nurture ourselves and believe in our worth, and to acquire skills in relating to other people. Because sexual addiction so often affects other people, recovery poses different challenges when it takes place within an ongoing relationship than when an addict is single. We asked women sex addicts for their views. They identified the following issues that an addict in a relationship has to deal with that a single recovering person does not:

- having to make ongoing decisions about sexual activities.
- having to deal with addiction and coaddiction simultaneously.
- having to deal with the added shame of having betrayed the partner.
- finding it easier to be dishonest about sexual activities.
- having a husband who believes it is only his wife's problem.
- having a husband who minimizes the problem.

**Having to Make Ongoing
Decisions About Sexual Activities**
"If your spouse had been a part of your sexual acting out, you have a constant trigger in front of your eyes," said a therapist who is an old-timer in sexual addiction recovery. Even if the sexual addiction did not involve the spouse, addicts in recovery need to make decisions about their sexual relationship. They need to ask themselves, *Do I want to be sexual now? Which sexual activities are comfortable for me and which are likely to trigger my addiction?* And if childhood sexual abuse occurred, they need to ask themselves, *Can I deal with my newly discovered abuse experience without distancing myself sexually from my spouse, or do I need to request some time out sexually?* At times, it may seem easier to be single and abstinent. After two years in sexual recovery, a married woman told us:

> I used to say in meetings that the single people were so lucky because they could just stop all sex. When you're married, you have to face whether or not you're going to work on having a healthy sexual relationship, and that was a painful thing for me, because when I decided I was going to get sexually sober, a lot of abuse memories came up during sex.

> We went through a period of abstinence; I could have gone on with that for a longer time. It was much easier for me not to deal with sex than to have sex, stay present, and be willing to feel the feelings that came up for me.

But now that I feel better about our sexual relationship, I feel really connected with my husband. I guess I'd have to say it's not easier for single people. The thought of even being single and having to know when it would be right to be sexual with a man—when a relationship would be safe enough and committed enough to be sexual—that really scares me.

Having to Deal with Addiction And Coaddiction Simultaneously

Sex addicts who are not in a marriage can focus totally on their individual recovery; married sex addicts have to also focus on their marriage. Married sex addicts cannot usually postpone working on their marriage because the relationship is often significantly damaged and requires immediate repair efforts. Sorting out their priorities becomes a difficult matter for recovering sex addicts who are married. Married women who begin recovery from sexual addiction can be sidetracked by the desire to please their husbands. One woman wrote:

In the beginning, I think recovery is harder for married women. The single women at meetings would say, "Well, at least you can have sex." And I'd be thinking, You don't know how hard it is to try to have sex and not know how to do it appropriately. And I would wish I didn't have a spouse who felt he had to have sex. Because I was married and wanted to keep the marriage together, I felt obligated to have sex, so for me it would have been easier to be a single person. My coaddict side is why I felt I had to have sex with him. But now that I'm in recovery and have a partner, I think it's probably easier because I don't have to go out and try dating.

Some couples may need to distance themselves from each other in order to work on their individual recovery. One woman wrote:

It's been very hard to stay in the marriage during our individual recovery. For about six months, we slept in separate bedrooms and lived totally separate lives. We had to find out who we were, not attached to the other person. Sometimes, I still need some time out—when I get so involved in making this relationship work that I forget who I am. It's so easy and so subtle to get all enmeshed in his life again.

Having to Deal with the Added Shame
Of Having Betrayed the Partner

Single women may feel shame about what they have done sexually, about inappropriate conversations, or about time spent fantasizing or obsessing. Married women who have had affairs feel additional shame. One woman wrote:

> *I think society feels like it's okay if you're single and sleeping around a lot. It's even more okay now for women than it used to be. But I feel there's more shame in sleeping around if you're married than if you're single. You've betrayed the commitment to the other person, you've betrayed the trust.*

Finding it Easier to Be
Dishonest About Sexual Activities

A sex addict's wife who eventually recognized her own sexual addiction was able to ignore it for a long time by telling herself she was watching pornography and engaging in various sexual activities only to please her husband. This problem was echoed by an older woman who recognized her sexual addiction only when in a treatment program for her coaddiction. She wrote:

> *We need to take responsibility for our own sexuality. Women tend to say, "It was them that wanted it, the men." It's a lot harder for women to get honest about our sexual behavior. Men usually initiate, so we can always blame it on them.*

Having a Husband Who Believes
It Is Only His Wife's Problem

When a man has affairs, his wife's first reaction often is, "Where did *I* fail?" And society often concurs that if a man cheats on his wife, it must be his wife's fault. If a woman cheats on her husband, the usual assumption is again that it was her fault. This double standard works against the rebuilding of marriages in which the woman is the sex addict. The result is that men whose wives have affairs are more likely to divorce them than are women whose husbands are unfaithful. A recovering alcoholic commented:

> *There's no question in my mind that it's a double standard. I could easily have divorced my wife, and society, my parents, everyone else, would have said, "She deserved it." I would have been completely exonerated, and no one would have looked at the obvious and asked, "What involvement did* you *have in it?" Even though I didn't advocate it, my behavior was involved in it.*

This husband would have gotten a lot of support for leaving his wife, because his friends and parents condemned her behavior. If he had not had the experience of his chemical dependency treatment and the years of AA, which made it easier for him to accept his wife's behavior as an addictive disorder, he might have been persuaded to leave her rather than work things out. Even if they decide against a divorce, some men find it easier to believe that the problem is exclusively their wife's.

The wife of a recovering alcoholic went to SLAA meetings to work on her "sexual anorexia." She related:

> *The first time I asked my husband to do anything related to sexual recovery was to go to the couples' meeting, and he flatly said no. Later, I suggested we go to a sex therapist. We wound up arguing about it, and he finally agreed reluctantly, but I could tell he was uncomfortable with it, so we didn't go. We don't talk much about sex, and my husband hasn't said how he feels about my going to the SLAA meetings.*
>
> *I'm a little sad and disappointed that my husband doesn't want to be involved, but I'm not controlled by that. I would like him to be involved, but I can't take responsibility for him. All I can do is work on myself.*

Having partners who believe the addiction is not their problem is not unique to women. Al-Anon has a smaller membership than AA, as do the programs dealing with sexual coaddiction. Thousands of men, too, are involved in recovery programs while their wives stand on the sidelines waiting for them to be fixed.

Having a Husband Who Minimizes the Problem

A woman with several years of recovery from sexual addiction pointed out:

> *Married women have some extra burdens. What they often talk about is how their husbands don't want them to go to meetings. Their husbands don't want to believe their wife has a problem. It's too threatening to them. Codependency is the biggest problem the women have. They're still into pleasing their husband.*

> *My husband wants to deny my whole addiction. He'd rather that we just forget it and go on with our lives. He used to go to S-Anon meetings, and he was often the only guy in the room. It was very hard for him. Somehow, because I'm an addict, it affects the way he views himself, how masculine he is. I'd like to feel he was more supportive of our couple recovery. Instead he says, "Well, you needed to be cured, and now you're cured, so can we get on with our lives?"*

Mixed Versus Women-Only Meetings

As the sexual addiction recovery movement grows, a woman can often choose between mixed and women-only meetings for sex addicts. The women we interviewed had differing opinions on the value of these two types of meetings. Some women were more comfortable in a women-only group. A thirty-two-year-old homemaker had had multiple sexual partners until she married; then she lost interest in sex. She wrote:

> *I feel more comfortable in women's meetings. I find that I feel less shame in talking about my particular situation. When I go to the mixed SAA meetings, I feel like I'm not a good enough sex addict, because I've been acting in instead of acting out. When I go to the SLAA women's meetings, I feel like it's okay that I act in.*

A twenty-eight-year-old woman whose husband is also a recovering sex addict related:

For me, the women's meeting is a very safe place. It's very shaming for me to go to mixed meetings. I went to a mixed meeting because about six months ago my counselor suggested I go to see how I felt about it. She asked me to write down my feelings about the men in the room, what I was uncomfortable with. One night I shared at the meeting and said, "I'm really scared here, I'm really uncomfortable." Once I got honest, I felt more comfortable.

I don't get sexually aroused by what the men say at the meeting, but listening to them gives me extreme power. My coaddict totally gets off on believing I know how to fix them, especially when they're talking about their relationships with their wives.

I'm finding it's not healthy for me at this time to go to the mixed meetings.

Risks of Mixed Meetings

When the wife of a sex addict discovers she is also sexually addicted, going to mixed meetings can present some problems. A woman who is both a sex addict and coaddict may respond as one or the other depending on the situation. In a meeting for addicts, she may respond as a coaddict, wanting to rescue and fix the crowd of needy addicts. Attending meetings with men can also be risky for a woman whose sexual sobriety is very shaky.

When she first began attending SA meetings, a married thirty-eight-year-old woman was the only woman there. This was no problem for her, however, because she said she had always been more comfortable with men than with women. She became very close friends with a man she met there, and they began seeing more and more of each other outside the meeting.

Finding a potential sex partner at a meeting is a risk and it is a wonder that it does not happen more often. For addicts, the easy solution would appear to be to attend only meetings where they are not attracted to anyone. But since no one can avoid encountering attractive people in their everyday life, the meetings can teach them how to relate to such people nonsexually. A woman talked about her experience:

> *The good thing for me about having mixed groups is that it's the first time in my life I've ever related to men on a nonsexual level, even though we're talking about sex. It was very good for me to hear their side of it. I am learning to be intimate with men through the program. They, in turn, are learning to be intimate with me in nonsexual ways.*
>
> *I'm working on my relationships with women. When a woman would come to our meeting, I felt almost jealous. I had gotten to be the center of attention because I was the only woman, and I liked it. Once, several women came to our meeting together, and they were all dressed up. I'm at the point in my sobriety where I can't wear makeup and I can't really primp, because that's tied into my addiction. So there I was, plain-Jane, and these women came in wearing a lot of makeup and tight clothes, and my coaddict really kicked in.*
>
> *I've gotten past that. What I do now, even though it's uncomfortable for me, is the minute a woman comes into the meeting, I talk with her and give her my telephone number and try to make her feel more welcome.*

Being the Only One

Although some people are uncomfortable being the only man or woman at a Twelve Step meeting, others thrive on the uniqueness they feel, and on the real or imagined extra attention. A man who attended S-Anon meetings and was often the only man there sheepishly admitted, "When another man comes in, I automatically go up to him, but I also feel like my domain is being invaded. It's not so much the maleness as the feeling that I'm unique at the meeting."

Some women attended both types of meetings and decided they were better off in the mixed meetings. One woman wrote:

> *I went to a women-only SLAA meeting and felt really irritated because they would soften their addiction by saying, "I'm a relation-*

*ship addict." I would get triggered at those meetings. I would lis-
ten to somebody talk about her latest struggle of trying to stay
away from this person and how she had to resist a seductive scene,
and I'd find myself thinking about buying some shrimp and putting it on cracked ice and personally delivering it to some man's
door . . . and I would leave the meeting to do it. Clearly, it was
not the place for me to be.*

*After two months there, I went to SA and SAA instead. Even
though there were men there, I found the men to be more on target
as far as the parallels between my acting out and theirs.*

*Initially, I found it hard to share anything more than my name
and that I was glad to be there. There are some things that I still
won't do at meetings. For example, I've been asked to be a greeter
and to take men to another room and share part of my story. I'm
not comfortable with that unless there's another man addict to go
with me and share a little bit of his story as well. After the meeting, a lot of times people hug each other. I've had to say to a guy,
"I'm glad to see you, but I don't want you to hug me. I can't hug
you." That was real progress for me. Before, anybody that wanted
to hug me, I was ready to be hugged!*

Another woman talked about the importance of noticing similari-
ties rather than focusing on differences. She wrote:

*At the first mixed meeting I went to, there was a roomful of men.
I couldn't relate to them because I thought, I don't do that. But
the more meetings I went to, the more at home I felt.*

*I would encourage women to go to mixed meetings and talk to
different people afterward. A lot of times, things don't come out
in the meeting. For me, it was easy to say to myself,* Oh, gosh,
that guy's a child molester. I don't have anything remotely
in common with him; *or,* That person is gay and cruises gay
bars. How can I be like that? *It's very easy for women to think,*
I'm not an addict because I'm not like that, *instead of thinking,* He is feeling pain because of what he did and I'm feel-

ing pain because of what I did; maybe we're more alike than different.

I would also encourage women to look for other women in the mixed meetings. It's my own bias that women who attend mixed meetings are probably a little more open than women who attend women-only meetings.

An old-timer in SA learned that, for her, women's meetings had certain advantages and mixed meetings others. She wrote:

What I liked in the meetings with men was recognizing that they were people with the same feelings I had. I realized I could talk with a man intimately and not have any sexual fantasy, feeling, or thought, and not do any flirting.

For a long time, my group had no women. So, when I went to the national conferences, I set up women's meetings so I could have a chance to get close to women. I needed the contact with women on occasion.

How Did Husbands React to the Disclosure
Of Their Wife's Sexual Addiction?

The two most important factors that determined a man's reaction to the disclosure of his wife's sexual addiction was whether or not he himself was a recovering sex addict and whether or not his partner had been sexual with other people.

When the Husband Is Not a Sex Addict

Husbands who were not sex addicts naturally reacted with a great deal of anger to the disclosure of their wife's affairs. Several considered having affairs themselves, including a man with no identified addictions. He wrote:

After she told me about her affairs, I felt angry at being betrayed, but most of my anger was from feeling ripped off and left out. I had given up open sexual relationships in order to be married to her, and then she went out and had affairs. There was a part of me that would have liked to do that myself. Several months later, I decided maybe I do need to go out and get it out of my system—be sexual with other women.

My wife wouldn't tolerate my living with her and doing that, so we separated for about two weeks. I spent time thinking about it, planning it, and thinking about my past relationships. What I found out was that the women I had been sexual with were usually my friends, people I cared about. I found I couldn't do it. So, I wasn't sexual with anybody else during that time, and still haven't been.

Another man with no apparent addictions had a similar reaction. He wrote:

I found out from a neighbor that a man had been visiting my wife at home. When he told me, I felt physically sick. I confronted her and she confessed a little. She told me the rest later on in counseling. I was really mad and really hurt. When she told me she's an addict, I thought, She's going for treatment. I'll see how it goes. *Divorce is no picnic, so I wanted to give her a chance.*

I didn't question my masculinity—I didn't think the problem was me. I thought it was her. One night when I came home, one of her old boyfriends was in the neighborhood. He had stopped by and was pulling out of the driveway. I pulled up next to him and stared at him, and he backed out real quick and took off.

I wanted to get him, not so much for revenge, but to send him back with a message for any others who might have ideas. After all, men talk; they compare notes. She went to bed with one man on the job and I'm sure he talked and the others saw it as an opportunity.

If she doesn't stay monogamous, it'll be my *turn to have sex with other people. When we were separated, I had opportunities, but I turned them down. I behaved myself. I figured I might find somebody nice who would really try to latch on. Then I'd have a mess. I've dated two people at once; I can't take the stress.*

Both husbands felt angry and both considered having sex with other women, but decided against it. It is interesting that the two husbands perceived sex as part of a relationship with another person and were not ready for sex as merely revenge or recreation.

One way in which mens' reactions differed from those of most women who learned about their husband's infidelities was that the men were generally more able to express their anger and wanted to lash out. One man described his reaction to the disclosure:

> *One night she told me she wanted to talk with me. She told me she had been molested by her brother when she was a kid and that that was the start of her preoccupation with sex. She proceeded to tell me about several affairs, including one I had not even suspected—with a guy who had just built a bookcase for us.*
>
> *I immediately went into deep anger and sadness and crying and rage at the same time. I pulled the bookcase off the wall and threw it off the balcony. Then I got my ax and chopped it into small pieces. The next day, I built a fire and burned the pieces. Looking back, I realize that helped me get rid of a lot of anger.*
>
> *By the end of a couple of months, I had worked out all my anger with my wife and all the other people except the last guy she was in an affair with. I wrote a letter to him because I was afraid to run into him; I was afraid I might do something I would regret if I saw him. I ran it by my counselor and my S-Anon group, made some changes in it, and mailed it. I told him I had felt violated, angry, and hurt, and I said I didn't want to be around him at an upcoming convention.*
>
> *Because of this whole thing, I feel a part of my sexuality has been taken away. I'm uncomfortable anytime anyone talks about sex.*

Another man wrote:

> *When she told me about her affairs during family week, I went into a jealous rage. One night in a parking lot, I tried to run down a man she'd been with. I'd go visit some of the bars she used to hang out in and they'd say, "You sure have a nice wife. She acts like a real lady." And I knew full well they were lying.*

At first, I felt shame and embarrassment that my wife was a sex addict. I came to the gradual realization that it was a disease and that she was in recovery from a disease.

I never blamed it on my own sexual performance. However, I've had some problems with impotence. My doctors say there's nothing physically wrong with me, so I wonder whether there's some repressed hostility that hasn't been dealt with.

Some husbands were more in touch with their pain than their anger. In this sense, their reaction was more like a woman's reaction. A salesperson who had separated from his wife and small children wrote:

When she told me about the last affair, she confessed without any sense of repentance, and in fact asked me to leave. I had been blind to what was going on right under my nose. I didn't suspect a thing, but that was partly because I was so out of touch with my own feelings; I don't pick things up very well. I was extremely jealous. It took me about one day to figure out who it was. My self-esteem was, of course, crushed, and I was in tremendous gut-wrenching pain. I had never understood before what emotional pain was like because I had so effectively isolated myself from that kind of hurt.

I felt I needed to confront the man. He was a member of our church, and I felt that if your brother sins, you should confront him. I told him how I felt about it and that I'd worked out a lot of anger. I admonished him to go confess it to his wife.

I still want to work on restoring my relationship with my wife, and I've been trying to let her know this, but so far she has not been interested.

It may be difficult for some men to accept their partner's sexual addiction, especially if they themselves are not recovering sex addicts. It may be more comfortable for them to regard their spouse as a relationship addict. A man whose wife had affairs told us:

I accept the therapist's explanation that she had a compulsion for relationships more than she had for sex. The sex was not the driving force. I think that if my wife had been really interested in sex, she'd have had more than five partners in seven years.

Other men may find it easier to believe that their wife has a character flaw rather than an addiction. A man whose wife told him she was a sex addict initially had difficulty accepting it. He wrote:

I wasn't totally convinced that it was a disease. I felt more like it was a character defect or a moral issue because I had had one affair right after we got married, with someone out of town. It was at the same time that I first suspected my wife was having an affair. I did some reading and I now do understand that it is a disease — that you're in recovery from it and you continue to get better, but you are never really cured.

When the Husband Is Also a Sex Addict

Men who were themselves recovering sex addicts usually had an easier time with their wife's disclosure than did men who were not. This was particularly true if the wife's behaviors did not include affairs.

A wife of a recovering sex addict was involved in making inappropriate telephone calls and in fantasizing about other men. After some time in S-Anon, she recognized her own sexual addiction. Her husband recalled:

When she first told me, I didn't know what to think about her being a sex addict. Now, I realize she is and I'm behind her recovery 100 percent. At first, I thought it might be because I wasn't a good enough lover. I fell immediately into my coaddict mode. I started asking a lot of questions about it — the same questions she asked me when I came home from my first meeting. I felt the roles changing very fast when she told me she was a sex addict.

Another wife of an old-timer told her husband she had a problem with emotional affairs and fantasizing about other people. He said:

My first reaction was not to believe she had any kind of addiction. She certainly didn't have it as bad as I did. But after maybe a half hour, I realized that there's only one person who can say if they're a sex addict or not, and she says she is. I realized I have to do for my wife what I would do for anybody. I felt that she's very lucky because she's got someone right here who has a lot of recovery and can help her. I realized that if I expect her to understand and accept my addiction, then I need to understand and accept hers.

In some ways, it's made me feel less guilty about my past behaviors because she's done some of those things too.

The wife of a sex addict felt humbled when she told her husband that she, too, was a sex addict, although she had not had any affairs during the marriage. She wrote:

Telling my husband was very humbling for me. For two years, I had been shaking my finger at him, shaming him. A lot of that wasn't even directed at my husband. I was looking into a mirror, and he was an easy scapegoat for me. I see that now, but at the time it sure sounded good to blame him! His first reaction was, "I don't think so." He didn't believe me. I was very angry. It had taken me a long time to get to that point and he wouldn't believe me.

Even when the husband himself is a recovering sex addict, it may take time for his wife to convince him of her addiction.

Did Men Tell Friends About Their Partners' Sexual Addiction?

Sharing with understanding friends can be healing. It may be difficult, however, for men to talk comfortably about something they feel to be shameful. Connecting at Twelve Step meetings with others who truly understand can break through their isolation. Typically, women find it easy to confide in other women, but men often find it hard to talk with other men about their feelings. And if they do talk about their feelings, they may get negative reactions instead of support. One man wrote:

I felt I owed an explanation to two of my closest friends who were supportive of me through the last two years. I gave them one, after they agreed to respect the confidentiality. Both condemned my wife's behavior. It required a great deal of tact and diplomacy on my part to show them the error of their ways.

The husband of a woman who had several affairs feared being judged. He wrote:

I haven't told my friends. It would be too embarrassing. It's not something that needs to get out. It would look bad for me. I don't think they would understand it.

It's more acceptable in society for men to talk about who they slept with. Many men don't condemn other men who talk about their sexual exploits; instead, they egg them on! They say, "How was she?" and compare notes.

Some men did confide in their male friends. Two nonaddicted husbands of sexually addicted women related their stories. One said:

I didn't suspect a thing about my wife's affairs, but for some reason I had been depressed for quite a while. When my wife confessed to me, I was so happy to figure out that there was something else going on. I instantly linked it to my depression and told all my friends, all of my co-workers, everyone I had any trust in.

The other said:

When I told my wife that I had told a friend, she got very upset and told me I had no right to do that. I told her that I was taking care of me. I also told someone else and my wife once again got very upset and said that I was violating her anonymity. I told her if I need to do that for my own recovery, I'll do it.

How can coaddicts tell their own stories without telling what their spouse did? Coaddicts cannot communicate their pain and anguish over their spouse's affairs without revealing some of what was actually going on. Too many coaddicts have spent years protecting and covering up someone else's behavior while blaming themselves and ignoring their own needs. Coaddicts' recovery mandates that they have the option of telling trusted friends. As addicts progress in their own recovery and begin to feel less shame, they often become more understanding of coaddicts' need to talk with others.

Some couples handled this sensitive area by agreeing that particular people — for example, parents or employers — will not be told.

What Men Said About Twelve Step Programs for Coaddicts

One survey respondent told us that attending S-Anon as a man is frustrating because men often feel out of place there, even when they know they need to be there for their own recovery. A man who attends a recovery program for sexual coaddicts is often the only man in the group. This can be uncomfortable, particularly if he is also a recovering sex addict.

After his wife recognized her own sex addiction, a forty-five-year-old man with several years of recovery from sexual addiction began attending S-Anon meetings. Initially, he was fearful of not being accepted by the group who knew his wife well. He wrote:

In some of these groups, the male sex is the enemy. Add to this the fact that they all know I'm a sexaholic, so I'm a little more of the enemy. Plus my wife had been in the program for two years when I started. But as it turned out, of maybe twenty women at the meeting, only one or two of them didn't seem to understand why I was there. The others have been really understanding. I've always felt a little bit like I was under the microscope. I have to be careful of what I say — I'm representing all men — but I think I've been as helpful to that program as they've been to me.

The major difficulty is that I have not been able to get a sponsor. Anybody who has any time in S-Anon has not felt comfortable being my sponsor. I take it that it's because I'm male. I wouldn't have a problem having a woman sponsor in S-Anon, although I would never consider it in SA.

I have to be careful about my fantasies in S-Anon. Some of those women should be in SA, but they don't know it. They'll wear the provocative clothing or talk about things and I'll catch the vibes. But at this point in my recovery, all it means is I have to do one more surrender. There are times when I have to do a lot of surrendering at the meetings. But truthfully, I thank my Higher Power for those times. He's teaching me a lesson.

Because of my time in S-Anon, I'm much more aware of my codependent issues. I've learned to set some boundaries as to what I won't accept about my wife's behavior. I think that every sex addict should have to attend three or four S-Anon meetings to see the havoc they wreak. I think it would help them in recovery.

Another husband, who was not an addict and had no prior Twelve Step experience, went to S-Anon when he began to suspect his wife of having another affair while she was attending SA. He wrote:

When my wife first joined SA, I went to one S-Anon meeting, but was uncomfortable and never went back. I felt it was my wife's problem. But after she began staying out late again and giving me excuses that I didn't believe, I became very despondent and my self-esteem got lower and lower. She said I didn't trust her and just wanted to control her. I felt like I was falling apart.

Finally, I went to another S-Anon meeting and found five women there. They made me realize I was not crazy, that I had the right to feel that my wife's behavior was unacceptable, and that I needed to work on myself. Had I not been at this low point, I would not have had the courage to go back to the S-Anon meetings. I still go. We may have some differences, but I've come to feel really close to my sisters in the program, and I really get a lot of support.

A thirty-three-year-old man, whose wife left him after she had a series of affairs, attended S-Anon meetings in which he was the only man for several months. He wrote:

I used to do almost anything to try to make peace, including making long lists of things that annoyed my wife and trying to remember to avoid all those things. Maybe then, *I thought,* she wouldn't be angry all the time. *I never did succeed.*

In S-Anon, I learned first that there wasn't anything I could do that was going to change her. Then, I learned that that doesn't absolve me from working on my own issues. The Twelve Steps have really helped me, for instance, with this "fearless moral inventory." I realize now that my wife hungered for an emotional connection that wasn't there. I was never vulnerable with her. And when there was conflict, I withdrew.

Some men who would like to attend S-Anon or COSA hesitate to go, fearing they will not be accepted. Of the men we interviewed, even the ones who were sex addicts told us they found acceptance at COSA and S-Anon meetings. We believe men can benefit from Twelve Step fellowships for sexual coaddicts. The gender issue disappears as people begin to heal together.

When Both Partners Attend
The Same Twelve Step Meeting

Because there may be no other meetings in some towns, two sex addicts married to each other may find themselves attending the same Twelve Step meetings. Most of the people we interviewed said they did better at separate meetings. "I've had a hard time going to meetings where I see my husband's friends. It's very shaming for me," wrote a twenty-eight-year-old woman. Her partner had already established friendships with other people in SA. The same woman felt invaded when her husband began attending S-Anon. She wrote:

For a long time, S-Anon was my meeting. I had gone there for two years. These were my friends. For the first time in my life, I had an identity. And I didn't want my husband coming into that meeting.

When his wife announced she was also a sex addict, one man did not want her to attend his meeting. He wrote:

SA had been my place. I was safe there. I could go talk about things. I had spent a lot of time building up a good support system, and I thought she was now going to be honing in on that. It upset me quite a bit. I didn't think she really had it that bad, and I didn't want her going to my meetings.

When a couple attends the same meeting, frequently one or both feel less free to talk. One couple reported:

HUSBAND: *When she is at my meeting, it inhibits me a little. For example, there are times when I want to make a comment or say, "Yes, I know what you mean," but I might not say anything now.*

WIFE: *I don't feel comfortable sharing in the same meeting as my husband. It's like I have to look for his approval about what I'm saying. My coaddiction is still a lot harder to deal with than my addiction. I think that coaddiction is every addict's underlying problem.*

This couple agreed to alternate attendance at SA and S-Anon meetings. This way, each was able to attend both meetings, but not at the same time.

Many people have felt inhibited when attending the same SA or S-Anon meeting as their partner. They say they found themselves censoring their words. For example, an addict who was told at home by his or her partner not to mention every struggle will be less likely to share in his or her partner's presence. Most sex addicts are codependents as well, so they want to look good to their partner. A second important point is the likely presence of coaddictive issues in a relationship between two sex addicts, including wanting to control, having difficulty detaching, and ignoring their own needs in an effort to please. Couples who fail to address these issues, believing that all they need to do is maintain sexual sobriety, are likely to have more difficulty in their relationship. Some partners have actually sponsored each other. A woman who was a therapist served as her husband's SA sponsor for a time. He wrote:

> When I bottomed out and had to go to someone for help, the one person I knew who had recovery was my wife. There were times I used her as a sponsor because there wasn't a man to talk to who had longer recovery than me. There was one big problem with using her as a sponsor—when the obsession would hit, my shame would keep me from going to her and I would eventually act out.
>
> I think it's really important that I know my wife's story and that she know mine. If you get to that point, you can go to the same meeting if you have to. And when you are honest, it's not quite so shaming to say, "I'm having a problem today." But you still need another sponsor. Don't sponsor each other.

Having a husband or a wife as a sponsor does not work. If there is no one else locally with sufficient time in recovery, addicts are better off obtaining a long-distance sponsor with whom they can communicate by telephone or letter.

How Do Couples Avoid Triggering Each Other's Addiction?

Sharing struggles with their spouse is particularly tricky for addicts when their spouse is also a sex addict. Material shared by one spouse can easily become a trigger for the other's addiction or coaddiction. When a recovering sex addict, whose bottom-line addiction was masochism, learned from her fiancé that his preferred sexual activity had been sadistic fantasies, she was triggered. She had to ask him not to share with her any further details. Another woman told us:

> I don't share details with my husband. I might say to him, "I'm having a hard time here at the mall today. I can't keep my eyes to

> *myself. I need to go home." But I don't go into detail about who*
> *the person is and what I'm having troubles with. With both of us*
> *being addicts, the details are real triggers. And then that brings*
> *out the coaddict in the other person. I've asked my husband not*
> *to share his stuff with me. It makes me want to go to bed with him*
> *because I'm scared that he's interested in somebody else.*

Particular sexual activities can also be a trigger. Addicts need to be honest with their partner about potential triggers. It may be necessary to stop certain activities during lovemaking. One man described how he handled this problem:

> *In recovery, I had no idea what I could do sexually with my spouse*
> *and no idea how to find out. I asked my sponsor and he told me,*
> *if I can't talk about it with my spouse before I do it, I probably don't*
> *need to do it. And if I can't pray about it and ask God if it's okay,*
> *then I probably don't need to do it. So if I'm unsure about a be-*
> *havior, I'll talk with my wife about it in advance and find out if*
> *she's okay with it.*

Final Comment

Women sex addicts are beginning to face their addiction and break through their shame, loneliness, and isolation. Many do so only after first recognizing their coaddiction and codependency.

It is often tempting, especially in early recovery, for women to label themselves as addicts as soon as they identify some compulsive behavior. Perhaps to feel acceptance in a Twelve Step program or to understand their emotional pain, they may be all too ready to find a simple answer to a more complicated problem. They may find themselves attending four or five different Twelve Step meetings, working on a host of issues rather than focusing on their primary addiction.

Women who recognize that some prior sexual behaviors were inappropriate need to ask themselves about the goal of the behaviors before deciding if they are sexually addicted. Chemically dependent women who were sexually inappropriate while drinking or using drugs need to look at their sexual behavior when sober. This will help determine whether the sexual acting out is part of an addictive pattern or was secondary to chemical use.

If you decide you are indeed sexually addicted, know that you are not alone and that recovery is possible.

CHAPTER TWELVE

Moving Forward

We live in the Arizona desert, but there is a neighborhood just to the east of ours that is quite uncharacteristic of the desert. Its narrow lanes are shaded by towering trees and foliage usually seen in New England. Nearby is a man-made lake where ducks take refuge from the Arizona heat. On the summer days when the early morning temperatures dip below ninety degrees, we begin our day by walking the path around the lake. We sometimes talk about living there instead of in our Santa Fe-style townhouse with its desert landscape. Sometimes, the grass looks greener on the other side of the fence. When we come back to reality, we think about what it takes to maintain this oasis in the desert—the extravagant use of water to keep the lawns green and the high fees that homeowners must pay. We realize that what most attracts us to the area may also be the area's biggest drawback. And so it is with relationships.

The Toughest Problems

In previous chapters, we focused on several problems that recovering couples typically face. To learn which problems were most significant at the time they completed the survey, we asked respondents to write a list of their problems and rank them.

Twenty-three percent of men ranked rebuilding trust as their number one concern; intimacy was listed by 20 percent. Women cited the same issues—19 percent ranked intimacy first; 18 percent placed rebuilding trust first. Spirituality was the chief concern for 14 percent of the men, while 8 percent cited setting limits, sexuality, forgiveness, or conflict resolution as their number one concern. The results for women were similar. Only 8 percent of men and 5 percent of women believed that sex was their most important problem, and fewer than one-third of respondents considered sex to be among their top three problems.

Conflict Resolution

Conflict resolution was regarded as one of the most significant problems by almost one-third of the men and by about one-fifth of the women. Based on responses to other survey questions, however, it was apparent that handling conflict was a crucial issue for most couples.

We believe how we handle day-to-day conflict is a barometer of our overall satisfaction in our relationship. Conflict is inevitable. In our own marriage, we had to negotiate solutions that gave each of us the freedom to be the kind of person that had attracted the other, and yet meet the other's needs.

By trial and error, we have adopted some tools for conflict resolution. One of the most helpful is the quiet listening technique. When one of us needs to express a concern, we ask the other to say nothing until we are finished talking. This may take five minutes or twenty minutes, but we know we will be heard without the other interrupting with defensive statements. When the first speaker is finished, it is the listener's turn to reply without interruption, taking as much time as needed. The process is then repeated if necessary. By the end of several exchanges, emotions have usually cooled and calm discourse is possible.

We have also learned that, for us, waiting several hours to talk about an event works better than immediately taking it apart. Jennifer usually needs time to sort things out. Burt, who is more emotional, is often too upset initially to be able to hear Jennifer's point of view.

Rules for Fair Fighting

All of us have had the experience of having the same fight over and over again. The details may change, but we recognize we are basically arguing about the same problem. At a weekend for recovering couples, we were invited to examine our own fighting patterns. Jennifer would analyze Burt's behavior, reminding him of past mistakes and quoting experts to back up her interpretation. Burt would start fights in the morning just before Jennifer had to leave for work, thus leaving the issue hanging. He would begin a fight about matters over which we had no control, such as the behavior of our former spouses. When he became discouraged and angry, he would announce that he felt like leaving the marriage. No wonder our fights were often unproductive!

In consultation with other recovering couples, we drafted some new rules for fair fighting. They are:

1. Do announce that we want to have a fight.
2. Do be specific—stick to the issue at hand.
3. Do use "I" statements.
4. Don't use "always" and "never."
5. Don't quote expert sources.
6. Don't analyze or label.
7. Don't start a fight in the morning before work.
8. Don't fight about issues over which we have no control.
9. Do decide whether you can live with the decision or not.
10. Don't make statements about wanting to flee or get divorced.
11. Don't fight over chronic issues, unless agreed to by both parties or unless there are new facts.
12. Do finish the fight—resolve the issue, table it, or agree to disagree.

These rules keep us from going around in circles, even though in the heat of the moment we sometimes forget to stick to them.

Many recovering addicts and coaddicts are in the helping professions and have a great deal of knowledge about psychology and addiction. It is natural for us to want to use that knowledge to understand our partner's behavior, then explain to them what we have discovered. Most of the time, it is better to let our partner discover these things for him- or herself. It's exasperating to get instant analysis in the midst of an argument.

Recognizing Root Feelings

Often, the arguments with the greatest emotional content are those that have to do with unresolved childhood issues. A friend told us: "When I get very angry over some minor thing, it usually means it's about something deep inside me. Then, I have to look at my own old stuff." If we can recognize the basis for these strong feelings, we can resolve them more quickly. For example, when Jennifer talked on the telephone for an hour one evening, Burt told her, with a lot of emotion, "I really get annoyed when you spend so much time on the phone." Later, Burt told her that he had been thinking about his highly charged reaction and recalled that when he was a child his mother was frequently on the phone in the evening talking to parents of children who attended the boarding school his parents ran. Burt wanted to be the center of attention. Listening to Jennifer talking on the phone reminded him of the feelings of neglect he felt as a child. Understanding this defused his anger at Jennifer.

Housekeeping is another problem tied to childhood issues in our household. Burt is more fastidious about housekeeping; Jennifer is often unreasonably resistant to his suggestions to help. Jennifer eventually recognized that she was digging in her heels because of her own childhood experience. As the oldest daughter in the home of two working parents, she had the major responsibility for cooking, cleaning, and housekeeping for a family of five. When her parents divorced, she and her sister remained with their father and Jennifer continued being Cinderella until she left home for college. As a result, she would rather do almost anything than cook or clean. Although they still need to negotiate about who does what, Burt now understands Jennifer's reluctance to participate in running the house.

How Other Couples Handle Conflict

In our survey, we asked other couples how they handle conflict. A thirty-one-year-old man wrote, "We don't talk; we draw our own outrageous conclusions, threaten divorce, and then when we're at the end of our ropes, we'll talk and laugh and make love." A fifty-five-year-old housewife described what happened in her thirty-year marriage: "We don't handle disagreements well. We both withdraw and things are strained for a few days, but we never resolve the problem."

Marriage counseling can help establish new patterns of fair fighting when arguing tends to degenerate into blaming and defending, and when one partner frequently feels attacked and reacts by shutting down.

Handling Anger
Anger prevented some couples from resolving conflict. One woman wrote, "I rage, he shuts down." Another said, "He gets angry, I run off." Many of us have difficulty handling anger in a balanced way. Some of us are frightened of making others angry or feeling anger because of childhood experiences. Respondents wrote: "My father showed only one emotion – anger. I learned to do everything to avoid his anger. Now, I do everything I can to prevent people from getting angry." . . . "I have a hard time expressing anger, so what I do is get other people angry. Then, I'm still in control and I'm not the bad guy. I don't like losing control." Some respondents said they were able to feel anger only at certain people. One wrote:

> It's very easy for me to get angry at the addicts, but it's very hard for me to get angry at the victims in my life – for example, I can't get angry at my mother, who always plays the martyr role. I'm afraid to get angry at victims. I'm afraid I'll destroy them. The woman who had an affair with my husband – she had an even worse childhood than I did, so I can't feel anger toward her, only hurt.

Some have the opposite problem – their predominant emotion is anger. One man wrote:

> Anger is my only way of feeling alive, so I do it a lot. The adrenaline rush I get lets me know I'm alive. When I'm in a rage, I release everything. Normally, I'm very cerebral. The only other way I've gotten out of my head is by riding a roller coaster – all you worry

*about is staying alive. I need to find smaller ways to feel alive—
learning to play, for example.*

Yet, some anger is appropriate. One woman wrote:

*I'm angry at him. I'm also angry at myself for having believed him,
and for feeling guilty when I was suspicious instead of trusting my
instincts. I'm angry that I have to spend my nights at meetings
getting better.*

When we are unable to handle anger appropriately, conflict resolution becomes difficult. A thirty-four-year-old woman who has
been married fourteen years wrote:

*We argue over how to handle finances, how to organize household
responsibilities, and how to discipline the children. The hardest
thing we struggle with is expressing negative feelings to each
other. We usually can't talk about our feelings, so we are very quiet
and swallow a lot of the problem without resolving it.*

It is helpful to understand how anger was handled in our family
of origin. With a therapist or in a group, we can explore who it was
in our family that got angry and how that anger was expressed. In
some families, physical violence accompanied anger—the rule was
to avoid parents' anger at all costs. In other families, it wasn't polite
to be angry and we learned to wear frozen smiles. When we understand the basis for our difficulties in handling anger, we can begin
to make changes.

Agreeing to Disagree
No matter how well couples communicate, there may be areas in
which agreement is not possible. It is just not true that every conflict
must end in agreement; sometimes the best a couple can do is
recognize that they do not see eye-to-eye about a subject and never
will.

We each bring different values and beliefs into the couple relationship. In our own marriage, we learned that we each had differ-

ent priorities for our children. Jennifer valued book learning and wanted her children to get the best education they could. Burt placed a higher value on social skills than on scholarship. Our children were half-grown by the time we married, so each set was growing up with the different priorities they had been taught. After numerous arguments over how to raise the children, we finally recognized that peace would require our agreeing to disagree.

We also asked ourselves, "Can I live with it?" and recognized that there are some areas in which we cannot agree to disagree. For example, we could not live with disagreement over the issue of fidelity. If Jennifer felt extramarital affairs were not acceptable, but Burt felt he needed to express himself sexually outside the marriage, Jennifer's boundaries would be violated and she may decide to end the relationship. Or if Burt wanted more of Jennifer's attention, but she was committed to working sixteen hours per day, we would most likely separate.

When couples reach an impasse, an outside person—a therapist or even a friend—can often help resolve the conflict. An uninvolved person can help a couple look at the problem in a new light, help them recognize that they may be reacting out of childhood pain, or help them brainstorm new solutions.

Working to Improve Conflict Resolution

Many survey respondents were working on better ways to handle conflict and improve communication. They reported trying to be honest and open, trying to talk about their feelings, and trying to compromise. A couple married almost thirty years reported:

HUSBAND: *We didn't handle conflict well in the past. We are working on this. I am trying to learn not to hide my feelings and not to take criticism as a personal failure.*

WIFE: *We are in the process of learning to communicate. We talk it out now without my husband building up walls and isolating himself, and without me feeling hurt and wondering if I caused the problem by talking about it and blaming. We used to be out of touch for days.*

Couples need to be willing to risk fighting fairly, even if it means arousing angry feelings in themselves or their partner. They need to be specific about what is bothering them and what changes they would prefer.

Parent/Child Interactions Between Adults

Most of us interact with other adults as peers, but who of us has not had the experience of feeling like a misbehaving child when our boss announces he or she wants to see us about something we have done? At times of stress, many of us have wanted to crawl into the arms of our partner and be hugged and comforted like a child. On other occasions, we may have found ourselves taking the parental role, berating an employee, a friend, or our partner. We might have given them unsolicited advice or attempted to change their behavior in some other way. Frequent parent/child interactions between adults can harm a relationship. One couple wrote:

HUSBAND: *I married a woman very much like my mother. Susan is a lawyer and so is Mom. Both of them are competent, hardworking, goal-oriented women. Both are logical and rational. There are times when I look at Susan and I think I'm seeing Mom's face—it's scary. The more competent Susan seems to be, the more incompetent I feel. When I was out seeing other women, I used to feel like a little boy sneaking out behind Mom's back. I'd view Susan like a controlling mother, and I would want to rebel. In my recovery, I've had to try to separate my reactions to Susan from my reactions to my mother.*

WIFE: *I've heard addicts say that their emotional growth stopped when they started acting out—say at age twelve or fourteen. And there have certainly been many times when Mike seemed to have the maturity of a twelve-year-old. I know there were times when I treated him like a twelve-year-old, but I don't want to be married to a child.*

Control is one of my big character defects, and I often think I know the right way to do things. In the past, I was very willing to give advice about everything. But ever since Mike told me about react-

ing to me like his mother, I've had to be very aware not to behave in ways that would make him see me in the mother role. I've really had to work on my control issues. Now that we both understand what's going on and talk about it when it happens, it's getting to be less of a problem.

It is not uncommon for addicts to feel like bad little boys or bad little girls who have misbehaved, and the more coaddicts assume the victim or martyr role, the more likely this is to happen. When a couple's interactions are more frequently parent/child rather than adult/adult, resentment, anger, and rebellion are sure to follow.

We asked our survey respondents whether their interactions have followed this pattern, and if so, how they handle it. Two-thirds of the men and almost 80 percent of the women said yes. Some said this had been a problem but was no longer. In some relationships, the wife tended to take on the parental role. One couple wrote:

WIFE: *My spouse will bring it to my attention when I'm behaving like his mother rather than his wife. He calls me "Joan," which is a humorous way of letting me know I'm behaving like one of his aunts who is very controlling and domineering.*

HUSBAND: *Building my self-esteem and separating from my mother is extremely important so that I don't feel a need to make my wife a substitute mom.*

In other relationships, the husband took on the parental role. A woman addict wrote:

Sometimes, I feel he's behaving like my father. I tell him to back off and I try to make my own choices and behave like an adult.

The codependent role is essentially that of a child needing validation from powerful others. This was recognized by one woman who wrote:

Sometimes, I feel like a needy child looking for approval and reassurance. I am trying to find that approval from within by working my program.

Communication is healthiest when it is primarily in the adult/adult mode, although child/child interactions can be fun in playful situations. When one partner feels like a child in need of nurturing, the other can become supportive; at other times, these roles can reverse. But when we recognize that our predominant interactions are not adult/adult, we can begin to make changes. Professional therapy can facilitate this process.

Balancing Individual and Couple Recovery
Our first priority must be our individual recovery. Only when we have succeeded in improving our self-esteem will we be able to be in a relationship truly by choice and not out of dependency. The health of our relationships is a reflection of our individual recovery. At times, this can cause problems. To find out how often the needs of the individual and the needs of the relationship conflict, we asked survey respondents how they felt about the amount of time their partner spent on his or her own recovery.

The majority of addicts (64 percent) and of coaddicts (60 percent) thought their partner was spending about the right amount of time on their recovery or that only their partner could judge if the time they were spending was adequate. Typical comments were: "He spends as much time as he needs. He seems very dedicated to recovery." . . . "I'm so grateful she is sober and also in S-Anon. I don't care how much time it takes. Without SA and S-Anon, we would have nothing." . . . "At first I was jealous, but now I feel good about the time he spends at meetings."

A large minority (30 percent of addicts and 24 percent of coaddicts) believed his or her partner was not spending enough time on individual recovery. Several addicts complained that their spouse was not working on their own problems. They wrote: "She has not come to full grips with being a coaddict." . . . "She has issues she's afraid of. S-Anon can help." . . . "When she's active in the program, she seems healthier. When she is not, she seems sick."

Coaddicts, too, complained that their spouse was not active enough in recovery programs. They wrote: "He still turns to me more than I would like. There are times I feel he should call his sponsor." . . . "Two meetings a week and thirty to thirty-five hours a week in front of the television set doesn't seem like a good recovery balance to me."

Although some coaddicts appeared to have legitimate concerns, others seemed to be influenced by their own insecurity. A thirty-five-year-old woman who had been in recovery for almost two years recognized that her concern about her husband's program was rooted in her own coaddiction. She wrote:

> *He attends one SA meeting and group therapy; it seems marginal to me. I want more "activity" because it is an outward sign to me of his growth, and this calms my fears. It's my control and codependence running rampant.*

Three addicts and ten coaddicts believed their spouse was spending too much time on individual recovery. In seven of these cases, the other partner believed that the spouse was not spending enough time on recovery. For example, a middle-aged couple had been in recovery for four months. She attended five meetings a week, he three. They wrote:

> HUSBAND: *She spends too much time on her recovery. She must start thinking about other things in life.*

> WIFE: *Not enough time. He doesn't call friends in the program. He would rather golf than study program literature.*

It is easy for one partner to feel left out when the other partner enthusiastically begins to attend meetings and hang out with a new group of friends. It is important to recognize, however, that rebuilding the couple relationship rests on the foundation of individual recovery. Consequently, both partners need to encourage the other's involvement in individual recovery.

Other couples who disagreed on the time spent on individual and couple recovery had been in recovery for a long time. One such couple was a therapist and his wife, in recovery over five years. She was attending four Twelve Step meetings per week, he over ten. He believed she wasn't spending enough time on her recovery. She wrote:

> *He spends too much time. The phone is always ringing, and when the kids are over he is often on the phone with other people. He can't seem to say no to new sponsees.*

Another woman, whose husband had been in recovery almost four years, had a similar complaint. She wrote: "Sometimes I resent all the time he spends trying to help other people. We have talked about this and it is in the process of getting better."

Although there is a demand for sponsorship and support from the relatively few old-timers in the Twelve Step programs for sexual addiction and coaddiction, there is also a need to balance the desire to help others with the need for time alone and with family. Learning to say no is a good exercise in boundary setting.

Monitoring Our Spouse's Recovery Program

As we grow in our individual recovery, it is natural to want to bring our spouse along with us on our journey. And as we learn about concepts such as denial, control, and acting out, we can't help but notice when these behaviors and attitudes surface in our partner. We also come to associate attending Twelve Step meetings, talking to others on the telephone, meditating, and reading program literature with the recovery process. Naturally, we notice to what extent our partner is following the program. As a result, it is difficult to avoid monitoring them, especially in early recovery.

We asked people whether they found themselves monitoring their partner's recovery. As expected, more coaddicts (51 percent) than addicts (37 percent) said they were monitoring their partner's recovery. One addict admitted:

> *I think,* Why isn't he doing a Fourth Step inventory? *I say to him: "Have you called your sponsor? You need a meeting."*

Some people who had been in recovery longer than their spouse wanted their partner to catch up. After six months in recovery, one man wrote, "I want to rush her through Twelve Step crises I've already had and worked through, but that's nearly impossible." Coaddicts admitted:

> . . . *I've looked through his things since being in recovery to see if there's anything that I think he shouldn't have. Also, every once in a while I watch his eyes to see how long he stares at other women.*
>
> . . . *When he expresses pain or anxiety, I suggest tools he's not using—writing, sponsor, phone. When he isolates himself, I nag him to identify what he's avoiding.*

Even after many years of recovery, it is sometimes difficult to let go of old reactions. Although both members of a couple were active in recovery for almost four years, the wife admitted:

> *When there are problems or stress, I still worry that he might give up and lose his sobriety. Sometimes, when he's extremely late and hasn't called, I wonder if he's going to run off with someone else or has acted out.*

Some coaddicts recognized that their attempts to control their partner were counterproductive. A psychotherapist whose husband was in recovery for over a year wrote: "I keep trying to get him to look into the issues that caused the compulsive behavior. The harder I try, the more he resists. I must stop." As coaddicts progress in their own recovery, they tend to stop monitoring their spouse's program. They learn to trust the process, focus on their own growth, and let go of the need to monitor their partner. And with decreasing control comes increased intimacy.

The Present and the Future
Some of the problems couples were dealing with were so significant that we wondered if they were discouraged about their future

together. To gain perspective on the overall relationship, we asked each person to rate their present relationship from very poor to excellent. We also asked them to use the same scale to rate the likelihood that they would be together in five years.

Overall, respondents were surprisingly positive about the present condition of their relationship, and were optimistic about the future. Despite their current struggles, the majority of respondents (61 percent of the men and 57 percent of the women) felt their relationship was very good or excellent. Only 9 percent of men and 11 percent of women felt their current relationship was very poor or poor.

When asked to imagine their future together, 85 percent of men and 77 percent of women thought it was very likely or definite that they would still be partners in five years. None thought they would definitely be apart, and only 3 percent of men and 4 percent of women rated their future chances as poor. Several respondents were reluctant to predict that they would definitely be together in five years. One man wrote, "Anyone who says definitely does not live in the same universe I inhabit." This man rated his current relationship as excellent. A woman who rated the probability of a future together with her husband as very likely said: "I'd say it's certain, but all we have is today, right? There just aren't any definites in life, at least not with addicts and coaddicts." Another woman stated: "'Definitely' is really an expression of hope. We are married one day at a time now."

Surely these results are a triumph of hope over experience. They indicate that if we desire to restore our marriage, we can. By working our individual recovery, taking responsibility for our actions, being honest and open in our communication, nurturing each other, and seeking professional help when necessary, we *can* rebuild our relationships. We also need to remember that being in a relationship is difficult, whether or not there is the problem of addiction. We cannot blame the addiction for all our problems. We also need to understand the part childhood messages play in our present interactions.

As we move forward in recovery, we each can develop techniques that help us restore our relationships. Here are some ideas that other couples have shared with us:

- Compromise. And if you can't do that, agree to disagree.
- Practice saying, "I was wrong."
- Have fun. Don't forget why you chose your partner. Take turns planning dates and weekends for just the two of you.
- Encourage the special talents and interests that each partner has.
- Do something spiritual together. Read aloud. Get out in nature.
- Share household tasks willingly.
- Attend meetings and retreats with other recovering couples.
- Above all, be honest.

A Final Word

A forty-one-year-old man summarized his experience in one and a half years of recovery from sexual addiction. He wrote:

I believe that I am only beginning recovery and that recovery proves itself in a series of stages. Like life, learning, and growth, the process never ends.

Sometimes I feel as though the past will never rest, that I can and will never really be forgiven, and that I am destined to be cast as someone who is less than whole. There is a double whammy of guilt, regret, and shame while being a sexaholic in a relationship that holds to traditional mores and values. That is, not only do I ride the roller coaster of self-blame and shame, but I go through a second wave for the hurt I've caused my partner and for the secrets I've kept.

Regarding therapy and therapists—I've listened to men who discount the value of therapy while citing their success in a Twelve Step program. I might have found the SA program without my therapist, but she expedited the process through her referral. On the other hand, I have sensed that some therapists are reluctant to embrace SA or Twelve Step programs for fear of losing control or seeing their patients abandon therapy.

I have learned many things about myself and my place in the world through SA that I may not have perceived in therapy, but I also embraced several ideas and facts through therapy when I needed a more focused direction with professional guidance. In the program, one guides oneself through practicing the Twelve Steps and by listening and talking at meetings. In therapy, the therapist is a guiding hand helping one to focus on pertinent data and possible cause-effect relationships. In therapy, I was persuaded more than once to encounter some of the feelings about people, events, and things that I have avoided all my life. Therapy helped me to see the patterns in my life. I am grateful for both therapy and SA!

Some of your questions dealt with spirituality. For many years I have felt this has been a missing piece of my puzzle, and yet I have found it very hard to practice a religion. The program seems to bring me spiritual enlightenment in more of an informal and comfortable way.

Making commitments and taking responsibility have always been difficult for me. Even now I do it, but it seems a struggle. Out of all this gray comes some special hope and light. I see improvement and ways to effect change. There is still some, but much less chaos in our home. There are reasons for things. There are answers. I keep coming back.

Endnotes

Chapter One: Overview

1. *Diagnostic and Statistical Manual of Mental Disorders, 3rd ed., Revised* (Washington, D.C.: American Psychiatric Association, 1987).
2. Patrick Carnes, *Don't Call It Love: Sex Addiction in America* (New York: Bantam, 1991).
3. Patrick Carnes, *Out of the Shadows: Understanding Sexual Addiction* (Minneapolis: CompCare, 1983), 9.
4. From the National Conference on Codependency held in Scottsdale, Arizona, September 8–10, 1989.

Chapter Two: Who We Are

1. Arnold M. Washton, "Cocaine Abuse and Compulsive Sexuality," *Medical Aspects of Human Sexuality* (December 1989): 32–39.
2. Mary Ann Klausner and Bobbie Hasselbring, *Aching for Love: The Sexual Drama of the Adult Child* (New York: Harper & Row, 1990), 84.
3. Richard F. Salmon, *Twelve Step Resources for Sexual Addicts & Co-Addicts* (Boulder, Colo.: National Council on Sexual Addiction, 1989).
4. *Abstinence and Boundaries in SAA* (Minneapolis: Sex Addicts Anonymous, 1986), 1.
5. *Statement of Purpose* (New York: Sexual Compulsives Anonymous, 1986).

Chapter Three: The Quagmire Before Recovery

1. Jennifer P. Schneider, M.D., *Back from Betrayal: Recovering from His Affairs* (Center City, Minn.: Hazelden Educational Materials, 1988), 182.

Chapter Four: Getting Help

1. N. Gattrell et al., "Psychiatrist/Patient Sexual Contact: Results of a National Survey," *American Journal of Psychiatry* 143 (October 1986), 1121–26.
2. S. H. Kardener et al., "A Survey of Physicians' Attitudes and Practices Regarding Erotic and Nonerotic Contact with Patients," *American Journal of Psychiatry* 130 (September 1973): 1077–81.
3. Peter Rutter, *Sex in the Forbidden Zone* (Los Angeles: Jeremy Tarcher, 1989), 25.
4. Ibid., 43.
5. N. Gattrell et al., "Psychiatrist/Patient Sexual Contact: Results of a National Survey," *American Journal of Psychiatry* 143 (October 1986), 1121–26.

Chapter Six: Sexuality in Recovery

1. *The Statement of the Problem* (Simi Valley, Calif.: Sexaholics Anonymous, 1985).
2. Consumers Union, *Love, Sex, and Aging* (Boston: Little, Brown & Co., 1984), 317.

Chapter Eight: Sobriety and Relapse

1. Patrick Carnes, *Contrary to Love: Helping the Sexual Addict* (Minneapolis: CompCare, 1989), 260.
2. Arnold M. Washton and Donna Boundy, *Willpower's Not Enough: Recovering from Addictions of Every Kind* (New York: Harper & Row, 1989), 197–99.

Chapter Ten: Gay or Bisexual Husbands

1. A. C. Kinsey, W. B. Pomeroy, and C. E. Martin, *Sexual Behavior in the Human Male,* (Philadelphia: W. B. Saunders, 1948), 289.
2. Ibid., 638.

3. Jean Gochros, *When Husbands Come Out of the Closet* (New York: Harrington Park Press, 1989), 132.
4. Ibid., 133.
5. Ibid.

Chapter Eleven: The Woman Addict and Her Partner

1. Mary Ann Klausner and Bobbie Hasselbring, *Aching for Love: The Sexual Drama of the Adult Child* (New York: Harper & Row, 1990), 82.
2. Charlotte Kasl, *Women, Sex, and Addiction* (New York: Ticknor & Fields, 1989), 46.

Suggested Reading

Sexual Addiction and Coaddiction

Carnes, Patrick. *Out of the Shadows: Understanding Sexual Addiction.* Minneapolis: CompCare, 1983.

Carnes, Patrick. *Contrary to Love: Helping the Sexual Addict.* Minneapolis: CompCare, 1989.

Carnes, Patrick. *Don't Call It Love: Sex Addiction in America.* New York: Bantam, 1991.

Diamond, Jed. *Looking for Love in All the Wrong Places.* New York: Avon Books, 1988.

Earle, Ralph, and Gregory Crow. *Lonely All the Time.* New York: Pocket Books, 1989.

Hope and Recovery. Minneapolis: CompCare, 1987.

Kasl, Charlotte. *Women, Sex, and Addiction.* New York: Ticknor & Fields, 1989.

Schneider, Jennifer P. *Back from Betrayal: Recovering from His Affairs.* Center City, Minn.: Hazelden Educational Materials, 1988.

Schneider, Jennifer P., and Burt Schneider. *Rebuilding Trust: For Couples Committed to Recovery.* Center City, Minn.: Hazelden Educational Materials, 1989.

Sex and Love Addicts Anonymous. Boston: Sex & Love Addicts Anonymous, 1986.

Sexaholics Anonymous. Simi Valley, Calif.: Sexaholics Anonymous, 1989.

Sexuality

Barbach, Lonnie. *For Each Other: Sharing Sexual Intimacy.* Garden City, N.J.: Anchor Press, 1982.

Blumstein, Philip, and Pepper Schwartz. *American Couples: Money, Work, Sex.* New York: William Morrow, 1983.

Consumers Union. *Sex, Love, and Aging.* Boston: Little, Brown, & Co., 1984.

Gochros, Jean. *When Husbands Come Out of the Closet.* New York: Harrington Park Press, 1989.

Hill, Ivan, ed. *The Bisexual Spouse.* McLean, Va.: Barlina Books, 1987.

Maltz, Wendy, and Beverly Holman. *Incest and Sexuality: A Guide to Understanding and Healing.* Lexington, Mass.: Lexington Books, 1987.

Woititz, Janet. *Healing Your Sexual Self.* Pompano Beach, Fla.: Health Communications, 1989.

Yaffe, Maurice, and Elizabeth Fenwick. *Sexual Happiness for Men — A Practical Approach.* New York: Henry Holt & Co., 1988.

Yaffe, Maurice, and Elizabeth Fenwick. *Sexual Happiness for Women — A Practical Approach.* New York: Henry Holt & Co., 1988.

Resources

**Twelve Step Programs For
Sex Addicts and Coaddicts**

Sexaholics Anonymous
P.O. Box 300
Simi Valley, CA 93062

Sex Addicts Anonymous
P.O. Box 3038
Minneapolis, MN 55403

Sex & Love Addicts Anonymous
P.O. Box 88, New Town Branch
Boston, MA 02258

S-Anon (for families of sex addicts)
P.O. Box 5117
Sherman Oaks, CA 91413

INDEX

when both are sex addicts
252–253
when husband is bisexual
183–222
when wife is sex addict
223–255
— D —
Denial 145
Dysfunctional family 10–11,
28, 178, 252
— E —
Enabling 33
Estrogen replacement therapy
107
— F —
Forgiveness 91–95
and time in recovery 93
definition 79, 91
steps of 91–92
— G —
Gochros, Jean 188, 214, 217
— H —
Hasselbring, Bobbie 229
Higher Power 4
**Homosexual men, sex
addiction in (See Sex
addiction in bisexual and
gay men)**
— I —
**Incest (See Sexual abuse,
childhood)**
Intimacy 78–79, 88, 124
definition 78
— K —
Kasl, Charlotte 232
Kinsey, Alfred 185
Klauser, Mary Ann 229
— M —
Masturbation 64

**Molestation (See Sexual
abuse, childhood)**
Multiple addictions
cocaine addicts 16, 17
switching addictions 17
— O —
**Obsessive-compulsive dis-
order** 9
— P —
Psychotherapy (See Therapy)
— R —
Relationship addicts 11
Relapse
definition 140–143, 151–154
in sexual coaddicts 151–159
myths about 146–147
prevention 141–143, 145–146,
155, 158
relationship to chemical use
144
spouse's reaction to 148–149
Rutter, Peter 70–71
— S —
Self-esteem 30, 34, 86, 157
Sex addiction
addictive cycle 9–10
behavior types 8, 19
diagnosis of 5–7
disclosure to family 162–182
telling only some children
170
telling young children
171–172
dishonesty 25, 33, 72–73, 79
fantasy, role of 104
in adolescents 181
in bisexual and gay men
183–222
in women 223–255
characteristics 226–232

Burt and Jennifer would welcome hearing from you. You can write us c/o El Dorado Medical Associates, 1500 North Wilmot Rd., Suite B-250, Tucson, AZ 85712